To James Gordon

with regards and all good wishes

Bellamy Partridge

Big Family

Books by

BELLAMY PARTRIDGE

SIR BILLY HOWE
Life of the Gay Revolutionary General

AMUNDSEN
The Splendid Norseman

THE ROOSEVELT FAMILY IN AMERICA
An Imperial Saga

COUNTRY LAWYER
The Story of My Father

The Big Family at the dinner table.

BELLAMY PARTRIDGE

<<<<<<<<<<<<<<<<<<<<<<<<<<<<<<<<<<<<<<<<<<<<<<

Big
Family

ILLUSTRATED BY

STEPHEN J. VOORHIES

<<<<<<<<<<<<<<<<<<<<<<<<<<<<<<<<<<<<<<<<<<<<<<

New York   WHITTLESEY HOUSE   London

MC GRAW-HILL BOOK COMPANY, INC.

BIG FAMILY

Copyright, 1941, *by* BELLAMY PARTRIDGE

First printing, August, 1941
Second printing, August, 1941

PUBLISHED BY WHITTLESEY HOUSE

A Division of the McGraw-Hill Book Company, Inc.

Printed in the United States of America by Quinn & Boden Company, Inc., Rahway, N. J.

FOR
THE REST OF THE FAMILY

Foreword

When, soon after the close of the Civil War, Father hung up his shingle as a cub lawyer in a country town he found the building shortage so acute that only one home on Main Street was for sale. This was not exactly what he thought he wanted, but since it was the best he could do he bought it. It was a big barn of a house that had never been occupied until Father moved in with the puny beginnings of what was destined to become a sizable family.

The builder, a man named Brush, had intended the place for his own use, but before it was ready for occupancy he became financially involved and had to sell it. Brush had bought doorknobs and other hardware for the place, but since they had not been attached to the freehold he carried them away before giving possession. Father understood this perfectly; the hardware had not become a fixture and so remained the personal property of the seller. Mother never could understand it, and all her life she regarded Mr. Brush as a petty thief who had as good as stolen the doorknobs right off her doors.

Though the front porch had been finished when the family took possession, the grounds had not been graded, and the steps could be reached only by walking up a plank. The water supply for the house was furnished by a cistern under the back kitchen, and for drinking purposes water was carried in a bucket from the well of a neighbor across the street until Father could have a well of his own dug. People could not greatly have minded the inconvenience of carrying their drinking water in those days, for fully ten years had passed before we had a well of our own.

Heat was provided on the ground floor by parlor stoves, but the only heat on the second floor was that which came up the stair well from below. To have heated bedrooms was supposed at the time to be detrimental to health, and to break the ice in the water pitcher on a winter morning was regarded as an invigorating way to start the day. Of course, the parlor stoves were eventually displaced by a furnace, the heat of which came up through the floors by means of large ornamental registers whose design several of the younger children will carry to their final resting place, for these registers used to become so hot as to act as a very efficient branding iron to anyone trusting enough to sit down on them. During the winter months it was customary to have the newest baby sleep downstairs, where walking the floor or administering the midnight bottle could be done with a little less discomfort than in the unheated rooms above.

With an average of something like two years between the new arrivals, it will be seen that the oldest child was nearing maturity when the birth of the last was announced at the breakfast table. Since I was the sixth child, many of my most vivid recollections of the period when all eight of us were there together are confined to the time when I was comparatively young. It is for this reason that so much of the story is seen through the eyes of a younger son.

I am well aware of the fact that there are even now many families throughout the land as large as ours and some even larger. But in these days the raising of a big family is regarded as an exploit, an achievement. Only the very poor or the very wealthy can afford such a preposterous luxury. Back in the eighties a family of eight children was no curiosity; it was as common as the eight-cylinder car of the present period. In those days food was cheap, children's demands were modest, land was still to be had for a dollar an acre, building costs were low, rents were reasonable. No monthly payments were due on this or that, since installment buying had not yet been contrived. "Miles per gallon" would have been an empty phrase, and the first income tax blank was yet to be printed. Father came home to dinner at noon, and Mother was still proud to be listed by the census taker as a housewife.

It is not my contention that life then was any better or any easier, but at least it was more leisurely and more simple, and by turning back to it we may find some worthwhile things that we have overlooked.

B. P.

Contents

Big Family

1. Enter the Stork

WE WERE seated at the breakfast table one autumn morning in the early eighties, Father, Grandmother Bellamy, and the seven of us, busy with our ham and eggs, and hash-brown potatoes, which ordinarily preceded the steaming stacks of buckwheat pancakes. Once started, the cakes continued to come in an endless chain as long as there was any demand for them. Usually the breakfast table was noisy and jovial, but on this particular morning a strange silence hung over it like a cloud, for Mother was sick in bed.

Our house was big, much too big when Father had bought it some years before, but it had gradually filled until now it was so crowded that, as Father said, there was no room to be decently sick upstairs. Only the day before he and Gra Richardson, who always came and took charge of the family when Mother was sick, had put up a bed in the back parlor which they were now calling the Emergency Ward. And they were just in time, for that same night Mother was taken violently ill. Father ran for the doctor while Gra Richardson started up the kitchen range to heat a clothes boiler of hot water. The next morning was one of the few I can remember when the breakfast bell did not ring. Father was afraid the sound would disturb Mother, so he came to our doors and called us. We dressed and went downstairs very quietly, for the doctor and Gra Richardson were still working over Mother as we sat down to breakfast.

I could see that Father was worried; his eyes, usually so bright, were listless, and he kept passing his hand slowly over the bald space on the top of his head. It was bewildering to see him so subdued, for Father, with all his buoyancy in the face of danger and distress, was always helpless and ineffective whenever anything was wrong with Mother. We watched him as he sat staring into his plate and not saying a word. Every little while he would take out his big gold watch, open it, and put it back in his pocket without looking at it. There was a little entryway between the dining room and back parlor with two solid doors, and still we could hear a noise from in there which sounded almost like the wailing of a kitten. Various members of the family would look at one another and shake their heads, and Father would dart his eyes quickly at the door as if expecting somebody to come out. Then suddenly we heard those doors opening and shutting, and somebody did come out.

It was Gra Richardson, tall and commanding. She drew the door shut behind her and smiled, her black eyes sparkling with anticipation.

"Well," she announced, looking from one to another of us, "you've got a little brother in there."

Stan and I were the only ones who acted at all surprised. The rest of them seemed to have been expecting something of the sort, and Father positively beamed with a mixture of relief and delight.

"So it's a boy—splendid! Everything's all right, I suppose?"

Gra Richardson nodded her complete reassurance. "Both doing famously."

"Well, my dears," said Father, exuding great satisfaction, "his name is Leslie." He whipped out his watch, raised it to the limit of its heavy gold chain, and studied it intently. "Shall we call it seven fifty-seven?"

With a glance at the clock on the mantel Gra Richardson replied, "That'll be close enough."

Father closed the watch with a snap. "He's a big strong fellow, I suppose?"

The corners of Gra Richardson's mouth went humorously down. "Ten and a half pounds!"

As she opened the door leading into the passage to the kitchen Father drew a notebook and pencil from his pocket. "I'll make a note of the vital statistics," he said, "and enter them in the family Bible later on. Uncle Leslie will be delighted, I'm sure. I'm afraid he despaired of our ever having another boy."

"I don't know why not," said Louise who, as the oldest daughter, was trying with all the dignity her fourteen years could command to fill Mother's place at the end of the table opposite Father. Intensely loyal to the family she resented even Uncle Leslie's despair. "Let him do his worrying about people who need it." She gave her thick black braid a toss. "We don't!"

"But four boys in a row," said Elsie from her place on Father's right. "I'll tell you how it should have been done." Father smiled indulgently at her serious face. She was a tall leggy girl, not the beauty that Louise was— not yet, at any rate. A year younger than Louise, she was already full of ideas and would, he imagined, go through life telling people how. "There should have been two boys, then one girl, and after that two more boys."

Cecilia, twelve, and fairer than her sisters, let out a ripple of laughter. "Better take the baby back," she cried, "and exchange him for a pound of tea."

But Elsie was willing to give no ground. "My way would have been best," she insisted, "if it could only have been followed. Of course I love having another baby in the family—but four *boys* one right after another!"

"Can't get too many of 'em," Herb, nine, put in. "I hope little Leslie grows up to be a good fighter and a good ball player. The worst trouble with girls is they can't play ball."

"I can," Cecilia declared a little defiantly. "And I don't kick when I get put out."

This brought a smile, for Herb, though a good ball player for his nine years, was a notorious kicker and simply could not accept an adverse decision without protest.

My own reaction to the new baby was a little confused. At seven I was wondering where he came from, how the doctor happened to get hold of him, and what made him my brother. I was delighted to have another companion

6

and asked how long it would be before he could come out and play with us.

"If he walks as young as you did," said Father, "he'll be ready for your ball team in a year, and if he talks as soon as Herb did he'll be kicking on every decision about eighteen months from now."

"But, Papa! Papa!" Stan had been trying to make himself heard for some time. "Please listen to me!"

"Well—what is it, Stan?"

Stan, youngest of the flock, just turned four, was worried. "I don't want you to change the baby for a pound of tea."

We started to laugh, but Father silenced us with a wave of the hand. "Why not, Stan?" he asked.

" 'Cause if you're gonna change him I wish you'd change him for a horse."

In the laughter which followed Stan joined noisily though he had no idea what we were laughing about.

"Well, Thad," said Father, "I guess you're the only one who hasn't been heard from."

Thad, the oldest child, now a slender youth of seventeen, shook his head in mock seriousness. "Eight! It's a lot of family."

Father and Thad were physically much alike. Both had the wide forehead of the Selden ancestry and the firm jaw of Grandfather Partridge. They also had in common a sense of humor which was a little rare in our family. The rest of us always enjoyed their banter.

"And eight is a big number for mental arithmetic," Thad continued.

"I can still make it add up," said Father.

"And get the right answer every time?"

"Practically every time."

"Mind if I make a suggestion about the name?"

"It's all settled," said Father, "but go ahead."

7

"I think you ought to change the name from Leslie to Lastly."

Father shook with laughter, but Grandmother Bellamy compressed her lips into a grim rainbow of negation. "I wouldn't change it," she said defiantly. "Uncle Leslie's going to be very much pleased; he's never had a namesake."

By this time all the older children were giggling, but Grandmother folded her hands and settled back into her chair with the attitude of one who had seen her duty and had done it. For some time past we had been hearing the little mewling sound quite steadily, but suddenly it began to increase in volume. There was an opening and closing of doors again and Dr. Howard came out of the sickroom.

"You can go in now, Sam," he said. "She's asking for you."

Father nearly tipped over his chair in his haste to get on his feet. "Is everything as it should be?"

The doctor nodded wearily. "We're over the river all right. Frances came through in fine shape. Wait till you see that boy." He looked at Father, who was not a large man. "I don't know how you do it. Everybody praying for boys, and you get four in a row."

"Don't ask me," said Father. "I have no magic formula. Now if you'll just sit down there in my chair Louise will give you some breakfast—if there's any left." And he disappeared into the sickroom with a cautious opening and closing of the doors.

"Do sit down, Doctor," Louise urged, "and tell us all about it."

"Nothing much to tell," said the doctor. "Labor a little longer than usual, I'd say, and pretty severe. Your mother knows the business about as well as I do. Puerperium perfectly satisfactory. A little sleep would do wonders for her right now." He gulped down a cup of coffee and bolted out of the house just as Gra Richardson appeared to get us started for school.

"Can't we see the baby before we go?" we all began to ask.

She shook her head. "Not this morning. You can all see him as soon as school is over. Put your things on now and I'll get you off to school—your mother's worrying about it."

This was a task that Mother preferred to handle for herself so long as she was able. We were checked out of the house like guests departing from a hotel. She wanted to be sure that no traces of breakfast still lingered around our mouths, and that we had on the right hats and coats to suit the weather. The final step of this inspection was to see our handkerchiefs; we had to show a reasonably clean one to get out of the house. Gra Richardson didn't know our wardrobes as Mother did, and we were sometimes able to do a little cheating if we felt so inclined. This time we tried no trickery and Gra Richardson was about halfway through her inspection when a knock came on the door leading to the side veranda. It was Dave Conroy, our newest gardener, wanting to ask Father some questions. Gra Richardson called him from Mother's bedside and he went outside and talked to Dave for a few minutes. When he came in he was shaking his head dubiously.

"I'm afraid Dave isn't going to do. He always has to be told. I want a gardener who will go ahead by himself."

Gra Richardson smiled and rolled her eyes. "What you want is another Jerry Billings," she said.

"What I want is the real Jerry Billings," said Father, "and he won't be available for several years."

Jerry had been our gardener before I was born, and after a number of incendiary fires in town he had been

9

arrested for arson. Father's defense of Jerry on this charge proved to be the most sensational criminal trial of his career. It lasted for days, and though Jerry was eventually convicted and sent to Auburn prison for a long term Father always believed him innocent and through the years of his imprisonment often spoke of the case as the perfect miscarriage of justice. For the first year or two after the trial Father was very touchy on the subject and flew to Jerry's defense whenever anybody intimated that Jerry might have been guilty of the crime with which he had been charged—which was at the time the general belief of practically the entire population of the town.

Gra Richardson was one of the few persons in Phelps not afraid to cross swords with Father, and she did not hesitate to bait him a little now and then just to get him going. As a matter of fact, she was one of a handful who shared Father's belief in Jerry's innocence though she would not give him the satisfaction of having her tell him so.

"If Jerry never comes back," she said with a grim smile, "I know a lot of folks who'll be well suited."

"Sometimes people wake up to the fact that they have made a mistake," said Father as he started for the front hall to get his hat and cane. Halfway across the room he stopped at the sound of a whine from Belle, our spaniel. The dog was standing at the door of the sickroom asking very plainly to be admitted.

"She hears that new baby's voice," said Father with a smile, "and wants to get in there and see him. I suppose she'll be feeling responsible for him from now on. Best nurse girl we ever had in the house. Always the first one on hand when a baby cries in the night."

"Hm-m-m—smart dog." Gra Richardson did not care for dogs.

10

"Want to come, Belle?" said Father invitingly. "I'm going to the office. Want to come?"

Belle looked up at him and wagged her feathery tail, but she made no move to go with him.

Father watched her and nodded his head. "I agree with you, Belle. I'd rather stay here, too, with Mother and the new baby, but there's an office full of people waiting for me, and I've got to attend to them and catch the ten o'clock train." He took up his stick and put on his tall hat of gray felt, and went quietly out of the door. From the porch he could see the children trooping up the street towards school in a random column which was augmented at almost every house they passed. At the gate he stopped and looked back at the big square box of a house with its mansard roof. He remembered so well the day he had bought the place. It was the same day he decided to settle in town. Hobson, his predecessor, had handled the deal.

"Only house in town that will do at all," Hobson had said.

"But sixteen rooms," Father had protested, overwhelmed with the size of the place.

"How many in your family?"

"Two and expectations."

He still remembered Hobson's heart-warming smile. "If you're the man I think you are you'll fill every room in that house inside of ten years."

Father smiled back across the years. It had taken him thirteen—but the rooms were full. His glance fell across the window of the library on the left of the hall and he recalled the innumerable nights he had worked in that room until the lamps had burned themselves out. In his mind's eye he looked through the folding doors into the dining room just beyond and saw the big family gathered round the table; he could see across the hall into

11

the big front parlor, sometimes used as a nursery but just now serving as an anteroom to the Emergency Ward— where Frances lay nursing her new-born babe. His eyes swept the second floor, front chamber on right, blue chamber on left, with the less distinguished rooms crowding into the rear. There was hardly a room in the house that was without some significant memory for him. He had slept in them all. He had kept watch over the children sleeping in them. Many of those rooms he had paced with sick or croupy babies. He had sat through the night by a sickbed in almost every room. Children had been born in most of them, and in one or two of them members of the family had died.

His eyes ranged over the grounds. He had graded and planted them himself. With his own hands he had set out that Red Astrachan tree by the corner of the house and had seen it grow to maturity. He had planted the crabapple at the other end of the porch, the mountain ashes in the lawn, the umbrella tree. He had set out the Queen Anne cherry by the side of the house, the pear trees beyond, and the two rows of apple trees along the hardpacked garden path.

As he turned to go on his eye fell on the white painted fence. Some day, when the children were old enough not to ruin the foliage, he would plant a hedge where that fence now stood. He would tear up the old plank walk and replace it with flagstone—a broad flagstone pavement leading to the steps of the porch. The name PARTRIDGE should be engraved on that pavement just inside the property line. With one parting look at the old house he loved so well he opened the gate and stepped outside. As the gate whanged shut a vista of tree-lined street confronted him. Tall maples, graceful elms, gnarled locusts, some of them standing where they now were when General Sullivan's raiders passed along the ridge half a mile south of the town. Saplings then, now grizzled giants, they stood in silent majesty as he started up the street. Father loved a tree, and only when he was deeply preoccupied could he walk past a fine specimen without a feeling of recognition and appreciation. He was especially fond of the two towering elms which stood before the Hoskins house across the way. Each tree was guarded by a huge leaden dog, one looking east, the other west, with tails rampant (and easily broken off by children climbing up to take a ride on the dog's back). Father seldom saw the dogs, though he almost never missed the trees. A little farther on were two horse-chestnut trees standing before the Gothic portals of the Presbyterian church. Father did not see these trees—he did not like them and spoke of them as European hybrids of untidy habit. As he passed he looked between them and straight through the closed oaken doors of the church to a point before the altar where he could see himself standing, as he had already stood seven times before, while the man of God sprinkled drops of water on the hairless head of an astonished infant.

"Name this child."

"Leslie James."

Father smiled and walked on. In front of the big brick house on the next corner he stopped to chat with Charley Harger, the owner, who was wheeling out his lawn mower preparatory to cutting half an acre of lawn. As they stood talking Phineas Dodd, the eccentric moneylender of the town, drove past in a rickety buggy drawn by a mangy-looking horse. Dodd rode with one muddy boot dangling outside the wagon box and coming to rest now and then on the worn and battered crossbar. Father smiled in the direction of the vehicle, but the old usurer took no notice of him. He was still angry over the blistering cross-examination to which Father had submitted him in a

13

recent lawsuit. Si Peckham, however, who drove past a few moments later, made up for Dodd's slight by the booming tones of his greeting. Si was running for sheriff at the time and was taking pains to leave nobody ungreeted.

In front of Woodpecker Inn Father paused to pass the time of day with Old Tick, the portly proprietor who stood on the veranda in shirtsleeves and slippers.

"Jees Cri!" Old Tick exclaimed in his high-pitched voice. "You'd think Si was a-runnin' fer Pres't Unite' States the way he yells hello to folks." He lowered his voice. "Think he's got a chance of bein' 'lected?"

Father shook his head. "Not a chance."

Old Tick's fishlike mouth fell open. The rolls of flesh beneath his chin formed themselves into a series of meaty terraces. "Jees Cri!" he mouthed. "You say he ain't got a chance? Why, I almost put up ten dollars on him to win!"

Father raised his eyes to the picture of distress staring down at him from the rail of the porch. "No chance about it at all, Tick," he said. "His election's practically a certainty."

Old Tick blinked. "You mean you think he'll win?"

"How can he lose? The Republicans haven't lost an election in this county for thirty years."

"Then you—guess it's all right, do you?"

"I'd be glad to take it off your hands—if I had the ten dollars."

Old Tick cackled with laughter. "Then I guess it ain't such a bad bet after all."

He followed Father into the hotel office with its checkered floor of large black and white squares, and up to that part of the counter occupied by a small showcase containing tobacco and cigars. Father pointed at an open box of *At Home* cigars.

14

"That's my brand, right there," he said.

"How many? It's a five-cent straight."

"You might as well give me a full box."

Old Tick's eyes lit up. A smile passed slowly across his flabby face. "Boy or girl?" he demanded.

"Boy."

"Well, Jees Cri! Won't that make Charley Glimpse mad though."

"Why should it?"

"Because Charley's just finished takin' the census, and now he'll hafta open up his books again. I'll help myself to a cigar out of the new box, and I wish you luck."

Father paused a moment at the door of the Inn to look up and down the business section of the little town. There it was all in a cluster astride the old stage road. Most of the store buildings were of two stories, a few of only one, and even fewer of three. It was a Y-shaped town with a spike-roofed bandstand in the fork of the street. Twice since its settlement the town had been completely erased by fire, but with unsuspected vitality it had each time risen from its ruins a little better than it was before. Some of the old trees had suffered from the ravages of time, and some from the march of progress, though enough were still standing to afford the horses at the hitch rail as well as the passers-by some comfortable shade in summer. A few of the store signs were, as in years past, fastened to the trees, and Father noted with sentimental satisfaction that the limb from which he had first hung his shingle on coming to town was still hale and hearty. Life had looked so simple to him then; having found a place to hang his shingle all he had to do was build up a law practice and make his way in the world. As he walked on towards his office he realized that his problem was still the same—only there was more of it.

Father spent most of the day in Canandaigua at the

15

probate court, but on the arrival of his train in the evening he hurried home without stopping at the office. The old house with lights gleaming from its windows had a warm hospitable look as he came down the street. On entering the door he was enthusiastically mobbed by the younger children. They were dangling from both hands and from his coattails before he was halfway across the hall. He had a kiss for each, a hug, a pat, and as soon as he could disentangle himself he went in to see Mother and found her just waking from a long sleep. With her dark hair lying in two plaits over her shoulders she looked almost like a schoolgirl. It seemed incredible to him that she could be in her middle thirties and the mother of eight. Her vitality had come back with a rush, brightening her soft brown eyes and bringing color to her lips and cheeks. She was in fine spirits. All memory of the night before was gone, and to her it seemed that the new baby was the most wonderful child that had ever come to her. Father restrained a smile. She was always that way; each one as it came was the most wonderful. Leslie woke up and began to wail. Father was struck by the volume and the lusty quality of his voice.

Gra Richardson hurried over to take him up. "Looks like his mother," she said, "but he certainly has his father's voice. He's trying to make a speech already."

2. The More the Merrier

MOTHER was an enthusiastic advocate of the large family. She was always ready to tell people why they should have many children instead of a few. One of the reasons she used to give was that the older children helped to take care of the younger ones, and with a little well-advised training would so simplify life that it was, for all practical purposes, as easy to have seven or eight children as to have only one or two. Carried to its logical conclusion it should have been easier; for with enough well-trained older children the mother would have nothing to attend to but the biological preliminaries and the obstetrical eventualities. But there must have been a point of diminishing returns somewhere along the line, for that was not the way it worked in our family. The older children did help some with the younger, but they did not relish the job and shirked or sidestepped it whenever they could.

Another advantage of the large family that she used to cite was that the younger children developed much faster and easier by learning from the older ones. This contention was not without merit. I learned something from each of the five children ahead of me, and doubtless from the two behind me. Some of what I learned was good, and some of it was not so good. It seems to me now that I mastered their most deplorable faults before turn-

17

ing my attention to their nobler qualities. I had long since mastered greed before I caught even the most elementary inkling of generosity. The practical value of lies came to me long before the great and fundamental beauties of truth. I had learned the argumentative effectiveness of a well-aimed blow by the time I was three years old, though the vastly superior force of logic did not come to me with any great conviction until quite a little later.

I think that Mother may also have had some vague idea that by bringing children into the world she was helping to swell the armies of the Lord against the invasions and incursions of the Devil and the insidious infiltrations of Demon Rum. Of all the proposals for the betterment of man these were the two which claimed her most active attention. She would drop anything she happened to be doing—especially if it was something that she particularly enjoyed—to go out after recruits either for Christianity or for the cause of Temperance.

The danger of becoming a spoiled child is practically nil in a family of eight. There might be a slight chance for the last of the line to get a little indulgence since there is nobody crowding him from behind for whom he must make room and furnish gangway; but he is pretty sure to have a good training in patience if he has to wait for seven older children, all clamoring over their seniority rights, to go through the mill ahead of him.

The moral support which comes from belonging to a big family was another of the advantages Mother used to point out. Family loyalty can be a mighty influence in a small town. As one of the younger children I derived great comfort from the knowledge that no matter what kind of difficulties I might get into, one of the older children was pretty sure to come along before anything of a serious nature was likely to happen. Larger boys with a bullying nature were inclined to keep hands off when they remembered—or were reminded of—my older brothers; though for some strange reason I never was much of a target for bullies. The tendency of this reliance on family solidarity was to make me rash and adventurous. I would take long chances which, had I been entirely dependent on myself, I never would have taken. I used to venture out on thin ice knowing that Herb or Thad would haul me out if I happened to break through, and once I came very near going to a watery resting place because I tacitly relied on Herb when he was powerless to help me.

It was in the spring when the ice was just beginning to break up in the creek. There was already open water under Willing's bridge, and the larger boys were having great fun breaking off cakes of ice above the bridge and riding them until the occupant could catch the iron stringers which trussed the bridge from below. With the high water these were within easy reach of the boys, who would swing on them and make their way hand over hand to the shore while the abandoned cake of ice would go floating down the stream, through the rapids, and up against or under an ice jam some five hundred feet below the bridge. Nearly all the larger boys had taken one or more rides down to the bridge, which they found most exhilarating. Then quite by accident they broke off a smaller cake that did not look large enough to carry a big boy.

"Hey, kid," Herb shouted to me, "this one's just your size. Hop it and take a ride!"

I had not expected to get one. This was an older boy's game and I was just looking on. But here was my chance. I certainly would not get another. The cake of ice was moving. It was a foot away from the shore ice. There was no time to consider—and I jumped aboard just before the current caught it and whirled it into the rushing stream. Not until I was out in the swift water did I realize how small my raft was. I had to stand in the center of it to keep it from tipping, and even then the surface of it was awash much of the time. I glanced anxiously at the bridge which I had assumed would look far away. But it was not so far as I had thought, and it seemed to be coming toward me with a swoop. I hadn't realized how large and imposing an ordinary highway bridge could look. I could see the stringer rods clearly and began to focus my eyes on the spot where I was expecting to catch hold a few seconds later if all went well. But all did not go well. As I came nearer those stringer rods began to rise higher and higher, and when the moment arrived for the jump I discovered to my horror that they were at least three feet above my head, and with such a leap as I could make from my precarious footing I could not possibly hope to reach them. First one rod— then the other—passed swiftly over my head and in another moment my floundering craft was in the quick water.

I had embarked on that ice cake with the vague assurance in my mind that Herb was right there and would look after me. Now I knew he wouldn't. The swiftest arrow could not have moved fast enough to catch up with me. A wave of fear went over me when I realized that I had to depend entirely on myself to get out of a bad situation. My past life did not flicker before my eyes, though I had the feeling that I was being swept on by a relentless fate. I knew I was in for a wetting, and though the shores looked very far away I had a feeling that I was going to be able to reach the nearest one. Some fifty feet above the ice jam as my floe was passing a little point of land I made a flying leap for it, and had it not been for some willow branches that I caught, the day and year

would undoubtedly now be carved on a neat little head-
stone in our cemetery lot.

Herb was as white as a snowman when he came panting up to the place where I stood shivering and dripping,
but now that the prospects of a funeral in the family no
longer loomed he tried to cover himself by treating me
contemptuously.

"Why didn't you grab the rods?"

"I c-c-couldn't. They were t-t-too high."

"Aw, you didn't even try."

"It was n-n-no use."

"You'll never catch anything if you don't *try*—you
muffed two good chances."

"I tell you they were t-t-too *high!*"

"And I tell you g'wan home and get on some dry
clothes—and you needn't come back here. You ain't old
enough for this kind of stuff."

He did not have to tell me that. I was already pretty
well convinced of it. Of course as soon as I had dry
clothes on, and had recovered from my fright, I would
begin to tag around after the larger boys again. I must
have been a great annoyance to Herb, but no greater, I
am sure, than Stan was to me. I suppose I would have
felt slighted if Stan had not tried to follow me around;
but since he did I was in a position to treat him with the
contempt that all younger boys seem to deserve from
older boys.

In a large family there is a fine opportunity for teasing; someone is always available. Louise and Elsie were
too mature for me. I could not do much with them, but
Cecilia was different. Although she was more than four
years my senior I used to lead her a life. Leslie was too
young for most of my efforts, but Stan was just about
the right age. To him I passed on with great regularity
all the indignities handed from above. Anything that

21

Herb had devised which particularly annoyed me went into my repertory for future use against Stan. Occasionally I would invent some original tortures when I found unexpected chinks in Stan's armor. Perhaps the most dependable of these was the one about his being an orphan.

I had noticed the shock with which Stan had learned that one of the little girls in the neighborhood was not an "own" child, but was an orphan who had been adopted into the family with whom she lived. For some reason the foster parents did not get around to telling the child, until someone had beaten them to it. Father, who had handled the adoption proceedings some years before, had advised the parents to tell the child its real status as soon as she was able to understand. But his advice was not taken, and now that the inevitable had happened he was sounding off on the subject. Stan could not seem to get the painful occurrence out of his mind. Long afterward he kept talking about it.

"Why, it might happen to anybody," he said. "How could a person tell?"

It was at that moment when the idea came to me. I shook my head seriously. "You couldn't tell," I said. "Nobody could."

"But how does anybody know whether he's an own child or only adopted?"

I pulled a long face. "Stan," I said, "I hadn't intended to tell you this, but if I don't somebody else will."

Stan looked puzzled. "What do you mean?"

"I mean that you're not really my brother at all—you're an orphan."

Stan bristled. "Who—me? I don't believe it!"

I smiled a little sadly. "Alice didn't believe it either."

"But—but nobody ever said anything to me about it."

"Nobody ever said anything to Alice."

22

"But if I was born in another place I'd remember something about it."

"We got you too young for that; but you're an orphan just the same."

"But Father said—"

"Yeah, I know what he said. But you remember he spoke about an 'exceptional case'? Well, that's what you are—but I like you just as well as if you were my real brother."

Stan's lips were working. "I don't believe a word of it."

"I'm kinda sorry I told you," I said. "I suppose I shouldn't have done it. But I had the feeling that you oughta know before you were a day older."

Suddenly he burst out sobbing and ran into the house. When he came out he was disgusted with himself and angry at me. "You lied to me. Mother says there isn't a word of truth in what you said."

I smiled knowingly. "Of course they'd have to tell you that."

"Why would they hafta?"

"Because they've made up their minds that you're never to know the truth. That's why."

"I don't believe it—not a single word of it."

But he did. He did not want to believe it, but he could not help himself. And back to Mother he went again. This time she tried to laugh him out of it and apparently succeeded—until I began apologizing for having told him, and begging him to forget that I ever said anything about it, and aroused his suspicions again. The best of hoaxes usually grows stale and loses its power to provoke, but this one lasted so long that Mother finally forbade me ever to say again that Stan was an orphan. I never did say it again, but I was able to say other things which accomplished the same effect. When a visitor remarked that Stan did not look much like his brothers, I reminded

23

Stan of it afterwards and said, "Now you know why." And when Stan made the discovery that his thumb was unlike that of any other member of the family, all I had to do was to give him a significant look and say, "You're not surprised, are you?"

It seems to be as natural for children to be cruel to each other as it is for them to be loyal and to fight each other's bloodiest battles. Today they will break your heart with plaguing and pestering, and tomorrow they will save your life at the risk of their own.

A perfect job of family tantalizing can be done with two participants, but only the large family can produce the big, inclusive, rip-roaring farces that go echoing down the well-worn corridors of time as "family jokes"—the kind which gather force with the retelling, that become better and better, and bigger and bigger as the years go on. First and last our family had quite a few of these, some funny, some tenuous, and some plain dumb. Events that are very comical before a number of people are not at all funny with only a few. If the famous Coon Scare had happened in a two-seater family it never would have drawn a smile, and would in all probability have rated no higher than an ordinary bedtime nuisance. It was the fact that it happened in a big family with a house full of people that gave it the epic qualities which made it one of the most durable of our family jokes.

To begin with, it happened on a Friday night, and Friday nights were likely to be very lively at our house. Most of our parties were given on that night, and even if there was no party the three girls would certainly have callers, sometimes so many callers it was hard to be sure that it was not a party. Stan and I always liked to be definite about that, for if it was a party there would be refreshments, and we could stay up until the eating was over. There were, however, no refreshments the night of

24

the Coon Scare, so Stan and I were sent off to bed at nine o'clock.

We hated to leave the fun and the gaiety although we had little part in it, except when Ernie J. (now a noted cleric, perhaps even an archbishop) would romp with us. As we went reluctantly out the door one of the callers was beginning to finger the piano and we felt sure that soon they would take out the leaves, shove the dining-room table into the bay window, and begin dancing. The town was still without electric lights at this time, and Father in his zeal for fire protection had decreed that Stan and I should go to bed by lantern light. In addition to the safety feature this arrangement simplified matters considerably; for the lantern could be lighted before we started upstairs, and after we were undressed and ready to hop into bed it could be extinguished with no fire hazard whatever. The only difficulty with the arrangement was that the person who blew out the lantern had to go to bed in the dark. Our usual practice was to take turns putting it out; but on this occasion there had been a dispute about whose turn it was, and since neither of us was willing to yield to the other we had stubbornly decided to go up to bed without lighting the lantern; then nobody would have to blow it out. Both of us began to regret that decision before we had gone a third of the way up the back stairs, which were not only crooked and steep, but as dark as the Bottomless Pit. And even after we had reached the top of the stairs we still had a pitch-black hallway to grope through before coming to the door of our room, the last one in the rear wing. Once we got a hand on the knob of that door the going became easy, for the night outside was illumined to some extent by a pale summer moon which threw a slanting shaft of sallow light halfway across the room.

25

Inside our room we drew a long breath of relief and quickly closed the door behind us. We would have locked it, but Father, considering locked doors a fire hazard, had removed all the bolts from the upstairs rooms. Still a little shaky from the affrighted ascent of the dark and eerie stairway we began at once our preparation for bed. I dipped my toothbrush in the water pitcher, made a few passes at my teeth, and sat down on the left side of the bed, where I started to undress. I heard Stan rattle at the water pitcher and drop down in a chair on the other side near the foot. We were keeping up a steady conversation, a sort of verbal whistling in the dark, talking mostly of the baseball game we had seen that day and of the prowess of a gentleman named White-eye Fitts who had pounded out the winning run for our side.

White-eye was notoriously bandy-legged and was so pigeon-toed one might have thought he would be stepping on his own feet, which he most assuredly was not. His parenthetical contours fascinated us, however, and after I had removed the last of my clothes I held my bare arms out in front of me with hands turned inward in imitation of White-eye's nether extremities. There in the dimly lighted room I was struck with the excellence of the imitation and dropped to the floor on all fours to see if it would work. It worked to perfection, and I was so pleased with my discovery that I wanted to share it with Stan. So, still on all fours, I started for the corner of the bed intending to say, "Here's White-eye Fitts."

I started the sentence, but never quite finished it, for as I rounded the corner and came into the slanting strip of moonlight—Stan uttered a piercing shriek and flew at me, clutching his fingers in my bushy and then copious hair. He, too, had just finished his undressing and was completely in the buff.

26

"What's the matter—what's the *matter?*" I screamed at him as I fought to disengage his fingers.

He recognized my voice and screamed back something about seeing a coon, though he failed to recognize as mine the hair at which he was wrenching and tugging with all his strength.

"Where? Where is it?" I shrieked.

His reply was lost in the medley of screams.

It was as confusing as it was terrifying. Aside from the belief that a wild animal was there in the room with us, I don't know what I thought. It was a perfect example, in a small way, of mob hysteria. Stan's terror terrified me, and my terror terrified Stan. We threw each other into a panic, so unreasoning a panic that clutching and tearing at each other, and shrieking and screaming with all our power, we battled our way through the door and into the Stygian hallway that only a few moments before had paralyzed us both with fright. We must have been instinctively trying to reach help at any cost. How it happened that we did not go crashing down those treacherous back stairs is a mystery, for when the rescue squads arrived, one led by Father up the back stairs, the other by Ernie J. up the front, we were tottering and wrestling on the brink, and still shrieking to high heaven.

Behind Father, who had a lamp in his hand, came Mother and Herb and all the callers who happened to be in the library or dining room. Behind Ernie, who also carried a lamp he had snatched from the hall table, were all the miscellaneous company of youths and maidens who had been in the parlors when the blood-curdling screams had come floating down from the rear wing. Seeing us still locked in mortal combat the leaders of both rescue parties had set down their hand lamps and pulled us apart still screaming as hysterically as ever. We were so paralyzed with terror that for some moments after their ar-

27

rival we did not even know they were there. My first realization that we had been rescued came when Father clapped his hand over my mouth and shouted above the tumult:

"What is the matter? Tell me instantly!"

Meanwhile Ernie J. had silenced Stan with a powerful hand over his mouth. With a return of sanity came a resurgence of modesty, and like certain of our ancestors we knew we were naked and would have been glad to have aprons of fig leaves. But Father and Ernie J. held us in a viselike grip so that we could not even turn our backs to the gaping multitude, with Father still demanding in a voice of thunder that we tell him what the matter was.

"We're b-b-both scairt," I gasped out. "Stan saw a coon —in our room—"

"What!" demanded Father. "A coon in your room?"

"I did not," protested Stan. "I thought *you* were a coon!"

"Well, anyway," I explained, "we're both scairt—"

My explanation never went any further, for it was smothered in a shout of laughter. I have never been able to figure out what was so funny about my remark, but those grownups stood there and howled with laughter until the tears ran down their faces. Even our good friend Ernie J. laughed as hard as anybody. This was a blow, as he had always seemed to stick with us before; but grown-up humor was hard for us to grasp at that time as usually it did not make much sense. We eventually escaped to our room, where in great embarrassment we pulled on our little nightshirts before a mixed crowd of a dozen persons, and went to bed by the light of two lamps.

To this day merely mentioning the Coon Scare will start the family off into gales of laughter. With the passing of the years the story has gathered color and details along with the cobwebs and dusty flavor of most of our family jokes, though it isn't any funnier to me now than it was the night it happened. Perhaps one has to be on the right side of a family joke to get the most out of it.

3. We Stick Together

THOUGH he was only a little more than two years older than I, Herb took his seniority seriously. He went around with older boys and considered me a mere infant. It was only when he thought there was a possibility of his getting into a fight that he allowed me to go tagging along after him. Herb had a quick temper and a belligerent spirit that often precipitated him into combat. I never personally had very many fights of my own, though I must have taken part in no less than a score of Herb's battles. Whenever he engaged in a fight it was understood that I would hover near by waiting for the battle cry. If he was able to carry on without any help from me he preferred to do it, but when he felt the need for reinforcements his war cry was always the same:

"Jump in, Bill—!" He called me that because it was shorter than Bellamy.

At the sound of his voice I would fly into the conflict like a whirlwind, attacking his opponent in what seemed to me the most vulnerable spot. If the combatants were on their feet slugging I would try to catch the enemy by a leg and trip him up. If they were down and rolling on the ground I would sock his opponent in the face every time it came up. And if it so happened that the other fellow was sitting on Herb's chest I would do all I could to reverse their positions. Usually I would attack from the rear, unhorsing the foe by a sudden on-slaught. This seldom failed of success, but on one memorable occasion it did, with resulting circumstances that might easily have had me in the toils of the law or even brought me into court on a charge of homicide.

Bad blood had existed for some time between Herb, who was then about sixteen, and a much larger boy named Joe Stanley. Joe came from tough antecedents who were much better known for their physical prowess than their intellectual achievements. He was an inveterate fighter given to dirty tactics and was known in school as a hard boy to lick. I never knew the details of Herb's disagreement with him, though I had been sent ahead as a scout on more than one occasion to see if Joe was anywhere around before Herb would venture into a place where Joe was likely to be. It was my unexpressed opinion that Herb was afraid of Joe, though Herb said repeatedly that he wasn't. I did not really believe that even Herb's fiery temper would ever get him into a fight with so wicked an opponent. But I was wrong about that. The fight occurred one Saturday soon after Howe's pond froze over and when we were having the first good skating of the winter.

Joe was not on the ice when we arrived, though most of the other boys were, and the first I knew of his presence there was when I heard the cry of "Fight! Fight!" from the farther end of the pond. I skated to the scene with all speed and arrived just in time to see Herb go down on his back with Joe on top of him.

Herb had a tricky way of rolling an opponent who tried to pin him down; but Joe made no attempt to pin him— he simply began to hammer the living daylights out of him. I shouted encouragement to Herb who was trying to protect his face as well as he could, but he must have

31

been absorbing quite a drubbing, for the moment he heard my voice he called for help.

At his cry, "Jump in, Bill!" I made a ferocious rush at Joe from the rear; but Joe had a long reach and easily held me off with one fist while he belabored Herb with the other. Again Herb shouted, "Jump in, Bill!" and this time his voice sounded so muffled and so beaten as to alarm me. I redoubled my effort to get in some deadly work from behind Joe's back and received several vicious punches myself, enough to convince me that I could never get at him with my fists, and I began to look around for a weapon I could use on him. A short distance away on the ice I saw a sturdy wooden stake some three or four feet long and as thick as my arm. With a few hasty strokes I snatched it up, and returned to the conflict with all speed. Joe did not see me coming, and as I skated up behind him his head made a perfect target. I gripped the stake in both hands and put everything I had into my swing. It struck Joe's head with a sound like a home run—and the fight was over.

Joe collapsed and toppled over on the ice. The speed of my attack had carried me past, and by the time that I could stop myself and turn back he was lying prostrate in a pool of blood, surrounded by a crowd of horrified schoolboys. In the excitement nobody paid any attention to me and I skated slowly over to the bank and took off my skates. I knew without being told that Joe was dead, and it came to me with a numbing remorse that I was the one who had killed him. I hadn't meant to kill him. All I had meant to do was help Herb lick him— and yet, back there on the ice lay his still body with the head bashed in and bloody. I had an uncontrollable urge to get away from that place, and since nobody showed any intention of detaining me I picked up my skates, slung them over my shoulder, and walked away.

32

I don't know why I didn't go straight to my father. Being a lawyer he would no doubt have protected my constitutional rights to the last ditch. It now seems to me that throwing myself on his protection should have been the natural thing to do. But he was one of the people I most wanted to escape from. So instead of heading for his office I started for the railroad yards. Evidently what I craved at the moment was escape rather than protection. I did not have one cent of money in my pocket—I rarely had in those days—but I recalled that there was a freight train which usually went through during the forenoon, and I had a vague idea of hiding in a freight car and being mercifully carried off to some distant point where I could change my name and start life over again without any knowledge on the part of my neighbors that they were harboring a murderer in their midst.

As I walked down the path I met other boys on their way to the pond.

"How's the skating?" they asked.

"Fine."

"Then why don't you stay?"

"Gotta go. Got sump'n else to do."

I had gone halfway to the railroad yards before I realized that the stick slung over my shoulder on which I was carrying my skates was an important piece of evidence against me. For a moment I stopped and considered; then I retraced my steps to the bridge and threw the incriminating evidence into the brawling waters of the creek. On reaching the railroad yards I was dismayed to find that no trains were in sight. I hung around the station until I attracted the attention of Clem Underwood, the station agent, who came out to ask what I was doing there.

"Just hanging around," I said.

"Well, this ain't no place to hang around. Why ain't

you up on the pond skating with the rest of the boys—
I see you got your skates?"

"Been there. The skating's no good."

"Well, the hangin' around's no good neither. Your pa
told me not to let you boys hang around here, and you
better be gettin' along."

"Is that so," I muttered. "Guess I can stay and see the
freight go through if I want to."

Clem cackled with laughter. "The freight *went* through
an hour ago. Won't be another until late this afternoon—" He stopped and looked at me curiously. "What's
the matter with you? Y'ain't sick, be you?"

"No." I started down the tracks. "I'm all right."

"You don't look it."

This made me very nervous; I didn't know quite what
Clem meant. I had often heard my father say that "murder will out," and I now began to wonder if there was
something about the appearance of a murderer that would
give him away. I had never thought about such a thing
before, but I was taking no chances as I went along, and
I avoided people as much as I could, turning my face
away even when they were some distance off. I had to go
somewhere, and in pursuance of the affinity which seems
to exist between the escaping criminal and the railroad
I continued along the tracks. I had no intention of going
home, but just as I was passing our own back lot several
men came out of the coalyard up ahead and started in
my direction. In order to avoid meeting them I turned
in our back gate—and the next thing I knew I was facing my mother in our kitchen.

"What brings you home—?" she was asking in amaze-
ment. "You didn't break through the ice, did you?"

I shook my head. "Why, no—I didn't break through."

She began to look me all over. "But what happened?"

As I stood there before her the voice of conscience kept

34

whispering, "Murder will out! Murder will out!" For a moment I was terribly tempted to tell her the whole truth. All that stopped me was the family. I felt sure she wouldn't blame me unjustly when she understood the circumstances, but I knew how deeply she would feel the disgrace I had brought on the family, and I was afraid she would never live it down. Suddenly I became conscious that I was trembling like a wet dog, and I started to retreat into the passageway where we hung our coats and hats, but she stopped me.

"You're shivering," she said. "You must be having a chill!"

I couldn't keep my teeth from chattering as I assured her that I was as warm as toast.

She laid a hand on my cheek. "Why, you have a raging fever," she said. "I must get you into bed this very minute."

Mother was small, and though she was probably one of the gentlest persons in the world, she was as persistent as the quicksands. Once she made up her mind to do a thing it was almost impossible to stop her. I was not sick. I knew perfectly well I was not sick. I had no desire to go to bed. All I wanted to do was to make my escape and start life over again. But Mother had other plans for me, and as soon as I realized that, I knew that escape was, for the time being, impossible.

I protested feebly, but she dragged me off to my room and got me into bed. The thermometer confirmed her suspicions. She must have read it wrong, for I heard her telling my sister Cecilia that my temperature was up over a hundred, and to go for Dr. Howard right away. Cecilia hurried off but found that Dr. Howard was in the country on an emergency call, and his wife did not know when he would be back. I breathed again. At least I was to have a little respite before the testy old doctor would haul me out of bed and declare that there was nothing the matter with me.

I dreaded facing Father when he came home for our midday dinner. He was a hard man to deceive. I don't know that I ever told him a worth-while lie and made it stick. And when he came into my room and shut the door behind him I felt sure that the bad news had reached him. I was astonished as well as relieved when he sat down beside the bed with a, "Well, young man, Saturday's no day to be under the weather."

This did not fool me at all; I knew that I was in for a cross-examination and must be careful of my answers. "I guess that's right," I said.

Then he began to get down to business. "I thought you went skating."

"I—I did—for a while."

"How was the ice?"

"Fine."

"Why didn't you stay?"

"I—I—I got cold."

"But it isn't very cold today."

I realized at once that I had given the wrong answer and I began to hedge. "Well, anyway I didn't—I didn't feel like skating."

He looked at me with interest. *"You* didn't feel like skating?"

"Not the least bit. I—well, I got tired."

"You got tired of *skating?*" He couldn't believe it—and neither could I. I'd have to do better than this.

"And anyway my skates were dull," I added.

"But only yesterday I gave you ten cents to pay for having them sharpened."

"I know—but—but I guess Ezra didn't do a good job."

He slowly rose and walked to the foot of the bed so

that he could look at me a little more directly. "You didn't get hurt up there?"

"Who—me? No, sir."

"You didn't get a fall and strike your head?"

"No, sir, I didn't fall," I answered quickly.

"Nobody hit you with a shinny stick—or some similar object?"

He was coming closer to the point, but I held my ground. "I didn't play shinny."

"Have any trouble with anybody?"

It wasn't my fight so I answered, "No, sir."

"You just didn't feel like skating—is that it?"

"Guess that's right."

As he stood there stroking his beard and looking at me I heard the door slam and Herb's voice from downstairs asking where I was. Then I heard him come thundering up the stairs. I tried to think of a way to warn him of Father's presence so that he would not blurt out something that would give us away before he discovered that Father was there; but my mind would not work fast enough, and he came barging in the door before I could get out a word. I certainly admired the way he acted when he suddenly saw Father standing there. Such nerve. You wouldn't have known from his manner that anything out of the ordinary had happened to him.

"Hello, Pop," he said casually. "Didn't know you were home. When do we eat?" Then he dropped down on the foot of the bed and looked at me. "What's the matter with you?"

I tried to copy his nonchalant air. "Me? Not much, I guess."

"What'd you come home for?"

"Oh, I didn't feel like skating, I guess."

"Must have changed your mind in a hurry. Say, Pop, you ought to have seen that ice! The whole pond is glary.

37

Smooth as glass. Everybody in town was up there. We won't get such skating as this again all winter."

Father gave me a sympathetic smile. "Too bad Bellamy has to miss it."

Herb straightened up and looked at me. "What's the matter with you anyway?"

"He's running a little temperature," said Father. "Probably caught cold. The doctor will be in to see him later."

Herb squinted up his face. "You mean he's really got a fever?"

"That's what your mother says."

Herb shook his head. "That's funny. He was having as good a time as anybody up there—and the first thing I knew he was gone."

I looked at Herb with admiration. One never would have thought that he had just been involved in a killing. He was so calm, so unperturbed. I wondered if he would walk through the big iron gate with a smile, while I came after him cringing and crawling in terror. The dinner bell rang and Father started downstairs after assuring me that Mother would send up something for me. "Don't lag, Herb," he said as he went out the door, "and don't forget to wash your hands."

Herb listened at the door until he was sure Father was out of earshot, and then turned to me and said, "Joe never knew what hit him!"

He needn't have told me that. I knew it from the first. "What are we going to do now?" I asked.

"Do? What do you mean?"

"About Joe. Everybody must know who—"

"Everybody knows that Joe's got a beaut of a black eye! Boy, it's puffed up like a baked apple! You must have hit him an awful sock. He was unconscious for fifteen minutes. The boys had to throw water on him to

38

bring him out of it. And what do you think—Joe had the crazy notion that *I* did it and, when he came to, the first thing he did was to shake hands with me—he wanted to be friends. So we shook on it, and then we went down to the market together to get a piece of raw beef for his eye."

By this time I was out of bed and getting dressed. Having escaped a murderer's cell, all that I could think of was that I was missing the best skating of the year. Mother caught me at the bottom of the stairs and put me right back in bed in spite of my earnest appeals and protestations. It meant nothing to her that the thermometer now showed my temperature to be normal. She thought I was still slightly giddy from my attack in the morning, and she sat beside my bed all the rest of the day before the doctor came and pronounced me out of danger.

I couldn't explain the real situation to her, for she was fundamentally opposed to our fighting, especially with boys who lived on the questionable side of the tracks. She had no ambition to make us into Rollo Boys. All she wanted, as she used to assure us, was to have us behave like little gentlemen at all times, proud enough to stand up for the right, but too proud to fight. She actually believed that a boy should follow the teachings of the Bible and turn the other cheek. I tried it once, but it did not work. Father's attitude was quite the contrary. He thought that a good fight never did a boy any harm no matter who his opponent was, and he was always suspicious that the little gentlemen who were too proud to fight were very likely to be lacking in the long and complicated tangle of digestive organs supposed to occupy the abdominal cavity. If I had told Mother the truth about the fight with Joe Stanley she would have confined both Herb and me on the premises during all our spare time for at least a week.

39

There were other occasions when I responded to Herb's call for help, many of them. Sometimes we won, and sometimes we didn't. And I never had to call for help if Herb saw that I was getting the worst of it in any of the personal encounters I conducted in my own behalf. In fact, so confirmed a battler was he that he could hardly stay out of my fights long enough to let me show what I could do by myself.

4. Younger Son

FATHER was a systematic man. Given an opportunity he would reduce to a system almost anything that was likely to be repeated. He even systematized the business of becoming a father. Captain Jenks, who was one of his oldest friends, told me of going into Father's office the day after I was born and finding on the desk just inside the door an open box of cigars on which was a hand-printed sign:

IT'S A BOY!
TAKE ONE

This must have been a great timesaver, for it prevented endless palaver over congratulations, and removed the need for the witticisms which every man feels called upon to produce whenever another man announces that he is a father—and still more so when the announcement happens to be that he is *again* a father.

The Captain regarded it as just a little humorous incident, but it touched me on a tender spot, for I was, when he told me about it, pretty well fed up with being quite so much of a younger son as I had turned out to be. In a family the size of ours the younger members were kept strictly in their place. The general attitude towards them was somewhat the same as the attitude of a college towards the Freshmen. It is no doubt true that children must be kept well in hand if they are not to become un-

41

bearable; but with so many bossing me around I began to feel at a very early age that the lot of a younger son was decidedly no bed of roses.

The disadvantages of being a younger son are not so apparent during infancy as they afterward become. The fact is that so long as you are "the baby" you are to a certain extent important. It is after there has been a still later announcement at the breakfast table, and you learn that you have been superseded as the youngest child, that your troubles really start. From that time on you become subject to the seniority rule. Instead of being first, you have to await your turn, which means being last, and which was in my case a fairly long and dull interval. Of course, if you live you do eventually work your way to the head of the line, but by that time you will be eighteen or nineteen years old.

Practically all the toys I ever had were hand-me-downs. According to the records I was destructive when small, so few toys of any intrinsic worth ever came to me. I was also inventive, so was encouraged to make my own toys. One item of which I was particularly fond was the game of marbles, and though I tried for years I never succeeded in making a marble worthy of the name. All my early marbles were cast-offs from the older boys, and they were without exception defective. Some were oval, some oblate, a few elliptical, and practically all were lopsided. Not one was round; not one would roll in a true line. When I started a marble across the floor it would reel like a tipsy sailor. For some time I did not know that marbles were supposed to be round. I thought it was part of the game to have them crooked so their course would be unpredictable. Then one day I got hold of an agate that had formerly been Thad's—and the entire picture changed. Here was something I had never seen before, a

42

marble that was a true sphere, a marble that would roll as straight as a chalk line.

This particular marble happened to be a real moss agate. It was the only one Thad had ever possessed and had been very highly prized by him. Uncle Selden had brought it to him from abroad, and it was said to have cost a dollar. A dollar! My marbles came ten for a cent, and even at that were thoroughly culled before I got them.

I took the agate to Mother and asked if I could have one like it. She explained that such marbles could not be bought any more, and that Thad had very generously given it to Herb. When Herb had become too old to play marbles, she said, the moss agate would be handed down to me.

That should have been enough to satisfy anybody. Herb would probably not keep on playing marbles for more than four or five years longer, and then the moss agate would become my property until I was old enough to pass it on to Stan. It was that entailed moss agate which opened my eyes and brought me to the conclusion that if I had it to do over again I would prefer to be born at or near the top of the list.

To this day I always have a fellow feeling for a younger son. I have sounded out a great many of them and never yet have I found one who sooner or later has not told me of the hard going he had in his youth, and how the older children stood in his way. One of the most put-upon younger sons I ever knew was a big strapping fellow named Tom Bryson, who was the last child born in a family of seven sons. The Brysons lived over near the Wayne County line. They had a large farm, though a rather poor one, and being an unsocial lot they made few friends. None of the boys ever married, and none of them left home. It was a common saying in the neigh-

43

borhood that all seven of them were needed to make a living for one family from that farm. Old John, the father, though he never was known to do anything for the sake of appearances during his lifetime, showed in his old age a desire to make a good impression on posterity when he bought what he described to Father as one of the most desirable lots in the town cemetery, and erected a monument on it.

As it turned out he was not any too quick about it, for hardly had the monument been finished before Bryson remains began to take possession of the lot. Old John himself was the first to move in, followed in less than a year by his wife. In due time the sons began to follow, and three of them had been buried there before the surviving four discovered that there was room left on the lot for only three more interments, thus indicating that one of the family would have to be buried apart from the rest, since the lot was located in a populous part of the cemetery where additional land was not available.

Young Tom, as they called him, then a man in his forties, had proposed that since there were four of them left they might buy another lot that was for sale only a few hundred feet away, and start an annex there where the rest of them could be buried together. But the older brothers refused. They could see no point in a second lot and a second monument, being thrifty Scots, and they were content to take their chances on being the last.

"But what's going to happen to me," Young Tom had insisted, "supposing I outlive you all, as you seem to expect?"

"You can cross that bridge when you come to it," they said. "You know how uncertain life is—you may not be the last."

That was all the satisfaction they would give him. What

business had a younger son to be offering proposals anyway?

One by one Young Tom had seen them go, none of them, as he told Father, in a particular hurry about being off, and still somehow a little reconciled to the going by the fact that each was sure of a place in the family lot. Young Tom was in his sixties when Jeff, the last of his brothers, died.

"I was born with two strikes against me," he told my father. "In all my life I've never made an important decision. I've been cuffed around by all six of my brothers and done as I was told to do. Now there's nobody left to tell me—and I want to know my rights."

"Do you happen to know whether Jeff left a will?" Father asked.

"He told me that he had never made one. He could see no reason for the expense."

"Then you're free to do exactly as you wish."

Young Tom slowly nodded his head. "There's naught in the law to compel me to fulfill any expectations that my older brother may have had?"

"The expectations of the dead are not legally binding upon the living," said Father with a slight emphasis on the legal angle.

"I offered them a fair solution, but they would not hear of it. They preferred to take their chances, and left me to cross the bridge when I came to it." Young Tom rose and pulled on his hat with a determined air. "Well, I've come to the bridge, and since there's nobody left to tell me what to do I'm going to decide matters to please myself. Jeff took his chance same as the others, and those who take chances have got to be ready to lose. He's going to be buried with his mother's folks in Pinewood Cemetery, and not with his father's folks under the Bryson monument."

45

With a family of children, as with a regiment of soldiers, there can be no order and very little effectiveness without discipline. The first words I ever learned were "do" and "don't." And not long after I had mastered these two key words I learned that if I would wait, my "turn" would come. This was important, for in our family one's turn was almost as sacred as one's honor. Never was a union member more secure in his seniority rights than the members of our family. The oldest always came first. They were served first, heard first, considered first, and the rest of us came tagging along afterward in the order of age. If an older child went off to school or college we younger ones felt the pinch all the way down to the babe in arms. When Thad joined a fraternity Louise had to make her party slippers do for another season, Elsie couldn't have her muff and tippet done over, Cecilia's new winter coat was lined with sateen instead of silk, and I didn't get Herb's Barney & Berry skates handed down to me because he couldn't raise enough to buy the new Peck & Snyders.

With this preferential army lined up ahead of us younger ones there were times when we felt as if we had been born with two strikes on us. I still recall how I used to look up the table at a Thanksgiving turkey and count the number who must be served ahead of me. It was not so much a matter of choice as it was something to eat; down there in the lower brackets we took whatever was given us and were glad to get it. I make no pretense of being the legendary martyr who thought a turkey was all neck—though I might as well have been, for I was the victim of a curious family tradition that I *preferred* the neck.

"Father, be sure to save the neck for Bellamy," someone would say as he began to carve.

"That's right," somebody else would chime in, "Bellamy always wants the neck."

Guests were usually interested. "You mean that he prefers it?" they would ask.

By this time I would be glowing with importance. "It's the only part of a turkey worth eating," I would declare.

Since such opportunities to step out of the herd were rare I seized upon them and willingly paid the price. As I grew older, however, and found other ways of attracting attention I would gladly have surrendered my preferential claim to some younger member of the family. In fact, I tried to make a deal with Stan, but he was not interested.

It is very probable that both Father and Mother would have been astonished had they ever discovered my private and personal reactions to the working of their vaunted seniority rule. They were so sure they were right, Father with whole libraries of legal decisions behind him, and Mother with the authority of the Old Testament and her own bringing up to fall back on. There were rarely any exceptions to the rule. Father was against exceptions on principle; he thought they weakened the structure of any rule. And as long as this was the law of the house he was for enforcing it down to the last iota. It touched every phase of our life and liberty, big or little, and was so thoroughly inculcated in us that we seldom protested and never rebelled against it. We accepted this rule very much as the camel accepted the law of gravity, and while it never broke anybody's back with a straw it has left me feeling slightly bent and rebellious through the years over a trifle of no more importance than a piece of pie.

We seldom had round pies in our family. I don't recall that we ever had any round ones until after several of the older children had left home, and the family was reduced in size. These old square-cornered pans must have measured about nine inches one way by eighteen the other. Two of them standing side by side would exactly fill one level of the oven. Each pie would cut into twelve rectangu-

47

lar pieces with a base of three inches and a length of four and a half. Of course the corner cuts would have crust on two sides, which created a great demand for them. Naturally since the older children had the first choice of these corner pieces I seldom tasted one.

Now the older children could have their pick of the seats in church without a murmur from me; they could come first in the matter of clothes and education and music lessons without any objection on my part; but just because they happened to be born before I was never satisfied me as a sound reason why they should invariably get the corner cuts of pie. The customary argument that my turn would come later on was in this case a disappointing solution; for when I reached the age when I would have been entitled to a corner cut as a matter of household law, they had stopped making the square-cornered pies on the ground that with our reduced family the large tins were more than we could handle.

For a number of years Stan and I planned that when we grew up we would form a tin-plate company to put out a square pie tin just large enough to cut into four pieces, all of them with a double crust. We thought there was a fortune in the idea—and perhaps there still is.

5. The Little Brown Derby

ONE meal would do for all of us, one roof would cover our heads, but when it came to clothing the family Mother had to deal with individual needs. As a child I never was conscious of any great household strain in keeping the larder filled. With barrels of apples and bins of potatoes and other vegetables around it never occurred to me that such things might be hard to obtain. I realized that nothing was ever wasted; the campaign against extravagance and waste was waged so consistently and so vigorously that I could not help being conscious of it. Not even the crust of a piece of toast could be left on one's plate without hearing from it. And it was the same way with wearing apparel. After a garment had been used and re-used and cut down and remodeled and turned and mended and darned and converted, its original identity was lost entirely; and when it positively could not be made over into anything else to wear, the better pieces were put into patchwork and the rest cut into long strips for rag rugs and carpets. The old-clothes man never stopped at our house—unless he had something to sell.

When Father bought a new pair of trousers they were invariably good ones. They had to be to go through the routine expected of them. Father always felt that in his profession he must be well dressed, so his pants were usually in good condition when they were handed down for the first remake. This might be in the form of long pants. On the next remake they would be shortened for Herb. By the time they reached me, about the only original parts left would be the pockets. A pair of Father's pants seldom lasted long enough to be handed down to Stan or Leslie, who almost entirely escaped the curse of the hand-me-down though they certainly did miss some capacious man-size pockets.

The clothing of every reasonably thrifty family in town was handled in the same way—thrift being respectable at that time—though very few of them had as good pants to start with as we did, for Father was really very particular about his.

On the distaff side the same custom prevailed, Mother's clothes being made over for the girls, sometimes after turning or dyeing, and sometimes without making any effort to conceal the identity of the original material. And sometimes it was exciting to see one of Mother's sedate go-to-meeting gowns turned quite unexpectedly into a brilliant evening dress for one of my sisters.

With the exception of coats and wraps, ready-to-wear clothes for women and misses were not considered to be very good style in the social circles in which my mother and sisters moved. Nor would my father so much as look at a ready-made suit. He would stand for hours in a tailor's shop being measured and pinned and basted when he would not have accepted as a gift the most perfect store suit in the world. On the other hand he would buy a hat without ever looking at himself in the mirror. "I'll never see myself wearing it, so why should I care how it looks?" he used to say. He would examine the hat carefully, and would fit it to his head entirely by feeling, and then he would pay for it and walk off with it.

We boys shared none of this hostility towards store clothes. We were thrilled by them. And while Mother was a little offish about women's wear at first and felt that it was bordering on the "common" to wear clothes that were made in a factory by a lot of workmen, she found in the end that they were so satisfactory and so convenient that she was quite won over to them.

Mother's spring and fall shopping trips to Rochester had some of the flavor of a buyer's visit to the wholesale district. Complete outfits for five boys, underwear, shirts, suits, overcoats, hats, stockings, and a certain amount of haberdashery. For the girls the outfits were not so complete—underwear (girls wore it in those days), corsets or corset waists, bustles, coats and hats, though the local milliner was used for the more mature headgear, and a wide selection of yardage of all sorts for lingerie, petticoats, and dresses. I do not mention lounging clothes, for I don't seem to remember such a thing. Of course Father had his housecoat and Mother had her wrapper and a garment she used to call a "tea gown." But there was no lounging, as such, in our family. Father hated the word and seldom used it except as an epithet. Thrift and industry were fairly rubbed into us. Keeping everlastingly at it was almost as important as saying your prayers before going to bed. No lounging clothes, no sport clothes—and stranger still no work clothes. Work had at that time not been glorified to the extent of having clothes designed especially for it. There was plenty of work done, but it was done in old clothes that were no longer fit for anything else.

Shoes were handled in a different way. Because of the importance of proper fitting all our footgear (except party slippers for the girls) were bought from the local dealer. Mother would spend half an afternoon there going over the various shapes and styles, and then after school we children would come trooping in to be fitted. If it happened to be fall we boys each got shoes, overshoes, and rubber boots; and the girls got school shoes, house shoes, and galoshes.

Purchases in the spring would be correspondingly lighter with fewer exigencies of the weather to be met. But in either spring or fall our semi-annual visits to the shoe store never failed to overwhelm the proprietor, who was used to having only one customer at a time; and after the last child had left his place, carrying a large package of course, the old gentleman usually locked up and went home for a rest.

Where Father found the money to pay for all these things is a mystery. His only income was that derived from his law practice, and Mother had no separate property of her own. I did not know it at the time, but I have since learned from the papers and records I found in his office that there were times when he was deeply in debt and very hard-pressed. For years the house was mortgaged, and the rising or lowering of the amount of that mortgage furnished a reasonably accurate barometer of his financial situation. Always during the periods of national depression he found himself skating on very thin ice, and then was when Mother's thrift and good management counted the most. As I look back I realize that there were times when clothes were cut down and made over time and again until the material disintegrated and fell to pieces. Until I was in my teens there seldom was a time when my everyday clothes were not patched. The patches were not very conspicuous, and I never was given the idea that they were there because of financial embarrassment of the family. I was told that I was so hard on my clothes that it really was not worth while to get me new ones except for "very best"—which meant primarily for church.

Mother must have had a very accurate idea of the size and shape of each of us, for she very seldom had to exchange any of the clothes she bought for us on her shopping trips to the city. It is very probable that some of the things she bought for one child were found to be better suited or better fitted for another, but her ability to pick the right size was uncanny. And she seemed to know what we wanted, for we were usually pleased with her choice of a pattern or a style. Once I was not, and though I protested vociferously she refused to make a change. That was the time when she brought home from her spring buying trip a new Easter hat for me in the shape of a little brown derby.

Even while they were getting off the train on this occasion I noticed the bandbox and asked what was in it. Mother gave me a persuasive smile.

"Something that's going to please you very much."

"Me?" I looked at the bandbox with a scowl. "It isn't for *me*, is it?"

"Indeed it is."

"But what is it?" I asked, suspicious on principle of anything that came in a bandbox.

She did not answer, but soon after we reached home I began picking at the tapes to untie them.

"Is this thing a hat?" I asked.

"Yes, dear, it is a hat—the very latest style for boys of your age. The clerk in the store told me that every boy in Rochester is teasing for one."

As the cover came off I let out a groan. "Why, it's nuthin' but a brown derby hat!" I wouldn't even take it out of the box.

Mother lifted it out and told me to try it on. I sniffed and snorted and growled with disgust, but she insisted and firmly put the little brown derby on my head. I hoped against hope that it wouldn't fit—but it did, perfectly. My two younger brothers, Stan and Leslie, screamed with delight. They treated the affair as strictly a comedy act. But to me it was not comedy, it was tragedy of the bitterest sort. That thing was my new Easter hat, and I had a strange

53

presentiment that nothing short of an unheaval of Nature itself would save me from wearing it to church.

The older children also started in to guy me, but Mother put the soft pedal on them, and a little later Herb, who had been with her when she bought the monstrosity, came around and tried in private to ease my mind.

"The hat's all right, kid," he said. "Makes you look more grown up."

I didn't want to look grown up, I wanted to look like the other boys. "If they're so nice why didn't you get one for yourself?" I growled.

"Would if I could. They didn't have my size."

"I won't wear the darn thing."

"Sure you will. You want to show the rest of the kids the latest style, don't you?"

"What do I care about style? I'll wear my old cap."

He shook his head. "Not with your new clothes and new shoes."

"But I *will!*"

"Mother wouldn't let you do that. The hat's all right, kid. You're lucky to have it."

The importance of having new clothes to wear to church on Easter Sunday can hardly be overstated. The winters were long and severe to people so shut in by lack of transportation, and with few amusements not furnished by themselves. Winter clothing received hard wear, and by Palm Sunday would be looking quite shabby and threadbare. Then with the dullness of Lent and the gloom of Good Friday past, the urge to join in the joyousness of the Easter services and the burgeoning of spring by putting on new finery became almost a primary instinct, and there would be scarcely a person in church who did not have on something new.

As the church bell began to ring on Sunday morning and the family gathered, as was our custom, in our library for the final inspection before starting our procession for church we were a gay-looking crowd. The three girls had on whole new outfits so far as could be seen, for there must have been some hand-downs underneath. Mother looked very handsome in a new bonnet covered with violets. Father in his high hat was wearing new striped trousers and had a bright red geranium in his buttonhole. We boys all had new suits or coats, and all except me had new hats. I was carrying my old cap, but holding it behind me as Father ran his eyes down the line.

"What are you holding behind you?" he asked.

"Just my cap."

"But, Bellamy, you can't wear that!" said Mother. She turned to Father. "It's his old one, and it's a disgrace. I bought him a new hat, and he doesn't like it."

Father did not even look at the cap. He had his eyes on his watch which he was holding in his hand to clock us out of the house at the proper moment. There was no time for an argument. "Get your new hat, son, and put it on."

"But, Father—"

"No time for protests. Get the new hat. We're starting right now."

Stan and Leslie, while not daring to be hilarious, were delighted over my predicament and kept making little noises well understood by me to be indicative of their glee. The older children said nothing, but I could tell by the rolling of their eyes that they were very much amused. All this struck me as an ominous indication. If that little brown derby could create such a commotion in my own family what would it not do among the boys of the neighborhood? I began to receive my answer before I had gone very far on my way to church.

A young gentleman of my own age came out of the Humphrey house on the further side of the street. I pretended not to see him, but all the time I was watching him out of the corner of my eyes. First he gave a sort of donkey laugh with his head thrown back and wobbling. Then he pointed a finger at my hat and touched his own.

A little further on the two Bidwell boys came out of their yard. When they saw my hat they nudged each other, and even though it was Sunday they began to whistle softly *Where Did You Get That Hat?*

On the grassplot in front of the church were the Crosby boys, the Peckhams, and one or two others. I did not look their way at all, but as we passed they scuffed their feet or cleared their throats, or made some other sign indicative of derision. We took our accustomed seats in Pews 61 and 62, and all through the service I sat looking at that little brown derby and trying to think of the most effective way to get rid of it without arousing suspicion. I could think of plenty of delightful ways of destroying it, but not one that was likely to convince the family that it had been done without any cooperation on my part.

Usually I was one of the first persons to get out of church after the service was over. But on this bright Easter Day I was in no hurry, for I thought that if I could just manage to hang around in the vestibule until Sunday School was ready to begin I would not have to put on the little brown derby which seemed much less conspicuous if held in my hand. I carried the hat loosely as I moved along the crowded aisle, hoping optimistically that somebody might knock it out of my hand and step on it, or that the crowd would somehow become unmanageable enough to smash it. But this, alas, was not to be, and almost before I knew it the people ahead had reached the vestibule and the crowd was beginning to leave the church.

I stepped aside into a quiet corner of the vestibule to let the mass of humanity pass me by, which it was doing in a very satisfactory manner with a hum of voices and a

haze of indistinct faces . . . until suddenly out of the
haze the visage of young Mr. Humphrey began to mate-
rialize. As it caught sight of me a grotesque leer broke

over it. The eyes glistened with anticipation, the lips
parted in a jack-o'-lantern grin. Then came the fateful
words. They were uttered in scarcely more than a whisper,
and had gone no further than "Where did you get—"
when, without any volition on my part, my fist landed
squarely in the middle of that grin.

The force, or perhaps it was only the suddenness of the blow, knocked young Mr. Humphrey over, but he was quickly up and at me with a muffled cry of pain and rage. He did not succeed in reaching me, however, for at that point Benson, the usher, stepped between us. He caught young Mr. Humphrey by the coat collar with one hand and me by the shoulder with the other. With what seemed like a single motion he yanked Mr. Humphrey back into the church and shoved me most emphatically out of the front door and into the midst of the cluster of boys who stood there waiting for me. If he had thrown me into a pack of ravening wolves he could not have aroused a quicker reaction.

I had not yet regained my equilibrium when I crashed into the younger of the two Bidwell boys. At the sight of me his eyes lighted and he puckered up his lips to whistle. But he never finished that tune. He never even started it, for I landed a hard blow on the spot that was intended as the source of the whistle at the exact instant when his brother knocked the little brown derby out of my hand. Rube Peckham snatched it up and put it on, but before I could even reach him half a dozen other boys were trying to knock it off—quite successfully as it turned out. In no time at all the place was a riot, with small boys clawing, and slugging, and pulling, and kicking, and all of them yelling and screaming at the top of their voices. It was too confusing for any participant to know all that was going on. Herb didn't get into it. He had stopped in church to speak to some girl, and by the time he had heard the noise and come rushing out the battle was over and the casualties were being led off by indignant parents who brushed at the torn and rumpled clothes as they muttered rebukes and maledictions quite out of keeping with the festival of the Resurrection.

As Herb came running out Father had me by the

58

shoulder, but it was more to support me than to restrain me. The fight was all out of me. My new clothes were in ribbons, and I was holding in my hand all that remained of the little brown derby—and it was not very much. The brim was dangling like a wreath, and a large hole had been punched through the crown.

"What happened?" asked Herb excitedly. "Who you been fighting with?"

"Never mind about that now," said Father. "We'll talk it all over later. The important thing is to get you where Mother won't see you in this condition. Better go right home and change your clothes—and wash the blood and the dirt off from your hands and face." He turned to Herb. "You'll be late for Sunday School if you don't go in at once."

Mother, ordinarily the most calm and placid member of the family, had heard the news and came home from church in a state of mind fit to start a jehad. Nothing would arouse and upset her like an act of irreverence or disrespect of the Church of God. And to have one of her boys start a fight—in church—on Easter Sunday was almost more than she personally could bear or the honor of the family could survive. In her humiliation and distress, she declared acidly that she was going to send to Rochester for another brown derby exactly like the one that had caused the row, and that as part of my penance I was to wear it to school as well as to church.

The hat angle did not interest Grandmother at all. She was determined that I should be made to get up in church and apologize to the pastor and the congregation, after which I was to offer a public prayer in which I should ask the Lord's forgiveness and future guidance. She also insisted that as a further punishment I should be compelled to read a chapter in the Bible every day for the next year.

On second thought she felt that a chapter a day on week-days and two on Sundays would be better.

Father had sat in silence during the discussion, and when they asked him what he thought about the matter he said he thought it was time for me to be excused. After I had left the room he turned on Grandmother and disposed of her in short order. He said that to use the reading of the Bible as a punishment was to put the Word of God on a par with a dose of castor oil. He then smiled at Mother and remarked that the other angles of the case were of too personal a nature to be discussed in the presence of a third person.

I never heard anything more about a second little brown derby, for Father was strong in his belief that a boy should never be made to feel ridiculous in the eyes of his fellows. He explained long afterwards that he would never have ordered me to wear the hat in the first place if he had realized what kind it was. Another time Father came to our rescue when Mother tried to get us into kid gloves ahead of the other boys. "If anybody's going to be called a sissy around this neighborhood," he said, "I want our boys on the side that's doing the calling."

6. Our Germs and Epidemics

GERMS, like the weather, have no doubt changed since the good old days. I have only the faintest recollection of our ever having colds in the family. Father used to have an extraordinary cough every winter, but it was regarded as an heirloom. Both his father and his mother were bronchial, and his uncle, Judge Selden, had gone to Switzerland for a tracheotomy, after which he had installed in his throat a silver-tubed ventilator that moaned in the night like a navigator's whistling buoy. We had no interesting throats among the children, and our good health was habitual; if anybody brought home an epidemic, however, we were in for trouble.

Stan was born into an epidemic of measles. All the rest of us had it in one stage or another, and Stan broke out when he was two weeks old. We had mumps in the house when Herb was born, and he was under suspicion of having the disease for two or three months, for with his fat cheeks and his continuous bawling the doctor could not be sure whether he was dealing with mumps or grumps. Indeed, the uncertainty lasted for fourteen years before Herb came down with a case of mumps that rounded him out like a toy balloon.

Chicken pox swept over our family in a tidal wave. Not only did the children come down, but the hired girl and even the cat and the dog. Towards the end of the siege

61

Father thought that even the chickens were catching it, but their trouble turned out to be the roup. Mother had Gra Richardson in to help her, but even with two in attendance they found the problem of caring for us in private rooms altogether too much of a strain for them. The nursing, meals, and entertainment at such widely separated points finally beat them down, and they transferred us to cots in a temporary ward established in the parlor, where we could all be handled if need be by a single attendant.

Diphtheria and smallpox, though common in the town at various times, somehow managed to elude us. And scarlet fever, though it went slowly through the family, never flattened more than one or two of us a season. With whooping cough we were all involved at the same time. The disease—or perhaps it is only a form of nervous self-expression—began with the baby and worked its way up through the older children. Just how it leaped from the baby to Stan nobody seemed to know. They isolated the baby as soon as his bark was identified as a whoop, but a day or two later Stan had begun to make the same noise. Not long afterwards I joined them to make it a trio, and a week later when Herb came in we had a very creditable quartette. We were like hounds; if one gave a whoop the others were almost certain to begin. For a little while the girls seemed to be cough-repellent, and Mother was hoping that they might be immune; but one night after a fit of laughter Cecilia began to cough, and eventually ended with what was quite definitely a whoop. The other girls poked fun at her for catching a juvenile disease, but within a very short time they both had it themselves, and the family chorus was complete.

At first our coughing was entirely without organization. There was too much individual solo work and too little team play. But one day when Father started to admonish Herb for some misbehavior at dinner, Herb went into a violent coughing spell which robbed the admonition of much of its beneficial effect, and when suddenly Stan came in with a series of orotund whoops Father's guns were silenced entirely. This little experience brought home to us the fact that in union there is strength, and from that moment, so long as the malady lingered on, we coughed down anything and everything that we did not care to hear. Apologizing profusely, of course, but bursting into another paroxysm every time the speaker tried to resume.

Mother took the situation calmly. If she was skeptical about what was going on she never said so. Father was not so easy to trick. He suspected us from the first volley. His face would flush with anger every time we did it, and still he was helpless to stop us. There was no doubt that we all had the whooping cough, and if it so happened that several of us were seized with the impulse to cough at the same time—it was regrettable, unfortunate, too bad, but just what could he do about it?

It was at family prayers on Sunday morning when the big idea really came to us. These household devotions began with a selection from the Bible read by Father. He always went about it with the air of a man who is doing something that he did not wish to be doing, but he carried on just the same week after week, year after year. The reading was followed by verses from the Bible recited by those present, beginning with Grandmother and going down the line according to age.

We all disliked learning verses, but nobody disliked it any more than Thad. He hunted out short ones, meaningless ones, strange ones; we were always on the alert to see what he would recite. On this particular day Grandmother had given her verse. Mother came next, then Thad. He said only a word or two, which did not sound like any verse I ever heard, and then suddenly began to cough. Spasms and paroxysms shook his frame, and whoops that any Indian might have envied reverberated through the quiet room. Father finally waved him aside and called on Louise. It is probable that Louise knew more verses than any of us. She could, if so disposed, reel them off by the dozen. But this time she stumbled for a few words, and then went into a cough. Thad was still struggling to quiet himself, with only a random bark now and then, so Father would understand that he had not entirely recovered his powers of speech. For some time after Louise began coughing Father watched her closely out of the corner of his eye. He was evidently suspicious of the performance, but he controlled himself and after giving her a reasonable time in which to subdue her cough he waved her angrily aside and called on Elsie.

Elsie put on a very convincing act. She got well into her verse before the coughing began, and even after it started she seemed to be struggling valiantly to continue—but eventually the cough got away from her and she began to bay like a hound.

Cecilia didn't even start a verse. The moment Father waved Elsie aside and nodded to Cecilia to go ahead, she launched right into her cough. Instead of further irritating Father this led him to believe that a hysterical nervousness had come over them all. One nod at Herb was enough to confirm the hypothesis, for Herb responded with a sort of trombone blast that had been his specialty from the beginning of the siege. Father looked hopefully at me. I had not been afflicted with as violent a cough as the others—just why, I never understood, for I certainly tried hard enough. But this time I was ready for my cue, and I responded with a hearty salvo. Stan didn't even wait for Father to look at him. As soon as he heard my voice he let loose with everything he had, and little Leslie was not far behind.

64

Father finally raised his voice above the tumult. "We'll dispense with the verses for today," he said, but it was easy to see that he was irritated and annoyed.

Gradually the coughing subsided, and finally stopped entirely. We all went down on our knees while Father offered a rather wooden prayer, at the conclusion of which we dispersed. I did not know about it until afterwards, but Thad and the three girls put their heads together and decided that it looked like a wonderful opportunity for all of us to stay home from church, if properly handled. Louise was to bring up the matter casually, as if it had not been previously discussed, and then Thad was to come in and carry on from there. Roughly the argument was to be that with our throats in such a touchy condition it was an imposition on other worshipers for us to make even an attempt to sit all through the service without having a coughing spell. They put up what they considered a very competent presentation of their position—but met with a cold rebuff.

It was highly unlikely, said Father in what almost amounted to a threatening manner, that we would have another such severe attack that day. And cough or no cough the children were going to church. Naturally the discussion was carried no further, but future events proved quite conclusively that Father's prognostication was very wide of the mark.

There was hardly any coughing at all while we were getting on our wraps and being marshaled into line for the procession to church. And I don't believe there was a single cough while we were on the way. We went solemnly down the center aisle of the church without a bark and took our places in our two family pews near the center of the auditorium. The organ played softly and dreamily to cover the slight confusion caused by the entrance of so many worshipers at the same time, but at last the people seemed to be seated and the organist brought her prelude to an end. For a quiet moment nothing happened. Then the pastor, good old Dr. Portman, rose from his chair and advanced to the pulpit, where he stood for a time with hands upraised and far apart. After what he considered the proper interval he began his service as he always began it:

"The Lord is in His holy temple: let all the earth keep silence before Him."

At just that moment Stan began to cough. There was nothing prearranged about it. He said afterwards that a tickle came in his throat and he couldn't help it to begin with. Stan's cough was not unlike the sound of a machine gun, with the shots coming very close together until he had reached enough of a crescendo for a whoop. It was not by any means an ordinary cough; it would attract attention anywhere, and on this occasion it did. It attracted Dr. Portman's attention at once, and he looked to see where it was coming from. When the people in front of us saw the good doctor looking, they turned to look, too. And when Stan saw them looking he was enough of a showman not to disappoint them, and he began to put a few little flourishes into his coughing. I think Herb must have recognized the difference, and being an artistic cougher himself he let out a few of his trombone blasts.

Dr. Portman lowered his hands to the pulpit and gripped the edges of it as he waited for quiet to be restored. The organist who had been waiting for the announcement of the hymn, rose up on her bench and craned her neck to see what was going on. And all the worshipers in the front of the church who had not already turned around now did so—and at just that moment Elsie became very red in the face, clapped her handkerchief over her mouth, and began her cough with its characteristic baying sound.

By this time Father was scowling like a thundercloud and Mother was digging in her bag for a cough drop. Suddenly Thad began to fumble in his pocket for his handkerchief, and in another second or two he had gone into action. I could have waited longer, but this was good enough for me, and I opened up and joined the chorus with a will. I can't say just when the other girls came in, but they did. Whether it was before or after Dr. Portman signaled to the organist I can't be sure; but I saw him motion to her with his hand and nod his head, and she, sensing a disagreeable incident, pulled out the stops and let the organ roar.

Under cover of the barrage of sound Father rose from his seat and stepped into the aisle. He turned to us, held out one hand as if to include us all in it, and made one sweeping, violent gesture towards the vestibule. We instantly took the hint, and covering our faces with handkerchiefs or hats, we bowed our heads and tiptoed rapidly out of the church. We were nearly convulsed with laughter before we could get the doors closed behind us.

Mother was still flushed and scolding when she came home an hour and a half later. She was "mortified to death" and couldn't imagine what had ever come over us to let ourselves get started like that in the House of the Lord. Father was a little more reticent. He left us all in doubt—unpleasantly in doubt—as to what his reactions were so far as our performance was concerned. But he left no doubt at all about the fact that he had enjoyed for the first time in many years the sensation of sitting in our pew with Mother alone. Such a thing had not happened in so long, he said, that he did not know it was possible.

The next Sunday Father left it to the discretion of each of us whether to go to church or not. To my astonishment the two younger girls went. The rest of us did not. And verses were dispensed with at family prayers on Sunday morning. But soon after this the weather had turned warm, and with the change our coughs began to wear themselves out.

The next casualty in the household came when Herb was carried home on a shutter with an injured foot. Mother was afraid of a broken bone when she saw it, for his ankle was so swollen that she could hardly get off his shoe. She sent for the doctor, who pronounced it a bad sprain and wrapped it with a rubber bandage about fifteen feet long. That rubber bandage fascinated me, but not half as much as the pair of crutches that the doctor left there the next time he went past the house. Herb attracted a great deal of attention when he went out of the house on crutches. School was too far away for him to go, but he used to hobble to the neighbors', who gave him cake and candy and fruit; and whenever I was anywhere around he kept me busy waiting on him. Mother saw me one day making a pattern of Herb's crutches and asked me why I was doing it. I said they were good crutches and you never could tell when we might need another pair. This proved to be both premonition and prophecy.

I made the new crutches to my own measure and put them in the back of the dark closet for safekeeping. Strange as it may seem, it was on the very day that I finished them that I went over to the coalyard where Herb had sprained his ankle and became involved in a game of tag. There was one shed a little higher than the rest, from the roof of which nobody had ever dared to jump. If a boy was cornered on that particular roof, he just gave up and got caught. It was almost fatalistic, the way I found myself cornered there soon after the game started; but to the astonishment of everybody I did not give up. Instead I ran to the edge, wavered a moment, and took a flying leap for the ground. I landed on my feet, but immediately collapsed and began to moan. When the other boys came running up I gasped out that I was in terrible pain and thought I had broken my leg. They carried me home on an old shutter that was found near by. The funny part of it was that it was the same shutter on which Herb had been brought home, and I had thrown it there myself earlier in the day.

Mother was very much upset when they brought me in. To have another disabled boy on her hands seemed like a catastrophe. She did not know quite what to make of it when she found on removing my shoe that the injured foot had not yet begun to swell; but she started hot applications at once and sent Stan for the doctor. When Stan found the doctor was out he left a message on the slate; but after two hours had passed without any word from the doctor Mother sent Cecilia, who found that in his excitement Stan had forgotten to sign his message. Cecilia brought the doctor back with her.

I was very nervous when he came in, though my nervousness left me when I saw how seriously he was taking my injury. The extreme pain I described, together with the absence of swelling, worried him. He diagnosed and diagnosed and finally came to the conclusion that the pain might be coming from either an injury inside the ginglymoid, where the tibia and fibula join the astragalus, or from a comminuted fracture of some of the adjacent structures. When I asked him if I would be able to walk on it within a day or two he glowered at me.

"If you step on it within two weeks it will be a miracle," he growled.

"But how much longer have I got to have those old hot towels on it?"

The doctor took a firm hold on my arm. "Now don't be a squawker," he said. "Those hot towels are probably what kept your foot from swelling up like a balloon." The more

69

he thought about that the more convinced he became. "You started with those towels right after the injury?"

Mother nodded. "Immediately."

He rubbed his hands together. "Well, I guess that's the answer. You stopped the congestion—" he caught himself—"the hyperemia, before it had time to start."

When he began to fumble in his bag I said, "You aren't going to put on one of those long rubber bandages, are you?" I hoped he was. But he shook his head.

"Not with that kind of an injury. I may have to put a plaster cast on it later if it doesn't come along the way it should."

"A plaster cast!" That seemed like carrying the thing a little too far. I hadn't forgotten the terrible time Elsie had with a plaster cast when she broke her arm.

"Won't know about that for a week or ten days," he muttered.

"But how long have I got to keep my foot up like this?" I was thinking about my new crutches.

I didn't like his laugh as he said, "You can put it down any time you want to, but you won't keep it down. Will he, Herb?"

Herb shook his head. "Not if it feels the way mine did. The first time I put it down it felt as if I'd stuck it in a hornet's nest."

Father carried me up to bed that night, but the next morning I astonished them all by coming downstairs by myself—on my own crutches. Mother was not only surprised, but she was fearful that I might do my foot some permanent injury. Father took the situation with his usual calm.

"Where did the crutches come from?" he asked.

"I made them."

He looked at me with amusement. "When?"

"Finished them yesterday."

70

"How convenient," he said, and turned away and started for his office.

Of course with my injury I could not go to school. Herb and I were pretty good company for each other. We played checkers and other two-hand games, and along in the afternoon while Herb was reading the *Youth's Companion* —being older he got the first chance at it—I hobbled around and called on some of our nearest neighbors. They seemed very much surprised to see me on crutches, explaining that they thought Herb was the one who had been hurt. But when I told them all the particulars they brought me cake and made lemonade, and I went home with my pockets bulging with cookies and candy and apples. Herb was quite upset when he heard what I had been doing. He seemed to think that I had been trying to steal some of his customers.

On the whole I found the life of a cripple quite delightful. I didn't have to get up in the morning until I felt like it—no going on the carpet for inspection—no school— played around with Herb in the morning, and in the afternoon made a few calls—no errands to run, and somebody always ready to wait on me. It was a bother to be hobbling around on crutches, though on the whole I liked the change. I missed taking part in the ball games and other outdoor sports, but after all you can't have everything. One afternoon when the boys had come to play ball and I had gone out to watch them the fire bell suddenly began to ring. A fire alarm was always a matter of the first magnitude with us, and regardless of what anybody was doing when the bell rang, he stopped doing it and ran to see where the fire was. At the first tap of the bell the pitcher stepped out of the box, as if to hear better. The catcher pulled off his mitt, and the batter reluctantly lowered his bat. Just then we saw workmen running across the lot.

"Where's the fire?" we yelled.

"It's the drill works!" the shout came back.

The drill works! It was the largest, practically the only, factory in town. For years people had been predicting that some time it would burn. And now it was in flames. The batter threw aside his bat, the catcher dropped his mitt, the pitcher slipped the ball inside his blouse.

"Come on, boys! Let's go to the fire!"

At the first tap of the bell I had come to my feet. As I stood there I could feel my crutches under my arms. Suddenly I was a little sick of being a cripple. I could have a lame foot any day; but a fire in the drill works came but once in a lifetime. The other boys were starting. I must make up my mind. I tossed the crutches over the fence—they might come in handy again—and with a bound I joined the gang. Mother, who was coming out to bring me a cushion to sit on, opened the door just in time to see me go.

The next day found me in school hale and hearty and completely recovered from my lameness, though very careful of the manner in which I sat down. Herb was still confined to the house with his injury, but I no longer envied him. Having a sprained ankle was not without its good points, but it also had its disadvantages, for Herb did not get near enough the big fire to have any fun at all.

7. We Have to Eat

YEAR in and year out the average number sitting down at our table could not have been far from fourteen. There were times when it ran up to twenty, and it was almost never below ten. When you have so many to start with the addition of one or two seems unimportant. Grandmother Bellamy lived with us for years, and it was not unusual for an aunt or uncle to come and stay for a month or more. And of course during every vacation we entertained a steady stream of cousins who looked upon our house as a second home.

At this time in its history Phelps was highly favored as a summer resort. It was a sequestered village with all the joys of country life and none of the isolation of the farm, and accordingly our place was very popular with the relatives during the summer season. But whether the table was set with ten plates or twenty the commissary department of the household was expected to function with the punctuality of a well-regulated railway. There were delays and breakdowns from time to time, and occasionally there would be a serious culinary disaster, but ordinarily the meals came along fairly close to schedule, and if one item of a projected menu went wrong a substitute was quickly provided to take its place.

Mother always liked to have emergency rations on hand to which she could turn in case of contingency. Indeed, she never felt quite easy unless we had a pretty generous supply of food in the house. One year when Father was paid for some legal work by being given half a carcass of beef just as the cold weather was coming on in the fall she decided to put it in the attic and keep it for household use. We had previously kept quarters of beef there in the wintertime, for the attic was as cold in winter as an ice-box; but shortly after she had stored this extraordinary amount of meat there the weather turned warm, altogether too warm for the preservation of beef without the aid of refrigeration. It so happened that the public supply of ice from the winter before had been entirely exhausted in town, and without ice there was at that time no refrigeration. Mother tried to get the butcher to take the meat off her hands, but found that he, too, had been caught without ice. There was only one alternative—to eat that beef before it had time to spoil.

An orgy of beef-eating followed. We had it for breakfast, dinner, and supper; and if any of the children came home from school hungry, instead of being given a slice of bread and butter according to custom, with a little surreptitious sugar or molasses on the top, a nice roast-beef sandwich was promptly handed out. The real gravity of the situation was not immediately sensed when the mercury had begun to climb. The supposition was that after a little fling it would go back down again and resume its seasonal deportment; but this the mercury failed to do, with the result that somebody had to go up in the attic every hour or two with a pail of fresh well water to change the cold cloths that Mother was keeping on the meat.

At first the cuts of beef were taken as they came, but when the mild weather continued Mother began feeding us only the finer cuts, so as to be sure of saving them. Thick tender steaks and juicy prime roasts became a commonplace on our table. But even this was not enough to

74

relieve Mother's anxiety, and as one mild balmy day followed another she began paying off her social indebtedness by giving a big dinner party almost every night, hoping against hope that the weather would break and save the rest of her winter's supply of beef.

This went on for some time, and though we children enjoyed the parties we became very tired of the food. Finally Father took a hand in the salvage operations and one day brought three out-of-town lawyers home to dinner without notifying Mother in advance. He knew as soon as he was inside the house that it would have been better if he had let her know, for the place reeked of fried sausage. But, confirmed optimist that he was, he thought he could still handle the situation, and at the first opportunity he took Mother aside.

"I should have let you know," he began, "but with all that meat—"

"I suppose you know what we're having," she interrupted with a smile.

Father nodded. "Yes, yes, but let's forget all about that; the sausage will keep. I'll speed up the fire for you and make some nice coals, and we'll broil a couple of those big thick porterhouse cuts. It will make a great hit with them, and of course they won't realize that we are just trying to save the meat."

Mother smiled with annoyance. "If you'd only let me know an hour ago—"

"But it won't take long to broil a couple of steaks!"

"You mean it wouldn't take long if we had the steaks."

"Well, haven't we?"

"I cut up the last of the meat this morning and put it down in brine for corned beef, two barrels of it, but if they're not in too much of a hurry I could give them some of that—in about four weeks."

"That's too long for even a *lawyer* to wait for something

75

to eat. Bring on your sausage. Right now I'd rather have it than any piece of beef I ever saw."

The story of the beef should have ended right there on the cheerful note that all's well that ends well, but alas this was not so to be. For the next night the temperature began to go down. By morning everything was frozen up solid. In another day or two it had touched zero and there it lingered for more than a week. Then came a series of blizzards which kept the country buried under snowbanks almost until Easter Sunday. And we lived on corned beef.

In the matter of vegetables back in those pre-refrigeration days it was a case of every man for himself. Not a store or a stand in town handled them. Why offer for sale what every man could have in abundance simply by scattering a few seeds in his own backyard? Father was an enthusiastic gardener during his younger days. The lure of growing things had a strong appeal for him, and he was up at the first glow of morning light and worked until time to go to the office. His evenings were also spent among the seeds and the weeds, and all through his life he believed that nobody could make a garden grow quite as he could, although he admitted freely that Jerry Billings was a close second. Jerry had been put to work in our garden just as soon as the income from Father's practice could support such a luxury. From the first Mother never liked Jerry and never quite trusted him, though she could find nothing to complain of so far as his gardening went. He produced abundant crops during the summer and built a root cellar in which to "put down" for the winter a generous supply of beets, carrots, turnips, and onions. These he used to keep under sand, and cabbage and potatoes he kept on racks so that the air could get around them. The things that Jerry put away never spoiled, although Mother was always expecting them to. And when Jerry was sent to jail on the flimsy charge of arson which

76

Father considered such a miscarriage of justice, Mother insisted she was not at all surprised.

In building the potato cellar Jerry underestimated our family appetite and made provision for storing only twenty-five bushels, so the space had to be refilled at least once a winter. We raised our own apples and usually managed to get through the winter on twenty barrels. The only green vegetables we ever saw during the winter months were a limited supply of lettuce and celery during the holidays. Our winter pears lasted until the first of the year, and after that our fruit supply was confined to apples and an occasional orange or banana, neither of which was ever served on our table.

Mother always bought sugar and flour by the barrel. Corn meal she got by the hundred-pound sack. Butter was bought in twenty-pound crocks from some farmer's wife. We had the same butter woman for years at a time, and I remember what a protest Mother made when a new one tried to raise the yearly price from ten to twelve cents a pound. There was a year-round price of ten cents a dozen for eggs, which in the winter often went as high as fifteen cents a dozen and in the summer usually fell as low as eight cents. These prices seem low today, but back in the eighties, with money as scarce as it was in our family, they were not regarded as a particular bargain, and there was constant talk about the high cost of living.

One of the strictest rules in our household was that there should be no criticism of meals. We had our preferences of course, and liked some things better than others, but I do not recall that any of the children ever evaded eating a thing on the ground that he or she did not like it. We were brought up to believe that food was desirable to have and hard to get. We did not take the trouble to thank God for the clothes on our backs, the shoes on our feet, or the roof over our head, but we never sat down

77

to a meal that we did not thank God for the food on the table.

Punctuality for meals was another of the old-fashioned virtues with which my mother was unwilling to compromise. We had a large dinner bell standing on a little corner shelf in the passage between the kitchen and dining room. This bell was rung five minutes before a meal was served, and even if a boy was at the plate with two on and the score tied he was supposed to drop his bat and start for home. If he stayed for another pitch he was likely to lose his dessert, for there was always a forfeit of some sort for a late-comer. In the summertime this bell was rung lustily at the curfew hour of nine, and woe be unto the boy who was not home within five minutes, for he would not be able to leave the premises the following night, a form of detention we called being on the "jail limits."

Given a choice of desserts most of our children would have voted for ice-cream, as we did not often have it; but there is little doubt in my mind that Grandmother's Indian pudding would have been the unanimous second choice. Indian pudding as we knew it in those days is extinct. Some of the materials of which it was composed no longer exist. Two of the ingredients, coarse stone-ground corn meal and old-fashioned black-strap molasses, have not been obtainable in forty years—and even if they were to be found on the kitchen shelves in abundance nobody living today could produce one of Grandmother's Vermont Indian puddings. Every member of my family has the recipe, but not one has ever made—or probably ever will make—such a pudding as Grandmother used to toss off on a moment's notice.

To show how simple the pudding was to make I am giving the recipe as it was written down in Mother's *Receipt Book.*

GRANDMOTHER'S INDIAN PUDDING

Mix thoroughly in a large bowl

Mixture #1

1 cup sugar
1 cup molasses
2 whole raw eggs well beaten
1 cup melted butter
1 teaspoon cinnamon
1 teaspoon ginger
½ teaspoon cloves
½ teaspoon salt

Mixture #2

To a quart of milk add five heaping tablespoons of moistened corn meal, and cook 20 minutes, stirring all the while. When removed from stove add 1 pint of cold milk, then pour in Mixture #1, stirring thoroughly. Put in baking dish and bake in moderate oven until done, which will be from 3 to 4 hours.

When Grandmother first came to live with us she could throw one of these puddings together with her eyes shut. She couldn't fail. She never did fail, though she became so decrepit that we had to move her to the kitchen in her chair. She needn't have gone to the kitchen at all. She could as well have made it on the piano, for she never spilled so much as a grain of salt, and during her later years Mixture #2 was always stirred during the preparation by an apprentice.

Grandmother's version of this pudding was not made by any sort of accurate measurement—it was the result of the touch system. Roughly there were so many measures of this or that, but they were only a starter, there being, of course, no formula for a work of art. The really important part was done by the feel. Corn meal varied; sometimes it was coarser, sometimes finer. Often after feeling out Mixture #2 with a wooden spoon she would add another handful of meal, stirring until it felt just

79

right. For Mixture #1 she usually took the big yellow bowl into her lap. After the ingredients were all in and she had stirred awhile she would stop and reach for something.

"It wants a mite more molasses." Then she would stir a little more, sniffing carefully, and finally call for another pinch of ginger or cinnamon.

After the two mixtures had been combined and the result was ready for the oven she would not allow it to stand a moment; the baking must begin at once. And the baking of an Indian pudding is a delicate matter. Two minutes too long in the oven will spoil it, and if it comes out too soon you cannot put it in again. It was always a mystery how she could tell when it was done. Different members of the family had different theories about this. Mother thought that Grandmother used to recite to herself certain chapters of the Bible. Some of the children thought that she counted up to a million by fives or tens. Father insisted that she was telepathic and could read the mind of corn meal. Grandmother herself said that she went mainly by the smell. But in any event when she said, "Fannie, I think that puddin' should come out," you could be sure that the pudding was at that moment ready to come out.

Anyone should have been able to make a good Indian pudding, but Grandmother was the only one who ever did. That Mother failed to master the art was not her fault. Certainly she tried hard enough. She hung over Grandmother every time the old lady made one, alert for any little point she might have missed before. We used to eat the results of Mother's attempts, criticizing them freely, though, as I have hinted, criticism of other items on the menu was not encouraged. If one of Mother's Indian puddings got as far as the table it was sure to be reasonably palatable. But Heaven only knows how many of them went to the chickens unsung and unremembered. Corn meal was good for the chickens, so Mother must have felt that the ingredients were not entirely wasted. I came upon the remains of one of her abortive attempts in the chicken run at least five years after Grandmother's death, and realized that even then Mother was still trying. I think the last Indian pudding Grandmother ever made was one that I ordered on my birthday. By that time she was almost stone-deaf, her eyesight was failing, and she was confined to her rocking chair by her rheumatics. But she still had the touch. Her last pudding was as perfect as any she ever made.

Mother's puddings were not all flops; some of them were really excellent, though not one was supreme. I don't talk about Grandmother's puddings any more. Merely mentioning them usually makes trouble; every woman thinks *she* can make one, but no woman can. As I said when I first mentioned the subject, some of the ingredients are no longer obtainable. That is an airtight alibi today, though it was not in Mother's time. My matured conclusion is that Mother just did not have the corn-meal touch.

From the size of Mother's key ring and the number of keys on it one would have thought that she was surrounded by a pack of international thieves. She used to say that it was not because she suspected members of the household, but simply that she did not want to put temptation in anybody's way. In addition to the keys to all the cupboards there were keys to the sideboard, the linen shelves, to bureau drawers, to closets upstairs and down, and even to old trunks in the attic. Indeed, there were so many keys on her key ring that even after she had found the proper keyhole she could not always find a key to fit it. Nor could she always find her key ring. Often while busy at her tasks she would wear the key ring dangling from her belt. So long as it was fastened to her there was little chance of losing it, but as soon as she began to carry it around in her hand trouble was usually not far away. Either she would leave it dangling from the lock of one of her treasure keeps, or she would put it on a closet shelf while she pursued some object of her quest. Occasionally it would get buried in a bureau drawer, and then what a questing and hunting and searching there would be. I have annexed many a dime from finding them for her. Perhaps it is safe after all these years to admit that on one or two occasions when I was pressed for funds I turned my head the other way, so that I could truthfully say I did not know where they were, and poked something that sounded like the keys into a place where they were not likely to be seen. But there was one time when I found them after a reward had been offered, and was deprived—

I will not say cheated—of my reward on what have always seemed to me to be technical grounds.

It happened one day when we had unexpected but very particular guests for supper; at least they were so particular that Mother wanted to impress them. She had put on her best silver tea service, and it was not until we were seated at the table that she discovered that the sugar bowl was empty, the sugar was locked up, and the keys could not be found. After the maid had spent some time hunting for them without success Louise suggested half-humorously that they might use the icing from the cake with which to sweeten the tea. Mother's look seemed to indicate that she would die first. She excused herself from the table and fluttered upstairs and down again, opening drawers and looking under things, but eventually she returned empty-handed, and in the end, to Mother's extreme mortification, they had to use the icing. Immediately after supper she posted on the family bulletin board an offer of ten cents to anybody who would find the bunch of keys. I made the mistake of finding them too soon and of delivering them to her in the presence of the company. After they had gone she refused to pay me the reward on the alleged ground that I had sat there and watched her beautiful supper spoiled, just because I thought that if I told where the keys were I'd be sent up to get them.

That was only partly true. There were two other reasons. One was the possibility that she might offer a reward, and the other was that I wanted to see the fun when they used that frosting for sweetening their tea.

8. Diversion and Relaxation

FATHER was a great one to bring home things that he had bought on the train. Sometimes it would be a bag of peppermints, and again he would smuggle into the house among his legal papers a claptrap novel that he had not had time to finish on the train. He was a rapid reader and would consume one of these novels in a few hours, though nobody ever saw one of them again after he was through reading it.

Once he came home with a puzzle made of two bent nails. They were linked in together, and the trick was to get them apart without using force. He let each one of us try for ten minutes to work it, and when none of us was able to get the two apart he smiled with satisfaction and said that he would show us how it was done. He had learned the solution from the newsboy on the train. Doubtless it had seemed very simple to him at the time, but when he came to do it for himself his complete lack of the mechanical touch tripped him up and he could not get the two nails apart any more than we could. He would fuss and fume over it for a while and then throw it impatiently aside. A little later he would go back to it and try again. Mother solved it in a very few minutes, and after we were all in bed she spent an hour trying to teach him the trick. After we children had seen it done once or twice we all got so that we could do it, and we used to stand around where he could not help seeing us and take the two nails apart with a great flourish.

So far as I know he never solved that puzzle without a little guidance from my mother, and one night in an outburst of impatience he went to the front door and threw it far out into the night. Herb found it the next day, which was Sunday, and spent quite a little of the day working it where Father must have seen him. That night the puzzle disappeared from Herb's pocket—along with a dime novel and two cigarettes which had cost him plenty on a swap, and which he was saving to smoke out behind the church with the boys the night of a social. We never saw that particular puzzle again, but about two weeks later we came across a boy who had one just like it—except that his nails were copper-plated. After long negotiation we acquired it from him and put it on the library table where Father would find it when he sat down to smoke his first after-dinner cigar.

He looked a little surprised when he saw it, and for a few minutes he studiously avoided picking it up. He eventually succumbed, however, and soon we saw with satisfaction that he was wriggling his toes and giving other signs of extreme nervous anguish. Suddenly he fell back into his chair as if in partial collapse. I glanced up and saw that he had one of the nails in each hand. He had accidentally worked that puzzle without any help from anybody.

Without a word he tossed the pieces on the table and went over to his desk and began his evening's work. We surreptitiously put the pieces together and left the puzzle around for several days; but his pride, or his vanity, or his curiosity had been satisfied, for he never would look at it again.

The library table was not big enough for all of us, so in the evenings we used to sit around the dining-room table, an extension affair which normally had about six leaves in it. If it happened to be an evening when we were copying legal papers for Father none of us old enough to write was likely to get very far from that table until bedtime came. Before the coming of the typewriter Father kept a copyist in his office, a maiden lady named Libby Weston, but as he often needed twenty or more copies of long-winded legal papers from ten to forty pages in length Libby was unable to do more than a small amount of the necessary work. So Father used to bring the longer papers home to be copied by members of the family. Copying was as much a part of our work as hoeing in the garden or shoveling the winter snow from the sidewalk.

Fortunately for us not every night was a copying night. We usually had supper at six, and by six forty-five we would be through and ready for some fun before bedtime crept up on us. We had every game obtainable at the period. Backgammon, checkers, squails, pachisi, lotto, crokinole, tiddlywinks, authors, go-bang, a wide choice of travel games, and inescapably a game of Bible characters, played like authors, for use on Sunday. That Bible game was never popular—not even on Sundays, when other games were forbidden. Mother was always on the lookout for new games. Since no "homework" was brought from school in those days, for the younger children at least, games were indispensable.

Father urged chess on the older children, but was never able to arouse much interest in a game requiring so much work and so little play.

Immediately after supper the tots were put to bed and Mother tried to engross the nine-o'clocks in some quiet game. Sometimes she was successful, but just as often the nine-o'clocks preferred to play some noisy extemporaneous game of their own. The older children, left to them-

selves, might start some adult game, or they might read
or write letters, and almost certainly before the evening
was over there would be music of some sort. All three
girls could play the piano, and some of us could play
other musical instruments as well. Until ten o'clock there
was no ban on noise in our household and usually we
made plenty. Of course the biggest noise-makers were
the nine-o'clocks, and much of the confusion would cease
after they had gone upstairs to bed. This was sure to be
so if there were no callers in the house. But as I look back
it seems to me that there were not so very many evenings
when our doorbell did not ring at least once. When we
had a copying job on hand it did not ring at all, for we
used to hang a sign on the knob that said "Copying To-
night." But so long as the three girls remained at home,
one or another, and sometimes all three, would be entertaining callers on nearly every night when the copying
sign was not out.

Callers came early in those days, for they had to go
home early. Anyone who rang our doorbell after seven-
thirty o'clock was regarded as late. For many years the
curfew at our house rang promptly at ten, and if swains
were too dilatory about taking their departure they were
almost certain to hear from Father. He carried his enthusiasm for punctuality right upstairs with him when
he went to bed, and he firmly believed that the word applied to going on time as well as coming on time.

But the older children were not the only ones to have
company at night. The nine-o'clocks had almost as much
company as the tens, the big difference being that they
did not stay so long. This would give the tens an hour of
comparatively uninterrupted time for their courtship. We
were surrounded by neighbors with children of our own
age, and it was only natural that we should want to spend
our playtime together. Mother did not care how old or

how young our callers were, but the difference in ages must have caused her no end of trouble.

She had a system of segregation worked out, though she never enforced it very rigorously. The older girls—sixteen and upwards, say—received their callers in the back parlor, where they could sit and talk, playing the piano now and then, occasionally singing, and if there happened to be enough of them, doing a bit of dancing perhaps. The next younger section—thirteen to fifteen—would theoretically occupy the front parlor, where Mother would try to get them established at some game. She was tactful about it; she would not actually go in and organize them into a game unless it became necessary. She saw to it that the games were on hand and she tried to keep alive a healthy rivalry that would encourage the young visitors to play. She made a point of remembering what games the neighbors' children enjoyed. If a lad liked pachisi, the pachisi board showed up in the front parlor soon after he did. When even younger children came in, as they occasionally did, she would take the group under her own wing and confine their entertainment to the family circle in the dining room, where she could keep tabs on them and at the same time work at her huge basket of mending and darning.

The noise and confusion never seemed to bother Father at all. He would sit at his desk in the library and work with apparent unconcern while a train of human freight cars steamed up and down the length of the dining room, ding-donging, blowing off steam, and calling out station stops in a lusty and stentorian tone. He would not pay the slightest attention to the noisiest possible game of bean-bags or musical chairs in the front parlor just across the hall. No amount of "polly-wolly-doodle" or "upi-dee-i-da" seemed to penetrate his consciousness. He would pore over his books quite undisturbed, making notes in lead

88

pencil on a large ruled yellow pad, and keeping the room blue with cigar smoke.

But let the clock strike nine, and he was all attention. And if the nine-o'clocks paused too long to figure up a score he would soon be looking in the door to see what was detaining them.

It was perfectly natural for the neighbors' children to like to come to our house because there was always enough of a nucleus to start something. And Mother never objected to a reasonable number of them. She used to say that it was easier to watch her children than to worry about them.

Only the older children were ever allowed to go out at night during the winter months, and then they had to have some good reason for going, a party or dance, or possibly fine skating on the pond, and occasionally the great treat of coasting by moonlight. We younger children made no fuss when they went; we knew we couldn't go anyway. It was the rainy days that used to get us down; we felt that the time outdoors belonged to us and that we were being cheated by the weather. Many a time Mother bundled me up and told me to run the length of the garden path twenty times—a distance of some two hundred yards. And occasionally on rainy days, when the house would be a little too small to hold our animal spirits, she would send us little fellows to the barn for an afternoon. We had a flying trapeze there, and rings, and we staged some great Indian attacks against the early settlers who used to occupy the upper story and try to defend it against the bloodthirsty redskins. I well remember how we used to howl ourselves hoarse as we swarmed up the stairs, or craftily wormed our way through the polished feeding chutes where hay was shoved down to feed the horses.

We were not supposed to go into the box stalls of the

horses, and rarely did except to retrieve a tomahawk or war club which went in there by mistake. Father had made very stringent prohibitions against our visiting the horses in their stalls, and we were convinced that he meant business; so we intruded on the horses only under the most extreme necessity.

It was on one of those rainy days in the barn that the "coalheaver" game came into existence.

As I have intimated, Mother had little regard for the "manly art of self-defense," while Father had a very high opinion of it. He never rebuked us for standing up for our own rights. Indeed, he had a theory that personal combat possessed remarkable cleansing properties and was a catharsis second to none for taking the meanness out of a human animal. You didn't even have to lick the other fellow to get the benefit—it was the fighting itself that was the good medicine.

At some time in the dim past Father and Mother had gone together to see the *Bohemian Girl*. It was a very gala occasion to which people went in evening clothes. As Father and Mother drew up before the opera house—no doubt in a brougham or possibly a hack—another young couple were just stepping out of their carriage. A vagrant wind raised the lady's skirt immodestly high, disclosing her instep or possibly her ankle. Father did not go into details as to that. But a rough fellow who chanced to be in the crowd of onlookers, described by Father as a coalheaver weighing about 185 pounds, got what would now be called an eyeful, and made a pertinent or perhaps an impertinent remark.

The lady's escort, a rather dandified fellow weighing about 135 pounds, blushed for shame and promptly took up the gauge. He handed his high hat to the lady, asked to be excused for a moment, stepped aside and without removing the white kid gloves he had on administered a terrific drubbing to the insulting coalheaver. This little duty performed he retrieved his high hat, apologized for the delay, gave the lady his arm and together they proceeded into the theater, where presumably they enjoyed the opera the better because of the preliminary diversion.

We found the story fascinating. "What's a coalheaver, Father?" we asked eagerly.

"Oh, a rough, dirty fellow who delivers coal."

"Did he have the coal with him?"

"I don't know that he actually had any coal right there. But he was a rough fellow—a roustabout type."

"What's a roustabout type?"

"Big burly chap—strong, tough, hard as nails."

"But why did the little man keep on the white kid gloves? Did he need them?"

"Of course he didn't need them—he just happened to have them on. They were part of his evening costume."

"Oh, did he have on a costume?"

"Naturally not. What he had on has nothing to do with the point. The important part is that in spite of his small size and his physical inadequacy he was able to give his adversary fifty pounds' advantage and still punish the big loafer so unmercifully that he ran for his life."

"Was that because the little man had on white kid gloves?"

"It was because the small man understood the science of boxing and the big powerful fellow didn't."

But by this time Mother had heard enough about the distasteful art of fisticuffs, and she very firmly changed the subject. She was, however, a little late with her interruption; the harm, if any, had already been done.

Stan and I remembered the coalheaver again one rainy day when we had been sent to the barn to work off our animal spirits. I must have been about twelve years old at the time and Stan the usual amount younger. We had

91

exhausted all the old games and were trying to think of a new one when Stan happened to think of the coalheaver.

"Couldn't we make a game out of that somehow?" he asked.

"You bet we could," I said. "Just wait a minute while I run down to the house and get sump'n."

I raced through the rain to the house and up the back stairs. At the door of Father's room I stopped and listened to be sure nobody was inside, then slipped softly over and opened the bureau drawer where he kept the shirts, cuffs, and collars that went with his dress suit. Right on top was what I was looking for—a brand-new pair of white kid gloves wrapped in a piece of tissue paper. I grabbed them, tucked them into my pocket and had started out of the house when Mother intercepted me.

"What are you doing here?" She ran an eye over me looking for suspicious indications.

"Aw, can't a fellow even come in to get his own jack-knife without having a permit?" I groaned.

She smiled. "Of course you can. You looked so funny I thought it might be something else."

When I showed Stan the gloves he was delighted. The only trouble was he wanted to put them right on and play the part of the dude. But I told him that I had already selected that part for myself. Stan very wisely declined to play the part of the coalheaver. Thus matters stood until we happened to see Fred Burnham passing along the street. We called Fred in and invited him to play with us. By giving the coalheaver role a big build-up we finally got Fred to take the part, although he had no idea what he had let himself in for, as we said we would explain the action as we went along.

Stan, who was taking the part of the lady with a lap-robe wrapped around him for a skirt, stepped out of the canopy-top wagon on my arm.

"You're supposed to insult the lady," we prompted. "Go on, insult her!"

"Who's the skinny slut you got there?" he called out tauntingly. "You with the white gloves on—"

I removed one of Father's old silk hats from my head and handed it to Stan. "If you'll excuse me now, my dear, I have an unpleasant duty to perform." So saying I whirled around and socked Fred in the eye before he could so much as get his guard up.

Fred danced up and down with pain and rage. "I'll get even with you!" he howled. "You see if I don't!"

"There's nothing to get even for," we told him. "You insulted the lady, didn't you?"

Fred's eye was already beginning to swell before we got him calmed down by telling him that he could wear the white gloves and be the dude as soon as we could get hold of another coalheaver. Fred thought of a victim right away; he had long been wanting to take a sock at Bung Condit, but Bung would never give him a chance. Fred knew where Bung was to be found, so we sent Stan to get him. Stan pretended to be looking for another boy, but he managed to let out the news that there was a big game of tag going on over in our barn, and Bung came right over.

We did play tag for a while just so he would not suspect anything, but the game quickly became listless and Fred suggested that we play a game of coalheaver.

Bung showed an interest at once. "How do you play it?" he asked.

"Well," I explained, "first you have to pick out a good strong fellow for the coalheaver. After that you pick a little fellow for the dude—anybody can play that part. I'll be the coalheaver."

"What do you want me to do?" asked Bung.

"You can be the dude if you want to."

"And what if I don't want to?"

"Then you can take the lady's part that Stan was going to take."

"Huh! Lady's part. You can't work that on me. I'll tell you what I'll do—I'll be the coalheaver."

We protested loudly, but finally gave in. Then we had to put up a fake argument to get Fred to take the part of the dude. With a great show of reluctance Fred agreed to be the dude just this once. So while Fred put on the silk hat and white kid gloves and handed his lady into the carriage I climbed up in front as the driver and clucked to the horses.

Bung did a better job of insulting the lady than Fred had done, and Fred did an even better job on Bung's eye than I had done on his. Bung swore like a trooper when the blow first landed, but he was quick to catch the idea that he had been a dupe.

"So that's the way Burnham got his eye choppin' wood, hey? Say, listen, let's see if we can get Jim Baker in on this. He's got beautiful eyes—I'd like to put me fist into one of 'em."

And that was how it happened that Jim was the next victim. As the afternoon wore on the play became more and more elaborate. An old dress was purloined from our attic and the lady was put in costume. A flunky in a painter's jacket attended the carriage and assisted in handing the lady to the curb. A combined ticket-taker and barker was now stationed at the theater door. With each new victim the audience became larger and larger. Practically all the old scores in the neighborhood were settled that rainy afternoon. And no new ones were made; for the peculiar psychology of being a dupe is that you must always blame yourself for being stupid enough to be taken in.

Stan and I were the only boys in the neighborhood

94

without a black eye. Herb had been in a fight a few days before and already had one. He regarded himself as too grown up to take any part in the childish pranks of boys

three or four years younger than he, but I must say that he watched the slaughter with the keenest enjoyment. The white kid gloves were of course a complete ruin. We did not dare put them back where we had found them, so for a while we kept them hidden behind a beam in the barn hoping that another dupe would show up, but the news had gone out far and wide, and we never succeeded in finding even one more.

It was weeks later, and I had forgotten all about the white kid gloves, when I heard Father getting into his dress suit one night. He was growling around his bedroom like an English-speaking grizzly bear, asking where this or that had been put. I had come up to ask him some question, but as soon as I saw what he was doing I went right down again.

"What's the matter with Dad?" I asked Herb.

Herb smiled. "He's hunting for his white kid gloves."

"Well, I can tell him where they are." Stan chuckled and put his hand over his mouth.

Mother finally succeeded in finding a pair of pearl-gray gloves that were made to do. They were too small for Father to get on, and one had a split in the palm. Father scoffed when he saw them, but Mother said he could carry them—and he did, though he made quite certain that he would never have to carry them again by dropping them at the first opportunity.

I have always had a warm spot in my vocabulary for the word "coalheaver." It is my one contribution to the "manly art of etymology," for I helped to change it from a dreary symbol of toil into a glorious fighting word of which our language has all too few. Even to this day, in the purlieus of my youth, you can call a man a son of this, that, or the other thing without any very serious consequences; but before you call him a coalheaver—you'd better smile. Otherwise you may find yourself nursing a punch in the eye.

The rainy afternoons at the barn were not often so productive. Stan and I teased Father again and again to tell us another story like the one about the coalheaver, but he never could seem to do it; in fact he seemed a little hazy on the details of the coalheaver story when we pressed him to repeat it.

Our house was on a corner. It faced that great national artery known as Main Street, but the portion of the public domain which flanked the property was a rather obscure little roadway which was not even sure of its own name. It led to the coalyard and railroad tracks, and was all that kept Pleasant Street (which by rights should have been named Railroad Avenue) from coming to a dead end. To us this indispensable thoroughfare was always "the Side Road," and the boys who habitually played there were "the Side Road gang."

Father calmly christened the roadway Pearl Street by nailing a neatly painted sign to a tree on the corner. And Pearl Street it remained until some years later when a dastard who was making a lithograph map of the town, of which my father refused to order a copy, put it down as Coalyard Street. The family never forgave him. Personally I did not care. More than a map or a street sign would have been required to make that street anything but the Side Road to me.

There I played my first game of marbles—and lost the equivalent of my shirt. There I first fanned out, first walked a batter, and first got caught napping at a base; but it was there that I also hit my first home run. There I played my first game of pom-pom-pullaway, and was first thrilled by the shout of "Run sheep run!" The Side Road was our family playground. It ran the whole length of our lot, and it was within easy hearing of our big dinner bell. Near the Main Street end was a low place where a puddle used to form in the winter, which, when frozen over, made a good though none too large skating rink. Here all the family learned to skate, one after another taking their first uncertain steps on an old pair of wooden-soled skates, the runners of which turned up in front and

97

ended in a fancy scroll. These skates had belonged to Father, and had had a part, we used to think, in bringing him to Mother's favorable attention. The Side Road had everything but a hill, which, after all, was not important since there were plenty of good places to coast within walking distance.

There were practically no daytime restrictions on coasting. Most of our troubles in that particular sport came from the old fogies who preferred not to have their sidewalks used as a bobsled run and persisted in covering them with sand and ashes—which we lost no time in sweeping off. Pond's Hill, Hammond's Hill, Neighbor's Hill, Frisbie's Hill—all would be peopled with enthusiastic coasters after school hours on any fine day in winter. Frisbie's Hill had the steepest pitch and the longest run, and in my memory will ever remain the king of coasting places. The Frisbies owned the property at the top and the bottom, and in between were amiable families most of which had children who liked to slide downhill.

Several times during the winter the Frisbies would give moonlight coasting parties. Two or three big double-rippers would be on hand. The Frisbies had the largest and fastest of them all; but any one of them was fast enough to lift a coaster's heart well up into his throat. With a brilliant winter's moon above, the crisp snow creaking underfoot, the sled run well packed and lightning-fast, a rosy-cheeked girl in front to hold on to and another clutching you from behind to keep from falling off, with a good steersman at the helm and a powerful send-off man to administer the final shove, life could still be beautiful even though we were wearing made-over clothes and caps and mittens originally made for somebody else.

We always started off with shouts and laughter, but there would be a momentary hush, an involuntary gasp for breath on the steep pitch. If we came out of the great swoop at all we came on a strong vocal upsurge of exaltation—triumph of mind over matter; but if, as all too often happened, we lost our center of gravity and ended up in a snowbank with a great confusion of arms and legs, there would be an equally strong vocal upsurge, but it would denote the rather embarrassing triumph of matter over mind.

The Frisbie Hill run under average conditions was good for almost half a mile—and then came the long walk back to the top dragging the bobsled behind. If it was a regular party Mr. Frisbie would be out there with his horse and sleigh ready to tow the bobsleds back to the top. And after an hour or two of coasting there would be a hot supper in the Frisbies' spacious dining room.

Skating parties were not infrequent in the early part of the season before the ice had been covered with snow. But our girls were not allowed to go on a skating party at night without a chaperon, and skating chaperons were very difficult to find. That was one nice thing about the coasting on Frisbie's Hill—Mrs. Frisbie would chaperon the party without stepping out of the house.

The boys in the family always had much more liberty than the girls, and in the summer especially we had the run of the entire township with only the one limitation that until a boy was able to swim he was not allowed to venture into the waters of the creek or to ride upon them in a boat unless accompanied by an older brother who could swim. We found this regulation so great an annoyance that we learned to swim almost as soon as we learned the way to the old swimming hole. It was just as well that I learned to swim before I could skate, as I seemed to have a gift for combining the two accomplishments.

9. Remember the Sabbath Day

SUNDAY at our house began with breakfast at eight o'clock. How we reveled in this late breakfast, and luxuriated in the knowledge that we would not have to "go on the carpet" before sitting down at table. On weekdays going on the carpet meant a severe military inspection of hands, faces, necks, ears, clothing, and especially shoes. I suppose I was sent back to polish the heels of my shoes oftener than for any other oversight. On Sunday the inspection was doubly stiff, but it came much later since we did not start for church until Father's watch showed the time to be exactly ten twenty-five. It was his custom to snap the case shut on the minute.

The timing of meals was equally exact. We must be there on the tick or take the consequences, which meant a certain loss of privileges. When Father was in the house the bell rang whether the meal was ready or not. We then took our places behind our chairs and waited until grace had been said before sitting down. After we were seated— there we sat until the food was brought in from the kitchen. We were a noisy family, forever talking, teasing, joking, and gibing at each other. But if a meal was slow in coming in Father had little to say and usually sat with his watch in his hand as if he had to catch a train, when really there was nothing more pressing than reading the paper or walking out to look over the garden.

On Sunday morning immediately after breakfast we had family prayers in the library, the routine of which I have already described. Father's selections from the Bible were certainly good ones. He did not miss a homicide, a bit of intrigue, an illicit love affair, or any good story having plenty of plot and action. I think Mother used to squirm a little at some of these selections; she could see no good reason for bringing that particular subject up. Grandmother, however, never turned a hair; anything in the Bible was good enough for her.

After prayers we dispersed, went to our rooms, and began a leisurely preparation for church. Immediately following church we came home and had our Sunday dinner. The rest of the day we had to ourselves, except that the older children were expected to attend church in the evening. Mother usually went with them, but Father never stepped out of the house on Sunday evenings. One church service a day was enough for him. He would go once and go willingly; but he was a man who could be pushed just so far and no farther. Mother understood this perfectly, and while she would have derived great comfort from having him attend the evening service, she never made an effort so far as I know to get him to go. Grandmother tried once, but never again. Father told her off in a few well-chosen words.

I have seen an envious look in Mother's eye on a stormy winter's night as she saw Father sitting in his easy chair with a book as she was about to start for church. She would have been glad to stay there with him, but her conscience would not let her, and she would trudge dutifully off into the night.

No secular music was allowed at our house on Sunday. The girls used to play the piano, but they had to confine their music to the hymnbook. We were not supposed to whistle or even to hum anything but religious music. Usually the cover of the piano would remain down all day long, though occasionally on a Sunday one of the girls would go in and pound out a few doleful-sounding Gospel hymns. When Thad was in college he brought a boy home with him one Sunday who was a regular wizard on the piano. Father and Mother had retired to their room for an afternoon nap and had just dozed off when they were awakened by the sound of stirring martial music from our piano. There was thunder in its tones and swing in its rhythm, there was incitement to battle, and the shout of victory.

Mother bounded off the bed. She didn't know what the neighbors would think. She threw on her wrapper and was halfway down the front stairs to put an end to the sacrilege when she recognized the piece as a stepped-up version of *Onward, Christian Soldiers*. On another occasion this same boy was invited to play the organ at our Sunday morning service and gave the congregation a great thrill. He used stops and pedals that had probably never been disturbed since the organ was built, and his footwork shook the building to its foundation. But the piece that was liked best of all was the one that he played for a recessional. Mother especially admired it, and when she pressed him for the name he fenced around a bit and finally told her that it was something of his own. He did not quite dare to tell her that it was a variation on the tune of *Yankee Doodle*. He did tell the girls, however, and they thought he was a regular devil.

For exercise on Sunday we were allowed to take a walk, but it had to be a supervised walk with Father in charge. Mother, presumably because of her child-bearing, was not much of a walker. Our two favorite Sunday walks were to go past the Burdick farm, a stroll of about a mile and a half, or to visit the cemetery. Personally I preferred to go past the Burdick farm, for this took us into the

The Partridge family in 1892: *left to right* (seated) Thad, Leslie, Mother, Father, Cecilia; (standing) Bellamy, Herb, Stan, Elsie, Louise.

country, across four brooks into which things could be thrown, along shaded country roads, and between pastures and cultivated fields. It also took us up on the high ground south of the town from which we could see the "buttonhook tree," a deformed dendrological growth which stood on the skyline far to the north. I always thought that some day I would find that "buttonhook tree," but I never did. It looked like a buttonhook only from a distance and could not be distinguished from a dozen other trees when one visited the neighborhood where it was supposed to be, and tried to segregate it.

All our games and playthings were put under lock and key on Saturday night, all, that is, except the stereoscope. We could look through that as much as we wished on Sunday, for the only pictures that we had were scenes of the Holy Land and views illustrating the life of Christ.

Our Sunday dinner was a meal to reckon with, usually built around a large roast or a platter of fried or fricasseed chicken, but for Sunday night supper we all went into the kitchen to have a bowl of bread and milk, and a piece of cake or a cookie. In those days we all had our individual bread and milk bowls, some with initials and some with nothing but pictures on the sides. My outfit consisted of a wide, shallow bowl and a deep saucer almost as large as a soup plate. The capacity of the bowl was about a pint, and on an average Sunday night I would empty it twice. This bread and milk supper was partly an economy measure, for it made a fine way to get rid of the stale bread which had been accumulating, and partly a religious function designed to release all household help so that they could attend divine worship. In looking back on some of the things I used to hear about the Sunday night adventures of our maids I am not so sure that they did not contribute more to delinquency than to salvation.

As my sisters began to grow up those Sunday night suppers lost some of their austere, meager quality. A single warm supper dish made its appearance, chipped beef on toast, swimming in cream sauce, or perhaps creamed fish of some sort. It was at a Sunday night supper that I tasted my first Welsh rarebit. At the time I thought it a fine way to spoil good cheese, but after a few trials I became and have since remained an enthusiast.

The one thing that I always liked about the Sunday night supper was the complete absence of punctuality. You could come or you could go. You could take it or leave it. The bread was there on the large circular bread-board on the outer margin of which the words "Cut and Come Again" were carved in raised letters. Milk was plentiful, for we kept a cow that furnished us with about twenty quarts a day. You could sit down or you could eat standing. Nobody told you what you could or could not do. There were times when I found the punctuality of our household extremely annoying. Punctuality is, I am told, one of the elements of good conduct. Up to a certain point I heartily approve of it. Beyond that point it can become a nuisance, if not an instrument of torture.

With Father punctuality was the queen of the virtues. He believed in kindness, but there were times when to win a lawsuit he would skin a witness alive. He believed in standing up very straight with the shoulders thrown back; but he was never very erect himself. He believed in telling the absolute truth; though nobody could draw the long bow any more effectively than he. But in the case of punctuality he practiced what he preached, for he never deviated from it by so much as a hairbreadth. I do not believe that he ever missed a train in his life, and in all those years that he started the family for church he was late on only one occasion, and then it was really not his own fault.

It happened one Sunday in the early spring. The garden had just been made, but the cow had not yet been turned out to pasture. The family were all assembled in the library, had all passed muster, and were about to start when the hired girl called down from upstairs and said that the cow was loose and walking around in the yard. Quite naturally Father did not want her walking in his newly made garden, so he sent Thad out to catch her and shut her up.

As Thad went out of the room Father glanced at his watch. When, a few moments later, the church bell began to toll he glanced at it again. From time to time he kept on glancing at it, but Thad did not return. Father became very fidgety, and finally he turned to Mother.

"You start along with the children, Mother," he said, "and I'll go back and see what's happened to Thad. He probably can't catch that cow alone."

He did not wait for an answer, but strode rapidly through the door that led to the kitchen and thence to the back door. But Mother made no move to start for church. She was as anxious as Father to know what was going on in the backyard; and after two or three minutes had passed and he had not come back she went out that way to see for herself. She did not go as Father had gone, striding along and slamming the doors behind him with the abandon of careless haste. It could hardly be said that she went on tiptoe, but at least she made no unnecessary noise. All she wanted was to satisfy her curiosity as to what was going on, and she had no particular desire to be seen.

She found the kitchen quiet, for the hired girl was still engaged with the upstairs work. She listened a moment, and hearing nothing, tiptoed over to the door, slightly ajar, which led into the summer kitchen. Father was crouching and weaving in a most peculiar manner, his fists doubled, and the back of his neck a fiery red. He was making strange motions with his arms suggestive of a

105

boxer. She thought for a moment that he must be out of his head, must suddenly have lost his reason. Then as he crouched far over to one side as if to avoid a blow she saw outside the window what was apparently responsible for Father's pantomime—Thad locked in mortal combat with Red Brower, the boy who lived next door.

Another fight—and on Sunday—! Just an ordinary everyday fight over a sandlot ball game was enough to upset and unnerve her for a whole day, and I never could quite understand why she did not scream and rush out to separate Thad and young Brower. It may have been the responsibility for getting the children to church, or possibly the fact that Red Brower was perennially in need of a thrashing, but in any event she stayed for no more than a glance at what was going on, and without letting Father know of her presence she quietly retraced her steps to the library.

"Has Thad caught her yet?" we asked as she returned to the library.

"Who? Oh, you mean the cow—I don't think so. But Father's there to help him. They'll get her. And we'll go on now and let them come along later. Louise, you come up and walk with Mother. The rest of you can stay in your usual places."

We reached the church on the very last toll of the bell. Father came in almost half an hour late, but apparently so well satisfied with himself that I felt sure he must have caught the cow before she had done any damage to his garden. Thad didn't come at all. When we got home we found that he had been hurt. The story was that Father had met him coming into the house with a black eye, a bloody nose, and several buttons torn from his Sunday clothes. Father instantly guessed what had happened.

"I see the cow has been dragging you around by the rope. I hope you're not hurt."

Thad began to brush himself off. "No, I'm not hurt any—got a few buttons torn off, and I guess I'm kinda dirty."

"There's a little blood on your nose—she must have bumped you somehow."

"Yes, she bumped me two or three times—but I bumped her some pretty good ones, too."

"All right," said Father, "you go in there to the sink and wash the blood and dirt from your face and I'll see if I can handle the cow."

As it turned out he handled her very easily. She let him walk right up to her and take hold of the rope. All the mischief and meanness seemed to have gone out of her. After looking Thad over, however, Father decided that the boy had better stay home from church and hold a piece of raw meat on his eye.

Mother never had liked that cow, and when Thad and Father had finished telling how vicious the animal had been she pretended to believe the story and insisted that the cow must be sold at once. Father protested feebly, but after the gory tale of what had happened to Thad the cow didn't have a leg to stand on, and Father had to let her go. I never could quite square Mother's method of getting rid of the cow with her Christian principles of uprightness and honesty. It is true that she was taking them at their word, but it is also true that she knew their story was a complete fabric of lies. However, the ethics of the transaction never seemed to bother her, and a few years after the cow had been safely disposed of she laughingly boasted to me that she had paid them in their own coin.

Mother was one of the original Fundamentalists. She believed in the story of Creation literally as told in the Book of Genesis. She believed that it was an apple—not a pear, plum, prune, or peach—with which Eve tempted Adam. She never would say what kind of apple, because

107

the Bible did not say, but I am fairly certain that she thought it must have been a Spitzenberg, as that was her favorite apple. We were brought up to believe this story in all its simple beauty, and I always pictured Eve as luring Adam over into her side of the garden by holding a Spitzenberg just out of his reach until she had him where she wanted him. We were asked to swallow in its entirety the story of Noah and the Ark, although the soft pedal was always put on Noah's tippling, for with Mother one of the most active and ardent of the local temperance organization, had we known the truth we might have wondered why the Lord God Jehovah did not bear down on Noah to sign the pledge.

She believed with all her soul that the children of Israel walked dryshod through the Red Sea, that the whale swallowed Jonah verbatim and regurgitated him to the glory of God and the consternation of naturalists. She was as certain that Shadrach, Meshach, and Abednego came walking unharmed out of Nebuchadnezzar's fiery furnace as she was that Father threw coal into ours.

She even believed in a personal Devil, and she brought all her children up in that same belief. Father most distinctly did not believe in the Devil or in any other kind of ghosts, spooks, hobgoblins, apparitions, or fairies. "If I were going to believe in any supernatural beings," I once heard him say, "I would prefer to put my faith in wood nymphs and Palmer Cox's Brownies."

For some years I believed firmly in the Devil, and I must say that I found him most cooperative. He never said No to any wrongdoing I proposed, and never tried to take the credit for any of my successful deviltry. But with a Fundamentalist God standing around to see that I did no wrong, and the Devil always on hand to see that I did no right, I never seemed to have any privacy. With my belief in a personal God and a personal Devil so firmly established and so well documented I found it only a short step to a belief in ghosts, witches, imps, sprites, in fact practically anything that you could not see.

We never told ghost stories at our house; Father wouldn't have it. We never read ghost stories if he knew it. He had a set of Poe's works in the house, but he kept them locked up so we could not get at them, although he was a great admirer of Poe. All his life he was on the lookout for some psychic phenomena that could not be explained or duplicated by natural means. So far as I know he never found it, though I came very near finding it for him one night when I had been sent on an errand to the home of Uncle Albert, who lived about half a mile out of town. Stan went along with me for company.

It was in the fall shortly before Hallowe'en, when witches were supposed to be very plentiful, and it was an ideal night for them. There was a lowering sky with scuds of cloud moving ominously past. Off in the southwest a waning moon cast a dull and eerie glow which wrapped the earth in a mantle of gloom. A gusty wind from the west jostled against our backs as we went down the hill, passed the last flickering street lamp, and started along the gravel path which crossed the brook on a foot bridge. To the south of us the railroad tracks crossed this same brook on a high embankment carrying the water of the stream through a little black tunnel far below. I was always expecting some prehistoric monster to crawl out of that tunnel, and as we hurried along I glanced that way just to reassure myself. I saw no prehistoric monster in the tunnel—but I did see on the top of the embankment a witch in a high pointed cap.

She was all in black, tall and cadaverous, and as we went rapidly east she went just as rapidly west, leaning against the wind as if bent on getting somewhere in a hurry.

I caught Stan's arm. "Look—!"

Stan had already looked and had seen just what I saw. "Let's go home—!" he gasped.

I needed no second invitation. Our sudden reappearance with eyes popping and faces white as ghosts threw the household into an uproar. The other children blanched with terror when we told what we had seen. They pelted us with awed questions. Was she headed that way? Was she riding a broomstick? Where was she now? Instead of ridiculing us and calling us fraid-cats Father took our story seriously. "I've always wanted to see a witch," he said. "Just wait until I can get on my overcoat."

We were not any too anxious to go back, even though Father was going with us, but there seemed to be no way out of it, for he took hold of me with one hand and Stan with the other and started off down the hill with great strides as we trotted along beside him. He was talking learnedly as we hurried along, explaining that the human imagination had a way of jumping to conclusions that were wholly unwarranted by facts, and making people imagine that they were seeing something that they were really not seeing at all. We did not realize how rapidly we were covering the ground until suddenly we felt him stop dead in his tracks, nearly knocking us over.

"Great Jehovah—!" he exclaimed.

We glanced quickly up and saw that the witch was still there, still bending against the wind, a threatening and malignant silhouette against the dim light that was filtering through the troubled clouds.

"There it is!" we whispered. "That's where we saw it before."

"But—but—but it isn't walking any more," stammered Stan.

"That's because we're standing still," said Father, his composure completely recovered. "Don't you see what it is? It's a big pointed timber that the railroad company has set up as a brace for the telegraph lines which make a curve right there."

Of course we were relieved, but we were still pretty nervous, for we expected him to turn back and send us on to do our errand half a mile down the unlighted country road. But he evidently understood exactly how we felt, for without humiliating us by asking us if we were still afraid he remarked that since we had all come this far we might as well go on and do the errand together.

10. Literature in Our Family

FATHER never sat down in the dining room except at mealtime. I can't be sure that this was or was not intentional or that he ever gave the matter a single thought. It was probably just one of his minor habits. He sat in the library because it was his custom to sit there. His desk was there, his easy chair, the marble-topped table littered with magazines, and all around him his bookcases filled with books. An unabridged dictionary stood in a bent iron holder at one side of the desk. On the other side was a large wastepaper basket. Both were liberally patronized. The dictionary was the authority which he most frequently cited in court. Many of his will cases hinged on the exact meaning of a single word.

"Look it up in the dictionary," was his almost invariable answer when we would ask him the meaning of a word. "I'll write down what I think it means, and you can check on me and see if I'm anywhere near right."

He usually was, though occasionally we would catch him. I finally discovered it was the mechanical words that he did not know. Simple words like "lug," "cam," "spline" would have him helpless. Whenever I came across one that was not familiar to me I would save it up for him. Father personified the library. I used to feel his presence there even when I knew he was at the office. It may have been that what he personified was some of my brain cells;

but in any event courage was required to break any of the very serious rules in that room. I could break them very easily in the dining room, or the kitchen, or anywhere upstairs, but my criminal tendencies were of little use to me in the library.

Mother's favorite place to work during the day was in the dining room. This was a large, light room with a huge bay window, the panes of which came within a foot of the floor. Here the morning light streamed in, for the room was on the southeast corner of the house. Mother's sewing chair, a low sturdy rocker, and her darning basket usually stood in the bay window. Mending and darning were her pick-up work, and whenever she "had a moment" she would drop into that sewing chair and start in on the contents of the darning basket. Grandmother used to sit in the dining room, too. The only time she ever sat in the

113

library was when callers came; and as soon as they were out of the house she would quit the library in a hurry. She was a word-of-mouth person and the presence of so many silent books no doubt disturbed her. She liked company and was quite a lively conversationalist on the vital statistics and the goings and comings of the neighbors; but literature left her cold, and in all the years that she lived with us I never knew her to read any book but the Bible.

The nucleus of Father's library came to him from his own father. In the main it was pretty grim literature, based largely on thrift and the building of a Christian character. The ideas for most of these books were purloined from either *Poor Richard* or *Pilgrim's Progress*. Grandfather must have taken them for a bad debt. He certainly was too good a businessman to buy them, and he was born far too thrifty to need any books on how to save your money.

The two books of note in the collection were purchased by Grandfather himself. One was the original edition of *Birds of America* by one J. J. Audubon. The other was a leather-bound set of the etchings of William Hogarth. The Audubon set was kept under lock and key in one of the big bottom drawers of the high bookcase. I never saw those books more than half a dozen times in my life, though I had the satisfaction of knowing that they were there if I ever wanted to consult them during the brief period while I was making a collection of birds' eggs. The Hogarth book was much more familiar to me. It was a table book in the front parlor, and though it was supposed to be only a part of the interior decoration of the room, I often beguiled the time on Sunday by studying the details of *The Rake's Progress*.

Of all the self-improvement volumes from Grandfather's library I think my favorite item was a paper-covered book called *Shut Your Mouth*. I was attracted at

114

once by the title, and the book on closer acquaintance proved to be a fiery bit of propaganda against mouth breathing. It was copiously illustrated with *before* and *after* pictures, showing the facial advantages of sleeping with the mouth shut.

There was a vast set of Bulwer-Lytton in three-quarter morocco with marbled edges. Nobody ever read it. Nobody ever had read it. Nobody ever wanted to read it. I hesitated to bring the subject up for fear that I would be told this was something that I ought to read; but at last my curiosity got the better of me, and one night I asked Father where the set came from. He smiled and said that it was a wedding present. And that was that. That's the way libraries are made.

Father himself bought the set of Cooper's *Leatherstocking Tales*, the *Waverley Novels*, Thackeray's *Works*, and *The Complete Works* of Charles Dickens. He admired Thackeray, he tolerated Scott, he felt that as an American he ought to have Cooper—but Dickens he loved. There was probably not a novel of Dickens' that Father had not read from ten to twenty times. He could spot a character or a line out of Dickens and place it at once in the book— almost in the chapter—where it belonged. He would read to us out of Dickens when he would not read anything else. He would tell us Dickens tales and Dickens incidents without number. Tiny Tim and Little Dorrit were as real to us as the children over on the back street. The whole town was peopled with the characters of Dickens. Father was always hoping against hope that he would develop some real Dickens enthusiasts in the family, but he never succeeded in bringing out even one. Some of us read a book or two. I think that was the limit of complete performance with me, though I made an effort to skim through four or five. All in all we had the typical Victorian library. Just to look at those books was depressing.

115

Great sets of this or that in uniform bindings standing unused on the shelves and seldom disturbed except at house-cleaning time. "Father's library" was like something sacred. We spoke of it in a subdued voice. It was a possession to be proud of rather than to love. My own reactions to it were such as might have been aroused by a large bronze plaque or a wreath of artificial flowers. Until I came across Richardson, Fielding, and Smollett on a top shelf I had no idea that life and gaiety were to be found in any of the gloomy-looking books that lined Father's shelves.

There was little reading aloud in our household, probably because there were so many things going on at the same time. Once in a great while Father would read us something from Dickens. Everybody gathered around when Father read aloud, for it was a real treat. I do not believe that an entire book was ever read aloud at our house. With the magazines, however, it was a different matter. The *Youth's Companion* came on Thursday, and of course there was always a scramble to get it first; for during daylight hours the rule on the *Companion* was first come, first served. But after supper the seniority rule went into effect, and if the older children wanted it, they could have it. The theory was that they could read faster than the younger ones and thus hasten the circulation. There was one exception to this rule: if a serial was running in which we were all interested the current installment must be read aloud before any individual could settle down to a private reading of the rest of the magazine. That was how it happened that when *The Flamingo Feather* was running serially I never had to read a single installment for myself. It was the same with a number of the other world-shaking serials of the time, though I can now recall the name of only one more, a stirring tale called *Lost in Patagonia,* in which the principal characters lost their way while searching for apples in what was supposed to be a barren land.

The leading adult magazine in the household shifted from *Harper's* to *Century* and back again several times. Father really preferred *Century*, but as we always operated on an exchange basis with one of the neighbors he occasionally found it necessary to subscribe to *Harper's* for a year or two. But whether we subscribed or exchanged we had both magazines to read every month without fail. The real difference showed only in the attic, where the back numbers were stored, for we saved the magazine we subscribed to. Over a period of nearly half a century our files were chronologically complete, though the breed was badly mixed.

From the standpoint of the children the *Youth's Companion* was the most important magazine to come into the house. From time to time we tried *Harper's Young People* and *St. Nicholas,* though they never seemed to satisfy the whole family as the *Companion* did. This was no doubt partly because they had no premium list—and the premium list of the *Companion* was supreme. Indeed, it was far to be preferred to any story ever printed in the magazine itself. When the premium list came, spring and fall, the entire town was combed for new subscriptions. This process was as exciting as an election. I do not now recall that I ever turned up a single new subscription in my life except that of an uncle in California who wrote Father that he was getting along in years and wanted some light reading. I wrote back by return mail before anybody could stop me and booked him without any trouble at all. With this new subscription and one seventy-five in cash I bought my first camera, a Harvard, which had a pinhole lens and took plates two and a quarter by three and a half. Good camera, though not quite so speedy as some I have since had.

Mother, who tried hard to supervise our reading, drew the line at a periodical called *Golden Days*. She regarded it as too sensational to be an influence for good. Of course that did not keep us from reading it. We simply added a little more sensation by bootlegging it. Other children in the neighborhood took it, and I don't believe that I ever missed an issue so long as I was interested. For me, at least, *Golden Days* was a steppingstone to the Dime Novel. And after I had once made the acquaintance of "Deadshot Dave" and "Petey the Scout of the Cinnamon Twins," the pallid heroes of *Golden Days* could never satisfy me again. I wanted no more juvenile heroes. Nothing less than a big he-man with a pair of guns that he was not afraid to use could now hold my interest. For a year or more there was never a time when I did not have a Nick Carter or some comparable thriller in my hip pocket. We used to trade these novels around as we traded jackknives and marbles. I probably read fifty of them in the course of a year, and during that period I may have bought as many as two or three.

A curious little periodical called *Farm and Fireside* used to come to our house off and on. I do not believe that we ever subscribed to it, though I suspect that was the publisher's idea in sending it to us. I never read anything in the front of this paper, nor did I ever miss anything in its advertising pages. Here one could buy loaded cigars or cigarettes; or, if one preferred, a bouquet from which a jet of water could be squirted into the face of any friend trusting enough to come within range. These and many other "jokes and favors" covered several columns which I studied with great care, not so much with the idea of making purchases as of defending myself from friends and acquaintances who might try them on me.

The "Sweetheart Cards" were quite another matter. And about once a year I used to purchase a supply. These came twenty-four for a dime, assorted. Most of them were "May I See You Home?" though there were always a few "Would Like to Get Acquainted." I used to wonder if it was all right to send the latter through the mail, for they quite plainly hinted at a pick-up and never failed to fill me with rakehell reactions. There were also in each package a few "May I Call on You?" but these did not seem so bad to me. But perhaps the card that stirred me most was the one which said "I Love You!" Quite naturally there was never more than one of these in any assorted pack.

I used to sit and look at that "I Love You!" card by the hour. I would keep wondering if I would ever have the nerve to hand it to any girl. The truth is that I never did, and I eventually traded one "I Love You!" for five "May I See You Home?" That's the kind of youth I was—just a playboy.

11. Help Wanted

THE servant question was ever present in our family. Girls came and girls went. Mother could always get a girl; there were no factories or offices then to employ them. If a girl was smart enough she could become a teacher. If not, she had little chance for employment in our neighborhood except in domestic service. Now and then a girl would have gumption enough to become a milliner. There was a job that took gumption. It also took good taste and imagination and diplomacy, and it required definite sales ability. Of course there were milliners—and milliners. Some used their fur and feathers to cover their real profession. But we never had more than one or two of either kind in our town. Yes, Mother could always get a girl, but she could almost never get a servant.

Trained servants were not only scarce, they were nonexistent. The country girls were willing enough to work, but they knew nothing whatever of domestic service. Many of the girls we tried had never seen a tablecloth until they came into our house. Half of them did not know what napkins were for. We occasionally got hold of a girl who had never before encountered bed sheets and was as likely to put them on top of the bedclothes as under them. One girl had seen sheets used only to cover the dead, and she always referred to them as "dead sheets." These girls were exceptions, however, and came for the greater part from the poverty-stricken families of farm laborers who received at that time as little as ten dollars a month for a sixteen-hour day, seven days a week. There were always plenty of these girls to be had, for the drifting farm laborers almost without exception had large families; but it was only when we were in a desperate plight for help that Mother would try one of them. They were usually shiftless and sloppy. They had no standards to live up to, no future ahead, and no ambition except to get by.

Another source of domestic help at that time was the immigration of "green" Irish girls. These girls came in waves, and though we were not always able to get one when we really needed help, some of the most satisfactory servants in our whole galaxy of help came to us straight from the Emerald Isle. Mother liked these Irish girls because they had a social sense, or, as she used to put it, they knew their place. She never criticized the girls of American birth for wanting to eat with the family and participate in the family amusements and recreations. Rather she admired their democratic spirit; but she took the attitude that while they might make good citizens when they grew up, they did not make the kind of servants she liked to have in her household. Many of our friends had kitchen help who ate at the table with them and sat with the family in the evening. But this was one point on which Mother never compromised. She was considerate of her help though exacting in her requirements. She nearly always clothed them, saw to their spiritual needs by insisting upon their going to their church, furnished them with good living quarters and a place to entertain their friends, but she insisted upon the observance of the very definite line that then existed between master and servant.

The going wage at the time for an inexperienced or

121

green girl was a dollar and a half a week and board. An experienced girl, reasonably good at cooking and waiting on table, commanded two dollars and a half and found. Only a tip-top servant who could make bread and pastry in addition to the ordinary cooking, who was capable of the most perfect dining-room service, could ever hope to receive three dollars a week. These may seem like starvation wages, but all wages were low at that time. The very highest class of unskilled laborer was to be had for one dollar a day, and even the skilled laborer considered himself lucky to receive two dollars for a ten-hour day's work. During this same period Father was drawing wills for one dollar and trying cases in Justice Court for ten.

Mother always tried to keep an eye on the morals of her maids. If she found that they were running around with married men, or even unmarried men of bad reputation, she would take them aside and give them some motherly advice. If this failed to straighten them out she would begin to look for another girl. On one occasion she was nearly prostrated by the discovery that her unmarried maid was in a family way. There was no doubt or guesswork about it—Nellie came to her and confessed and asked for help. Very much in a quandary Mother went to her own mother for advice, Father being away somewhere trying a case.

Grandmother was in no quandary at all. "She deserves to be stoned out of the house." She gave a quick decisive nod. "Don't let her spend another night under your roof."

Mother shook her head. "But, my dear, she has no place to go."

Grandmother rocked slowly back and forth in her chair. "Is that your fault?"

"Why, no—but, Mother, we must show a little charity. Remember the woman in the Bible who was taken—under similar circumstances."

122

"That woman was in an entirely different situation. She was simply caught in an immoral act which concerned only herself. But this woman is going to bring into the world an innocent child that will be branded as an illegitimate all its days. And think of your own daughters sleeping under the same roof with such a woman!"

Mother did think about that, so she sent her daughters over to spend the night with Auntie Cad. When they came back the next day Nellie was gone and they were told that she had been taken to the County Hospital for treatment for some serious internal trouble.

"But wasn't it very sudden?" asked one of the girls.

Mother shook her head. "Oh, no, it's been coming on for some time."

In due time a lovely little girl was born, which Mother succeeded in getting into a good orphanage. In order to free the child of any sign of illegitimacy it was not only necessary for Nellie to sign away all maternal rights but to forego any knowledge of the child's whereabouts and future life. Nellie never knew even the name of the institution in which her child was placed.

In telling me the story, years after it had taken place, Father remarked with a smile that although Mother would not have such an immoral woman in her own house, she had no such compunction about the houses of her friends. It seems that finally by means of her gilt-edged recommendations she placed Nellie in service with one of the old South Main Street families in Geneva, where she remained for several years before marrying the milkman and going to live on a dairy farm.

One would think that with such a pretty denouement as this Mother would have been perfectly satisfied with her handling of the entire case; that in this instance she could accept the philosophy that all's well that ends well. But her Puritanical conscience would allow her to accept no such philosophical balderdash as this, and to the end of her days she used to wonder a little guiltily if she had not been a party to the perpetration of a wicked fraud on that milkman.

After the sudden departure of Nellie we had a number of short-lived and undistinguished incumbents in the kitchen, among whom was Hannah, the only colored lady who ever worked for us. Hannah was ample and buxom. She wore a bandanna around her head and weighed upwards of two hundred pounds, but she was the sole hired girl we ever had who could run down a rooster before breakfast, wring his neck, pick and parboil him, and serve him fricasseed on toast for breakfast, tender as a bit of filet. Hannah had a raft of coal-black boys who used to come and play with me in our yard. There may have been too many of them to suit Mother, who used to ask me every day if I couldn't find any white boys to play with. Or perhaps it was just that they came too often. She may even have thought that I was enriching my vocabulary along unnecessary or undesirable lines, for those boys certainly did have good words for just about everything. Be all that as it may, she finally reached the point where she thought that the easiest way to get rid of the little colored boys who were tumbling on our lawn, climbing in our trees, swinging in our swing, and teetering on our see-saw was to relieve Hannah of her command. Hannah hated to go, and I hated to have her, but Mother was right; after she left, the little colored boys never came there to play again. I saw them one day swarming over Dr. Howard's lawn, and heard that Hannah had gone there to work. A little later I saw them darkening Dan Richman's door and knew that she must be working there. The time came when Father met her on the street and she told him she was leaving town as there wasn't really room enough for her family to develop in such a small place.

After Hannah left we had a young girl from the Five Corners. She was really no more than an apprentice and served mostly as a nursegirl. I don't recall her name, and she was not there very long. All I can remember about her is that we boys nicknamed her "Dipperlip" and she taught me to dance the schottische.

We had one girl who came and went half a dozen times. Her name was Annie and she lived in Clifton Springs. Annie liked small babies, and as long as there was one in the house she would come and stay quite contentedly, but as soon as a baby began to walk and talk Annie would become restless, and when there was a birth in the family of another of her patrons she would leave us. Not without tears, I am happy to say, for Annie never ceased to love her nurslings, but she simply could not control herself where a little new baby was involved. Getting Annie back again was just a matter of time. She had an uncanny way of knowing when the stork was about to alight, and would call and make her arrangements some little time in advance. Of course the time came when the stork no longer stopped at our house. Annie was obviously disappointed when she dropped in for one of her period ical calls; it was the first time in years that her calculations had gone awry. She told Mother with many shakings of her head that she was sorry to lose so steady a customer, though she cheered up considerably when Mother told her that Louise, who had been married two years before, was "expecting." Annie took down the address, saying that she wanted to write to Louise and congratulate her, and the next thing we knew Annie had gone on to Westchester County where Louise then lived, and was in full charge of proceedings. She stayed on for a baby or two, but Annie could not keep pace with the new generation

125

who had their babies delivered in hospitals, fed them on precision formulas, and wrapped them in chuck-away diapers. After the completion of Louise's contribution to posterity Annie retired to her old home in Clifton Springs, where she finished her allotted time in comfort with occasional visits to the families where she had served so valiantly in her day.

Every maid under forty who entered our service was at once confronted by a menace in the person of Larry Hixon, who lived on the street which ran back of our property, in a little house facing the railroad tracks. To give Larry his due, he was industrious and good-natured. He was a good worker so long as somebody was present to tell him what to do. He did not earn very much, but it was enough to keep him from going into debt. Larry preferred to work at loading and unloading cars, and during the shipping season when farmers were bringing in their wheat and apples and cabbage, he was never out of a job. He was a painter of sorts and occupied the off-season for shipping by painting barns, and occasionally he would tackle a job of paperhanging. Larry's ruling passion was to be a lady's man, but by some strange perversity of Nature he seemed to be totally without attraction for women. He courted our cooks assiduously for years without making any impression on them. They poked fun at him, and refused almost without civility his invitations to go for a walk, or to stroll uptown and have a dish of ice cream at Walt's.

But if Nature had been stingy with her masculine charm in Larry's make-up she had been equally lavish in another direction, for she had given him patience without end. In spite of all rebuffs Larry would keep on trying. And at last his efforts were crowned with success. Reba, the homeliest and most unattractive girl we ever had in our kitchen, succumbed to his charms. And when

126

Reba succumbed she so completely capitulated that it was not long before the affair was the talk of the town, and Reba had to be discharged. This was apparently just what she wanted, for she promptly moved into Larry's little house without the formality of marriage and undertook to make it into a happy home for him. But for some reason things went badly with the affair, and in less than a month the two were quarreling. Then one night Larry stamped out of the house after a tiff and went uptown, where he spent the evening drinking beer in one saloon or another. When he came home after the saloons had closed he found Reba lying on the bed and thought she was asleep. But when he took hold of her hand to waken her, he found it stone cold. She had taken enough arsenic to kill an elephant.

This episode proved to be the turning point in Larry's life. From that moment he ceased to be an inoffensive nobody. Women peered out from behind the curtains as he passed, and men stopped him on the street to talk to him. Larry was always ready to talk freely about the suicide. He did not make a nuisance of himself, but anybody who was interested would have no difficulty in getting all the details. Larry always spoke nicely of Reba. She was a good girl. She had made him very happy. She was all right. There was nothing wrong with Reba. He thought she must have been temporarily insane. He admitted that they had had words before he went out. What man doesn't have words with his woman once in a while? Any woman worth her salt would put up an argument now and then. It was just a little spat, and he had gone out to give her a chance to cool off.

Men began to look at Larry in a different way. He was no longer merely a roustabout carloader; he was a man for whom a woman had given up her life. He must have something—something that they had never suspected. They

127

began to treat him like a person of consequence. When he spoke, instead of poking fun at him they listened. What he said always seemed to make sense, and they could not be sure whether his talk had changed or whether it was just that they had paid no attention to him before. The general opinion among the men was that he was quite a fellow. But it was in the attitude of the women that the greatest change had come. One might have thought that after the unfortunate affair with Reba all women would steer clear of him even more assiduously than before, but what happened was the exact opposite. Now he piqued their curiosity. They were a little afraid of him, and still they were drawn to him. If he invited one of our maids to go for a walk with him—she went. She might be blushing and palpitating as they started off, she might be troubled with shortness of breath and inability to carry on a conversation, but at least her eyes would be bright, and she would be on the alert for almost anything. One woman had died for this man, a maid of ours once told my mother, and there was no telling what some other woman might not do for him.

I guess our Sadie was the only girl we ever had after Larry came into his own who wouldn't even look at him. Sadie not only had beaux aplenty, but she had good looks to spare and she was ambitious. Mother was not given to picking out comely housemaids. This may have been entirely by accident and it may just as easily have been by design. With boys growing up and an attractive husband on the premises there was every reason why a prudent woman should exercise the greatest care in the choice of her household help. I can readily count up on my fingers more than twenty reasonably youthful maids who have come into our house as servants, and of them all Sadie was the only one who really compelled a second look. I thought so then, and I think so now. Whether her soul was as beautiful as her face and figure I would not be able to say. I was only a young boy at the time and knew very little about the romantic frailties of the gentler sex.

Strictly speaking, Sadie did not belong to the serving class. She was of the landed gentry. Her family had owned their own farm for many years, and when they died they left it to Sadie. The only trouble was that it was heavily mortgaged and there were numerous debts besides, and when the executor had finished with his seemingly endless computations the farm was gone, the old homestead was gone, and all that Sadie had left was a square piano that her family had bought for her when she was just old enough to begin taking music lessons.

We had been without a maid for a week or two. My sisters were quite content to make their own beds and keep their rooms in order; this was something that Mother insisted on whether there was any help in the house or not. But they were becoming very much bored with getting the meals and doing the dishes, and when old Dr. Howard told Mother that Sadie was looking for a job, Mother lost no time in driving down in the country to see her.

Sadie knew how to cook, she knew all about housework; the only thing she didn't understand about was waiting on the table, and she was sure she could learn that. The wages Mother offered were satisfactory, and she was all ready to strike a bargain when Sadie stopped her.

"There's one thing more," she said, "would there be any place for my instrument? It's about the only thing I have left. My father and mother gave it to me when I was a little girl, and I've always said that I'd never go anywhere without it. I've taken lessons and I can play quite a few pieces."

"What kind of an instrument is it?" asked Mother dubiously.

129

"A beautiful mahogany py-ano."

"Oh—is it a square or an upright?"

"It's a square, a lovely one, such a nice tone."

"Would you mind having it in your bedroom?"

"Oh, no; that's where I would like to have it."

Mother glanced around. "Well, the maid's bedroom is about the size of this room that we're in. Do you think that would be too crowded?"

"Why, I think that would be perfectly lovely."

"Then it's understood that you'll come?"

"Oh, yes, Mrs. Partridge. When will you be ready for me?"

"Your room is all ready now. Could you come tomorrow?"

Sadie looked thoughtful. "That depends entirely upon my instrument. If I can find somebody to handle it—I'll be there."

When Mother brought home the news the girls almost danced for joy. Father, too, was pleased with the prospect of some experienced kitchen help.

"Just when is this household paragon expected?" he asked.

"That depends entirely upon her instrument," said Mother.

Sadie's instrument arrived the next day in a hayrack with three husky farmers to carry it upstairs. And that night I drifted off to sleep to the tinny tinkling of *Little Brown Jug* and *The Prettiest Girl in the Room*.

12. New England Conscience

GRANDMOTHER BELLAMY, born Mahala Bayley, in Newbury, Vermont, in 1807, was married to Thomas Bellamy, September 16, 1828. The marriage was performed by her father, James Bayley, a Justice of the Peace in and for said township of Newbury, Orange County, in the state aforesaid.

For the marriage certificate the old justice used a scrap of paper torn from a larger sheet, on the back of which are computations continued from the unused portion. On such an occasion almost any bride would have made a splurge and used a whole sheet of paper for her marriage certificate. But not Mahala. She believed in thrift and frugality, and perhaps it is just as well that she did.

At the time of the marriage Thomas was pastor of a little white church in Bradford, Vermont. But he did not long remain in New England. He caught the western fever and started by easy stages toward the setting sun. He was, however, no real frontiersman, for when he had reached Monroe County, New York, he dropped out of the procession, and there he preached in one small town or another all the rest of his life.

He was a man with a calling. Born in England of a family of some discrimination he found it necessary to run away to America in order to satisfy his ambition to enter the ministry, although he had seven generations of ministers ahead of him, if the family traditions are to be relied on. For upwards of forty years he preached the Gospel, continually complaining in his journals of the indifference and lack of interest of his congregations. It seems never to have occurred to him that he might be partly to blame. The old parson never swerved from a firm belief that he had been called by the Almighty Lord God Jehovah to preach the Gospel unto every creature, and despite his precarious health he never missed a chance to ascend the pulpit and sermonize. But no man can butt his head against a stone wall year after year without getting a headache. Defeat and indifference, while unable to silence his exhortations and imprecations, were not without their effect on him. He became subdued and saddened and eventually arrived at the conclusion that this world was a very indifferent place in which to live. With his mind dwelling constantly on the joys of the existence to come it is not greatly stretching the truth to say that during the last few years of his life he lived more in the next world than in this.

He would not bother to put down in his journal any mention of the birth of one of his children, but he never missed noting the text of every sermon he preached. Nor did he mention a death unless he was asked to officiate at the funeral. Weddings were quite another matter, and it was his habit to enter in his journal a complete copy of the marriage certificate including the fee. His customary fee for uniting a couple was two dollars, or if they woke him up in the middle of the night, three. He once received ten dollars for performing a marriage in a lighthouse on Lake Ontario, adding with underscored words that the building was "built by the govt" as he noted the event in his journal. His largest fee, twenty dollars, was received for the marriage of Colonel Elisha Marshall and Miss Hannah Erickson of Rochester. The ceremony was performed in Charlotte, some ten miles from Rochester, at four o'clock on the morning of September 14, 1863.

Job C. Hedges, father of a son by the same name who came near being the governor of New York State, was one of the witnesses; and a P.S. following his entry of a certificate of the marriage adds, "Col Marshall stole Miss Erickson out of the window in the night because her Father was opposed to their marriage. The Con'l was in 14 Battles commanding the 19th Reg. of N. Y. Volenteres"—my father's old regiment, and Grandfather's only mention of the Civil War which was raging at the time.

With some financial pinch-hitting from her older sisters, who had married well, Mother achieved a large church wedding at St. Peter's in Rochester, during which, her father noted in his journal, the gas lights in the church flickered and burned with a dim and ghostly light. "Not a good omen," he writes. "I fear no good will come out of this marriage. If she lives one year I shall be glad. If she should not I should not be disapointed." In spite of the evil omen, however, the marriage proved to be not only fruitful but extremely happy, and missed reaching its golden anniversary by only a few months.

At the slightest indisposition Grandfather would note down in his journal, in a clear strong hand, such conclusions as, "I am sinking fast to my grave—the will of the Lord be done." Once he wrote, "I feel the seeds of death in me, my hold of life is broken & I stand wating." This sounds pretty serious, but a week later we find him performing a marriage at the American Hotel in Rochester, "before a large assemblage of people."

God was no Sunday visitor in that household; He was a steady boarder. After noting in his journal the purchase of a horse and carriage because his health "required riding (in a carriage) as exercise," Grandfather adds, "Lord, I hope to serve thee with this horse."

133

From other entries in the journal I learn that the horse cost one hundred dollars, the carriage twenty, and that he paid five cents per week for pasturage. His salary at this time was three hundred dollars a year, plus the Sunday collections, which ran from ninety-three cents up to three or four dollars, and an occasional donation party. Everything considered, the horse and carriage seem an extravagance, though the hiring of a maid on the same day at fifty cents a week was more in keeping with the family income.

With a provider of so much spiritual nourishment and so little medium of exchange it has long remained a mystery where the food came from to fill the hungry mouths of nine children, or the raiment to keep the wintry blasts from their little bodies. The family of the parson had a certain social position to maintain; they must be reasonably well dressed and well shod, and not only must appearances be kept up, but there was a certain amount of entertaining that had to be done. Without the rough-hewn, thrifty, and steadfast character of Grandmother at the tiller the family must almost certainly have gone on the rocks, or perhaps the rock pile. She could never have been very sweet-natured to live with—she was grim as winter, and immovable as a granite boulder. But as a household manager she had few equals. She knew how to cut all the corners, and she had a way of making things do. Her executive ability and her managerial resourcefulness she passed on to my mother; but she also passed on another legacy that was not quite so useful—that was, in fact, an annoyance to Mother all her life. It was her New England conscience.

By natural endowment Mother was light-hearted and gay. She loved fun and laughter and was always to be found in the midst of the music and dancing. Good company stimulated her and brought out all her gaiety. She did not, like Grandmother, believe that fun was a waste of time and in all probability sinful. She liked a good time too well to believe any such foolishness as that; but it was her firm conviction that to be happy you must be good. And it was in drawing the line between what was good and what was not good that the New England conscience got in its deadly work.

Fundamentally Grandmother was as religious as her husband. Her convictions were every bit as strong, and she shared wholeheartedly his belief that our sojourn here is a sort of training camp for the Life to Come. By the time she came to live with us she had already lost four of her children, though she felt perfectly secure in the knowledge that they had died in the faith and were among the elect patiently awaiting her arrival.

Grandmother could never be just a passive member of our household. She was too dominant a personality to sit and watch the world pass by. She was very free with her opinion on any problem of family discipline, and I never saw a person so wedded to the idea that every culprit was presumed to be guilty until proved innocent. I would not go so far as to say that she was vengeful, but I will say that if she had had her way not many offenses in our family would have gone unpunished. The thought of sparing the rod was something that apparently never came to her. So long as she lived she wielded a strong influence over Mother. Father was the only one who could hold her at bay. If she managed to get on his toes he silenced her with a blast; but Father had great respect for her and thought that her influence on the household, though somewhat Bourbon, was on the whole beneficial. Nobody could convince Grandmother—that was something she had to do for herself. She was in the main a doer, not a talker; and usually when she talked it was about doing. The one exception was the Lord's business. She felt that she had no choice but to talk about that whenever the occasion presented itself. On that subject she even argued back at the doctor on her deathbed and told him that he had no business to be there giving her pills when he ought to be in church saving his own immortal soul.

Grandmother had no conscientious scruples against either drinking or dancing. A little wine never hurt anybody, she said; and as for dancing, if a body wanted to hop around to music, she could see no reason to object. Somehow this surprises me. I would have expected her to regard dancing as a wicked vanity. But no, dancing was mentioned in the Bible and so was all right; and none of her five daughters was ever without an escort when there was any dancing to be done. The diversion that she abominated above all others was card-playing. Cards were a contrivance of the Devil.

When Grandmother, soon after she came to live with us, discovered that Mother allowed us to play cards, she was horrified. She couldn't have been any more astonished if she had discovered that Mother allowed us to play with matches and kerosene. Less, in all probability, for matches and kerosene would only burn down the house and consume our bodies, whereas playing cards most certainly would destroy our immortal souls.

Mother happened to be away from home the afternoon when Grandmother made her painful discovery. Two of Louise's classmates had dropped in after school and with Elsie to make a fourth were sitting quietly in the library playing a game of cassino while Grandmother sat in the bay window of the dining room in a low rocker she loved, with Mother's big darning basket beside her. The double doors between the two rooms were open, as they usually were. A coal fire was glowing in the dining-room grate, for it was a chilly fall day. Occasionally Grandmother would finish with a stocking, find its mate, roll the two together and put them on a pile of finished work on the windowsill.

Suddenly the word "ace" came to her ear like the warning hiss of a serpent. This was quickly followed by other words of a suspicious nature that might or might not be damning. "Spade" . . . "jack" . . . "trick" . . . Grandmother's needle paused in mid-air. Then came Louise's low-pitched voice:

"I had high, low, and game, but Linda had big cassino."

Grandmother dropped her work and went hobbling hastily into the library. "Heavenly Father, forgive them!" she gasped as she saw the playing cards scattered over the table. "They know not what they do!"

She scooped up the cards in her hands, awkwardly, as an inexpert player might do, her thimble which she had neglected to remove tapping irritably against the tabletop. The cards avoided her and she finally cleared the table by sweeping them impatiently into her apron.

"Why, Gramma!" Louise expostulated. "What's the matter?"

"Matter!" Grandmother stood trembling with indignation. "Four innocent young girls *playing cards* and you ask me the matter! You should be down on your knees begging God's forgiveness."

Abashed and embarrassed by this quite unexpected outburst in the presence of their friends Louise and Elsie blushed furiously. Louise finally pulled herself together.

"But Mother lets us play cassino."

"She even plays with us sometimes," said Elsie.

Grandmother stepped up to the grate and threw the cards into the fire. "A likely story—but at any rate nobody will ever play with *these* cards again."

She went calmly back to her darning, but the visitors did not stay long after that. The fur flew when Mother

137

came home, for she was just as positive that she was right as Grandmother was that she was wrong, the only difference between them being that Grandmother wanted to argue the question and Mother did not. Mother never would argue so long as she held the whip hand, and after a little Grandmother subsided into an indignant silence.

Having the law on our side we children took especial delight in flourishing a pack of cards around wherever Grandmother happened to be, and playing the simple card games we understood where she could not help seeing us. We had great fun at this. Even the older children derived a certain added pleasure from rubbing in the fact that Mother allowed us to do a thing of which Grandmother thoroughly disapproved. For a while Grandmother used to express her displeasure by dropping whatever she was doing and leaving the room. Sometimes, just to annoy her, we would move our card game wherever she went— except to her own room, which we were not allowed to enter without an invitation. There was nothing, however, to prevent us from snapping cards just outside her door, or even against it, where she could not help hearing the sound.

This teasing had to be done on the sly of course. Mother would have taken steps if she had known about it. It goes without saying, however, that Grandmother needed no help to protect herself from a host of children; and if we left our cards lying around, as we very frequently did, they had a way of disappearing. She must have burned them in the shiny round stove which stood in her bedroom. But the burning of an entire pack of cards is quite a bother. The stock from which they are made is not easily inflammable, and the tendency of cards to stick together excludes the draft that is necessary to good combustion. Then, too, there may be a decidedly noxious odor from the burning of such material, especially if the stove door has to be opened frequently for poking.

But Grandmother was resourceful, and she was not long in discovering that a pack of cards was as useless if minus a single card as if she had gone to the trouble of exterminating the entire pack, and from that time on it became almost impossible to keep a complete pack of cards in the house. A curious twist that developed was that when Grandmother ruined a pack in this way she always removed the same card—the ace of spades. For some reason this card had a peculiar significance for her. We children used to puzzle about it as we tried to invent games which could be played without this particular card. We never arrived at any very satisfactory conclusions, but I have since wondered if that black ace did not suggest to her an imprint of the Devil's hoof.

Grandmother was no nagger. She did not keep on going over the same ground after losing the initial decision. She took matters into her own hands so far as she was able, and she was doggedness itself at biding her time. On the playing-card issue she bided it long and well, but her day eventually came, and when it did she handled the situation in such a way that victory could not possibly escape from her grasp.

Thad, who was in Hobart College at the time, had come home for the week end and had brought one of his college friends with him. With three attractive sisters Thad was never at a loss for college friends to bring home with him, even though they knew that the old Sunday Blue Laws were strictly enforced in the household, and that they would have to submit to a dose of family prayers and at least two doses of church. The family had finished a large and rather overwhelming Sunday dinner, and the older members of the household had retired to their rooms for a siesta. There was an unwritten law in our household that during the Sunday rest period of one hour there should be no playing of musical instruments, no singing, and no loud or unseemly noises. This left little to be done except talking, reading, or the writing of letters.

Immediately after dinner the younger folk had drifted into the parlor, where they sat chatting and bantering about not much of anything, as young people will. Father and Mother had paused in the doorway for a pleasantry or two on the way to their room, and Grandmother had already gone to hers without stopping. The dinner table had been cleared and no sounds were emanating from the kitchen, where the hired girl was presumably eating her dinner.

For a time Father and Mother could hear a pleasant drone of voices from the parlor, and when these ceased they idly imagined that the young folks had retired to their rooms for a quiet period of reading or letter-writing. They were just dozing off when suddenly the door of their room burst open and Grandmother stood before them, her eyes blazing with excitement and indignation.

"Come with me—both of you!" she commanded in a subdued voice.

Father sat quickly up. "What's the trouble?"

"I'll show you what the trouble is," said Grandmother exultantly. "You come with me—and be still about it."

They followed her to the door of Thad's room where she stopped them with a motion of her hand. "Listen— they're all in there."

"But what of it?" asked Mother. "So long as they're quiet."

"Wait till you see what's going on! I could hear them from my closet." Grandmother threw open the door—and there they all sat in the midst of a card game. "Playing cards on the Sabbath Day! What did I tell you!"

It was an embarrassing moment for all concerned—that

is, all except Grandmother who gloried in her moment of triumph. The scene could easily have become extremely disagreeable had Mother let matters get out of hand; but

even though she agreed with Grandmother, her social sense would not allow her to have the guest made any more uncomfortable than he already was. She suggested that the young people go downstairs and sing hymns, as she felt sure the resting for the day was now over.

141

They were only too relieved to go. The subject was not mentioned again until the guest was out of the house—and then the playing of cards was summarily banished from the house forever. Mother had more sense than to tell us that we must never again play cards. Of course we would play cards in other places, and did, and we invented some ingenious subterfuges for use around home. Our game of domino euchre was played exactly as the card game is played, only we used a number instead of a suit as the trump. And we had a marked deck of "authors" containing fifty-two cards. We could play whist with these, or cassino, or any other card game, but the only thing I now remember about that deck is that Oliver Wendell Holmes was the deuce of spades—the "little cassino."

Father was an interested onlooker in this household interdiction against playing cards. He never liked to play, and so long as cards were not allowed in the house he knew that he never would be forced into a game against his will. My impression is that he must have thought the whole affair pretty silly, though he never said much about it. When the ban was finally lifted—it was Father who lifted it. He came upon a group of us one day playing pedro out back of the barn with a soiled and tattered pack of cards belonging to one of the boys who lived across the railroad tracks. If we had seen Father coming we would have put the cards out of sight, but he was upon us almost before we knew it. He stopped and watched us for a few minutes and went on. That night at supper he announced that playing cards were legal in the house once more after a moratorium of over seven years.

"If you boys want to play cards," he said, "you needn't go out back of the barn."

At first Mother was a little diffident about playing. After the long period of abolition she did not wish to have the appearance of being inconsistent, she said. But her diffidence wore off and in time she became the most enthusiastic card player in the family. There was one amusing repercussion, however. Upon the banning of cards from the house Mother had felt that she must resign from the card club, and not wishing to be out of the local club life entirely she had organized a literary society called the Periodical Club. This organization caught on among the non-card players and eventually became so popular and successful that she found it very much on her hands after the reason for its being had ceased to exist.

Grandmother did not live to see this great heresy and reprobation. For more than a year before it occurred she had been quietly sleeping the sleep of the elect on the hillside beyond the schoolhouse. But her enmity to playing cards lived on in our memories, and to this day I seldom pick up the ace of spades without a little thrill of surprise to find that it is still in the pack. And I may as well admit that of the fifty-two cards the ace of spades is my all-time favorite.

13. School and Hooky

THE morning line-up for inspection that we called "going on the carpet" was never anything but a nuisance to me, but I must admit that there was a certain rough justice about it. If you reached the line before the bell rang you were credited with being on time no matter how many times you might be sent back to remedy some minor defect in your sartorial—or ablutionary—arrangements. Many a time I have gone racing down with one shoe entirely unlaced or one stocking inside out. I knew I could never pass the inspection, but it was better to be sent back than to get a tardy mark. Occasionally I used to try getting in line without washing my face—but it almost never worked.

There was very little practical use in having the older children in the line-up. They never had to be sent back. Sometimes Mother would disagree with one of the girls over what was a proper ribbon or ruffle to be worn to school, but the change, if any, would not be made until after breakfast. Their presence on the carpet was academic; it was to impress the younger children with the importance of the morning inspection.

If we could have put right back on again the clothing we had taken off the night before the problem of dressing would have been greatly simplified. But we could not do that. Our school clothes were something special, and until we were of high school age we had to come home every day right after classes and change into our play clothes. I did not mind this very much; of course I begrudged the time wasted in making the change, but I was always rough on clothes, and it was a relief to have on something I did not have to be careful of. One of the worst troubles with playing hooky was the necessity of keeping track of the time so as to check in at the proper moment for a change of clothes. I think I was caught that way oftener than any other. But I kept right on trying.

In our family the children started school at the age of about five. I personally beat the gun in this event and began school when I was only four and a half. It was not, however, because of any great thirst for knowledge on my part, but rather because I was so much of a nuisance around home. The particular event that caused my initial enrollment in the public schools of the land had to do with my fondness for woodworking tools. We had a carpenter on the place mending the side porch, and when he went home to dinner he left a mallet and chisel lying on the floor of the porch. As soon as he was out of sight I picked up the tools and started to work on my own initiative. By the time that my father had reached home for his midday meal I had just finished carving my full name on the side of the house.

"Well, what do you think of that?" I asked him.

"I think that any boy who can do as good a job as that is old enough to go to school," he replied.

And when my brothers and sisters went back to school after dinner I went with them. Our house was in the eastern part of the village, and the school was in the western part, about three-quarters of a mile away. Mother never allowed us to take our lunch to school. She thought that school children required a hot meal in the middle of the day. She also thought that a lot of mischief could take place around the school in the one-hour intermission that was allowed for the midday meal. So we plowed back and forth twice a day through the snows of winter, and we sloshed back and forth through the rains in the spring and fall. We fumbled over our examination papers and grumbled over our report cards. I started regularly every fall in a back seat, but at the end of a week or ten days I never failed to find myself in a front seat, where the teacher could more easily keep me under surveillance.

We used to go trooping out of the house in the morning like a bunch of colts turned out to grass. The older children were supposed to take care of the younger, but they paid little attention to us so long as we kept going in the direction of school. The old schoolhouse was three stories high, with two stories of brick above a first story of cut stone. The main entrance to the upper floors was by curious twin stairways to the second floor. The original idea was to have separate stairways for the boys and the girls, coming together on the wide piazza before the second-floor entrance, but the plan was abandoned. Promotion in this school was really going upward, with the Primary Department on the ground floor and the Academic at the top.

With only six rooms in the schoolhouse and eight children in our family we had little difficulty in placing a child in every room, though with the passage of time the tendency was to have them concentrated in the upper rooms.

From the beginning of my school days I had trouble over excuses. Punctuality seemed unimportant to me in comparison with the importance of the various projects which caught my attention between the time of leaving home and arriving at school, especially after I was old enough to require no further overseeing by the others while I was en route. Tardiness became a regular habit with me, and there was an occasional case of hooky to be accounted for. With Father regarding punctuality as highly as he did I preferred to get my excuses from Mother, and made a practice of presenting them to her already written at times when she was too busy to investigate them very closely.

I once found her signature on a scrap of paper and put it away for future reference. The next time I needed an excuse to cover a case of hooky I wrote out the document myself according to the usual formula, and had a friendly grocery clerk copy her signature on it. The plan worked so well that I began to use it for tardiness, and once or twice a week I would write myself an excuse to be let out at two o'clock or two-thirty. Mother remarked one day that I must be doing better about getting to school on time and I modestly admitted that I was. A very comfortable future would have been assured had I continued to use the kind of paper we had at home; but success made me careless, and one day when I had been riding the rounds with the grocery clerk and needed an excuse—I presented one written on a cigarette paper, the only writing material he happened to have at hand. That afternoon the teacher stopped in to see Mother, and when I came in later I was confronted with all my forged excuses. Mother could hardly tell which signatures were genuine and which were spurious; she was frequently signing excuses for the children and could not possibly remember them all. I might have come out of my perfidy unscathed had it not been for the cigarette paper. Mother despised cigarettes, and to have me represent her to the teacher as a woman who would conduct her school correspondence on a cigarette paper so angered and embarrassed her that she disavowed all my excuses, the real along with the counterfeit. She was still so upset, even after Father had finished with me, that she turned me over to the principal of the school to be punished as a forger and an impostor. I had, however, scarcely finished with my expiation for these misdeeds before I became involved in another unfortunate affair.

Every year after the weather was warm enough the boys of the family would tease to be allowed to go barefooted to school. Our chances of receiving an affirmative answer would have been as good if we had asked Mother to let us go to church in a barrel. She was not averse to bare feet in our own backyard, but she would never let us be seen off the premises without shoes and stockings. No matter how nice the weather or how tempting the new blades of grass she always seemed shocked to have us ask her. Her attitude was that we should have known better than to ask. One year when the weather was particularly entrancing Herb and I made the customary request as we came home to lunch. We were both sullen over her instantaneous refusal, and on the way back to school we decided to take the matter into our own hands. We removed our shoes and stockings at the top of the schoolhouse hill and hid them in the end of a culvert built to carry the surface drainage under the crossing of an intersecting street.

We had a delightful time running around on the soft new grass of the schoolyard, though we were prudent enough to keep out of the sight of our older sisters so they would not have anything on us. It was no great trouble to avoid them, as the schoolyard was large and the children numerous, and as we were both in the Intermediate Department there was no danger of our seeing them after the session had begun. All went well until the middle of the afternoon, when a terrific thunderstorm blew up. The rain came down in torrents, turning the lawns into lakes and the streets into raging freshets, and when after school we went to the culvert to get our shoes—they were nowhere to be found.

I would have crawled into the tile in quest of them if

the opening had been a little larger, and when we found I couldn't get inside we offered five cents to one of the little Duffy boys to go in for us, but he did not care to undertake the job, especially since he was not to get the five cents if he did not get the shoes. Mr. Cooley, the store-keeper, came along and asked what we had lost and we told him a ball. Being a kind-hearted fellow he stopped and tried to help us get it. He borrowed a long piece of fencing wire somewhere in the neighborhood and pulled a short piece of fencepost all the way through the culvert. His apparatus brought out plenty of mud and leaves, but no ball—and worse yet, no shoes.

"How long ago did you lose that ball?" he asked finally. "Was it before the storm?"

When we said it was he laughed heartily. "Better look for it somewhere along the gutter," he cackled. "It may have been carried forty or fifty rod away—but it certainly ain't in that culvert."

He went on, and Herb and I made our way slowly down the gutter probing every likely-looking puddle with our questing toes. Finally we found an old shoe, but it was so soaked and muddy that we did not recognize it at first. Then Herb thought of washing it in the watering trough, and after he had cleaned it off he saw that it was one of his own. A little further on we found the mate, and eventually we found both of mine. We cleaned them as well as we could and Herb let his dry slowly under his bed, and they came through all right. I put mine under the kitchen stove, where they dried much more quickly, but they shrank so much I could hardly get them on. I had polished them carefully before going on the carpet, but Father saw at a glance that something was wrong.

"What's the matter with your feet?" he asked.

"Nothing. My feet are all right, I guess."

"You walk as if they were sore."

"Oh, it's nothing," I said. "Just a little tight."

"Your shoes don't look large enough."

This brought Mother into the discussion. She was the one who bought our shoes and saw to the sizes. "They were plenty large enough when I bought them," she said. "They must have shrunk."

"It's much more likely that his feet have grown."

"But I allowed for that," said Mother.

They had me take off the shoes and examined them carefully.

"Why, they're in a terrible state," said Mother. "I never knew a pair of Mr. Cooley's shoes to act like this. I'll take them right back to him this very day."

Mr. Cooley stood up for his shoes as best he could. He said they had received very hard treatment and that they looked to him as if they had recently been soaked through. Mother indignantly denied the soaking, and she insisted that a boy's shoes should be made to stand rough treatment. In the end she paid a small amount of money and I got a new pair of shoes. The old storekeeper fussed over the package until she had left the store. Then he gave me a very peculiar smile.

"Did you find your ball?" he asked.

"What ball?"

He held up one of the damaged shoes. "This ball right here."

"I don't know what you mean."

"Oh, yes, you do. The little Duffy kid told me you tried to get him to crawl into the culvert to get your shoes."

"Aw, you know what a liar he is."

"No use calling the kettle black," he said. "I did the best I could for you. The easiest thing for me would have been to tell your ma the truth. But I didn't give you away, I drove a good bargain for you—and now you got to work

150

out every danged cent it cost me, or I'll put the whole business up to your father."

He had me. I couldn't see any way out. "How much?" I asked.

"Oh, we'll call it two dollars."

That was how it happened that I ran his errands for the next two weeks, swept out his store, worked in his garden, and made myself generally useful. I found out later what a good businessman old Cooley really was, for he had figured in his regular profit on that pair of shoes.

Hooky was not for me the ever-present temptation it is supposed to be. There were times when I did not particularly hate to go to school. I could go all winter long with hardly a thought of running away, but with the first warm day of spring the four walls of that schoolroom made a prison from which I had an irresistible urge to escape. I can still remember the great upsurging of spirit that used to rise within me with the arrival of the first robin. Only a day or two of the vernal sunshine was needed to set my pulses to singing. Even before the snow was gone we would be haunting a sugarbush about a mile from town. We used to watch this place pretty closely until the "sugaring-down" was over, for there would be pans and kettles to scrape, and odds and ends of broken sugar that found its way into the pockets of the boys. By the end of the sugaring season an occasional bird would be seen, and soon afterwards mysterious little buds would come poking up out of the damp and chilly soil. This meant that we would soon begin going over to the Thicket.

The Thicket was an uncultivated hillside perhaps a quarter of a mile from the school. It extended from the top of Tiger Hill in a steep slope to the south bank of a creek called the Canandaigua Outlet. To call so sweet a stream an "outlet" has always seemed to me to put a lovely bit of Nature into the class with a feeder, a canal, and an irrigation ditch. As the name implies, this hillside was thickly overgrown with shrubbery, and out of its rich black soil grew every kind of wildflower imaginable. The children would go over there in droves and wading in the lush growth to their knees would pick huge bouquets of trillium and hepatica, Indian paint, violets, and a dozen other flowers we could not name. There was something about the smell of that soil that aroused and excited me. I could feel the call in my blood. I simply could not resist the place. I would take a chance on playing hooky to go over there when I was almost certain to be caught.

After school the place would be crowded, and during the noon hour; but a truant who managed to get there in the middle of the afternoon session would have the place all to himself—well, not quite, for there were almost sure to be one or two others who also had been unable to resist the magic spell. And the nice part of it was that girls were just as susceptible to this maddening spring fever as the boys.

Gradually it dawned on me—or possibly it was not so gradual—that the presence of the right girl, or almost any girl in fact, would arouse my inmost emotions more deeply than even the smell of the soil and the touch of the lush greenery. It was there in the Thicket that I had my first kiss. Why I did not expire on the spot of some sort of spontaneous combustion I never could quite understand. She was a lovely little girl—a halo of golden hair—wide blue eyes—lips as red as a cherry. I can't seem to remember her name, but there never was another girl in the world like her. Two or three times without any previous arrangement we played hooky together, so responsive was one to the call of the other. And then the hot weather came on; we no longer felt the call of the wild, and if I played hooky from school it was to go to a ball game.

In time the Thicket came to be a symbol. Girls who went there too often were likely to lose their good name, if nothing else. Our girls were strictly forbidden to go there, but of course they went. Touched by the madness of spring everybody in school went. But if my sisters picked flowers there, they had to give them away, for certainly they could not bring them home.

14. Mother Supports a Cause

OUTSIDE activities frequently made use of the school to further some cause. This might be patriotic or charitable. Sometimes it was no more than a ticket-selling scheme. But with at least one child in every room of the school there was little that our family missed. One of the most vigorous of these campaigns was conducted by the Women's League for Temperance, when Mother was a member of the Board of Directors. The great tidal surge of Prohibition was rising rapidly at the time, and the local churches were putting on the pressure to induce every church member to sign the pledge. Their efforts succeeded to such an extent that the League members went outside the churches and made an attempt to sign up every man in town regardless of religious affiliations. This was by no means so successful, but even before the results were known the League had invaded the public schools with a war cry of "Save the Boys!"

Teams of businesslike women went up and down the aisles with printed cards signing up the boys not to drink beer, wine, whiskey, or other alcoholic liquors as a beverage. I had never tasted beer, wine, whiskey, or any other alcoholic beverage at the time and did not suppose that I ever would, but I signed on the dotted line, as did every other boy in the room. Mother was delighted when we all came home and said we had signed the pledge, but Father was annoyed. He said that pledges of the sort made by children were an imposition; in the first place they were legally unenforceable and in the next place the signers were mentally incapable of understanding the meaning or consequences of signing such a unilateral instrument.

We were quite accustomed to this difference of opinion on the Temperance question. Mother had long been a Prohibition stalwart. Father on the other hand was a free thinker on the subject of strong waters. He did not believe that the taste for alcohol could be legislated out of the human race. It was his personal hope that the attempt would never be made, for under the right circumstances he enjoyed a drink himself. His defense of his position was usually amiable and bantering. He regarded the Temperance women as nuisances, and I think he was always a little ashamed to have Mother belong to the League. Mother on the other hand was proud of the connection. She not only took a high moral stand, but she also assumed the practical position that the mother of five boys could do no less than give her full support to so noble a movement.

Soon after we had enlisted in her fight against alcohol a gruesome double murder was committed in Auburn. A woman and a man, apparently her paramour, were found murdered in cold blood. Naturally the finger of suspicion pointed at the husband. When a pistol that had once belonged to him was found not far from the scene of the crime, he was arrested and tried. During the trial some prominence was given to the fact that the accused was a Temperance worker. It is quite probable that this emphasis was originally applied as a character build-up for the defendant; but with the defense in the hands of an unskilled and inept attorney little advantage had been gained from it.

The defendant was convicted by a bored and listless

155

jury, and would no doubt have met his fate at the end of a hempen rope had not a smart young newspaperman in Auburn seen some possibilities in this Temperance angle. No sooner had sentence been pronounced on the defendant than the Auburn *Sentinel* came out with screaming headlines about a miscarriage of justice. The defendant, it said, had been the victim of a political attack on the Temperance cause, and called upon Prohibitionists everywhere to rally to the defense of the wronged Temperance worker while there was still time to save him from the gallows.

The Temperance forces, always a little touchy and inclined to be on the defensive, rose gallantly to the bait. Contributions to a defense fund came in so rapidly that at the end of ten days or two weeks the *Sentinel* felt that it had enough to warrant hiring a better lawyer. It considered the matter for a day or two and then went to Rochester and retained one of the most brilliant and resourceful criminal lawyers in western New York. The record of the case was found to be in poor condition for an appeal, so the new defense lawyer promptly unearthed some newly discovered evidence, which was used as the basis of an application for a new trial.

The new trial was granted, whereupon a motion was promptly made to change the place of venue on the ground that public opinion in Cayuga County had been so aroused that the defendant could not possibly have a fair trial there. This, too, was granted and the case was sent to Wayne County for trial.

These maneuvers had been handled with little regard for expense, and the *Sentinel* defense fund was becoming depleted with a long and costly trial ahead. Quite naturally the *Sentinel* had turned up some business for itself, but the same bright young man who had started the appeal movement could see no reason why the Temperance

156

forces should not continue to bear the expense. Up to that time voluntary contributions had been sufficient; now he would see what some organized fund raising would do. He drew a circle of fifty miles around Auburn and began with a bombardment of literature softening up all chapters of the Women's League for Temperance found to be inside. When it was felt that they had been sufficiently prepared a fund-raising team was dispatched from Auburn to do the mopping up.

One day Mother came home from a meeting of the League very much aroused and excited. It had been a thrilling meeting, she said. The ladies had just learned the inside story of the terrible persecution of that poor Temperance worker in the Auburn double murder case— he was being unjustly driven to the gallows by the Liquor Interests. Two very keen, very forceful speakers from the Auburn Chapter had explained how the cause was being hurt by all the publicity that was being given to the fact that the convicted man was a Temperance worker. And after that a very brilliant talker from the Auburn *Sentinel* had explained all the fraud and trickery of the Liquor Interests, and how by directing suspicion at an innocent man they were making it appear that the Temperance cause was made up of a lot of thugs and murderers.

Father listened to a full report of the meeting and then said quietly, "Better not get mixed up in it."

"But I'm *already* mixed up in it," said Mother. "I'm chairman of the Fund Raising Committee of our chapter to get money to carry on the fight."

Father smiled in a placating way. "Why not let the matter rest for a few days?" he suggested. "I'm going to be in Auburn the first of the week and I'll find out what's back of all this activity."

"Auburn? What's taking you to Auburn—Jerry Billings again?"

Father nodded. "I'm going down to find out about the time he gets off for good behavior. I want to be sure that he is released as soon as he's entitled to be. They pay more attention to these things if they know somebody's interested."

"Gracious, he's not coming back here, is he?"

"Possibly. That's up to him."

No more was said at that time about the Fund Raising Committee, but when Father came back from Auburn he was quite insistent about Mother's resigning as chairman. But Mother was stubborn.

"I don't wish to resign," she said. "I want to see that innocent man cleared of a false charge—and a blot removed from the cause of Temperance."

"My dear," said Father patiently, "you're getting into something you don't understand. There are forces at work that don't appear on the surface. Frank Hilliard of the *Sentinel* is smart, but he's a scamp. He doesn't care a straw for the Temperance cause—all he wants is a lot of sensational stuff for his paper. Why do you suppose he retained George Haines to defend the case?"

"Because he wanted the best criminal lawyer he could get, I suppose."

"Not at all! He doesn't want a good lawyer, he wants a flashy lawyer who will make headlines for him."

"I think you're very unjust," said Mother.

Father shook his head. "I hope not, my dear. The man is undoubtedly guilty. The prosecution made a very strong case against him. But whether he gets off or not is irrelevant to our discussion. What I'm trying to tell you is that I thoroughly distrust this Hilliard-Haines combination. All I want is to keep you clear of what may be a very unsavory trial."

We children did not know what an unsavory trial was, but we thought Mother was right in standing up for her friends. Since signing the pledge we felt that our loyalties were with the Temperance forces and we wanted our side to win. We were glad when Mother refused to resign, and jubilant when her committee succeeded in reaching their quota, which they were not long in doing. When the case went to trial some time later Haines plunged at once into the paramour angle and ripped the character of the murdered woman to shreds. Whenever the court sessions became a little dull he would introduce another paramour. Unsavory from its opening day the case rapidly became malodorous.

At the beginning of the trial Father brought home a copy of the *Sentinel* every night. I think he must have done it just to tease Mother. But after the second or third paramour had come into the case we found no more *Sentinels* around the house. The other papers carried a running account of the trial, though they gave no such detailed particulars as the *Sentinel,* which regarded the battle that was going on in court as its own private property. Eventually the case went to the jury and Judge Crane had retired to his chambers to await their deliberation. He had been there only a short time when Jeremiah Collins, the sheriff, came to him and said that the prisoner would like to have a few words with him.

"What does he want?" asked the Judge.

Collins shook his head. "He wouldn't tell."

"All right," said the Judge, "bring him in, and ask the district attorney and Mr. Haines also to come in."

Collins nodded and went away. He came back shortly leading the prisoner and followed by the two attorneys.

The Judge glanced at the prisoner. "You wanted to speak to me?"

"Yessir."

"Well, what is it? What do you want?"

"I'm sick and tired of the whole business. I don't want to hear no more about it. I come in here to confess."

"You mean—you want to plead guilty?" asked the amazed jurist.

"Yessir. I killed 'em both."

These words were followed by a temporary paralysis on the part of all but the prisoner, who looked from one to another for some sort of reaction. Then suddenly came the hollow sound of three lusty raps from the jury room. *Thump! Thump! Thump!* At almost the same moment the bailiff appeared in the doorway.

"The jury has agreed," he said.

Judge Crane nodded. "Very well—bring them into court." He turned to the sheriff. "Return the prisoner to his dock." Alone with the two lawyers he put the question up to them: "Well, gentlemen—?"

"The jury can be discharged," the district attorney proposed, "I'll move for a new trial—and we can then receive the plea of the defendant."

"Impossible," growled the defendant's attorney. "You can't move for a mistrial after a jury has reached an agreement. The defendant is entitled to their verdict in spite of hell and high water. What he does after the verdict is returned is his own business. Of course—they may find him guilty."

Judge Crane nodded. "That's the law. This court has no other possible course than to receive the verdict of the jury."

In response to a question from the Judge as to whether they had agreed upon a verdict the foreman of the jury stood up.

"We have, your honor," he said. "We find the defendant not guilty."

This decision caused great consternation among the lawyers. For there could, of course, be no appeal from a verdict of acquittal; and since the defendant had been once in jeopardy he could not again be tried for the same offense; and without a trial no man may be punished for murder even though he admits his guilt. The district attorney stormed and thundered, but his efforts were in vain, and in spite of the defendant's readiness to plead guilty—he walked out of court a free man.

Mother was greatly relieved when she heard that the prisoner had been acquitted. "There!" she said. "The Temperance cause is exonerated."

"Hardly that," said Father. "The man is legally free, but I should say that the Temperance cause is still polluted."

Mother looked at him in surprise. "What do you mean by that?"

"He was only a convicted murderer before, but now he is a *confessed* murderer."

"But the jury acquitted him."

"Does that erase his admitted guilt?"

"Perhaps not," said Mother. "But I do think that a court decision by twelve men should carry more weight than the word of a poor hounded defendant who was probably so confused that he did not realize what he was saying."

Father did not prolong the argument. "The defendant's attorney could not have put it any more neatly," he said, and let it go at that.

We children were left in a rather ticklish position, for now we did not know which side to be on.

Father's trip to Auburn may have been futile so far as Mother was concerned, but it certainly was effective in getting Jerry Billings out of prison, and one morning when Father walked out into the garden he found Jerry at work there just as if he had never been away. But this was only a temporary job, for Jerry had learned a trade while in prison. He had become an expert meat-cutter and not long after his return Father set him up in a meat market of his own.

Mother was very skeptical of this venture. "Who do you think will dare to buy meat from an ex-convict?" she asked.

"We will," said Father.

And we did. Everybody in town did. His market was one of the most successful the town ever had. And though we boys were by this time getting large enough to take care of our garden Jerry saw to the planting and to the putting down of the winter vegetables. He bought the hay for our horses, he started the furnace in the fall, and as long as he lived he was our general factotum and handyman. Nobody could have done a better job or been more agreeable, and still Mother didn't like him. She was about the only person in town who didn't.

15. Life, Liberty, and the Pursuit of Happiness

ONE of the liveliest sources of patriotism was lost to our democracy with the passing of the torchlight procession. I have seen soldiers go marching off to war, and I have seen soldiers returning from battle, but never have marching men moved me as those men in the oilcloth capes. I have watched the flash of bayonets and sabers, both on parade and in actual warfare, but never has the gleaming of arms so thrilled me as the flares of those sputtering tin cans.

Down the street they came—ranks close-packed—swaying as they marched—flames from the torches leaping and dancing—bands blaring forth gloriously with *Yankee Doodle* or *Hail, Columbia, Happy Land*—and the *tramp-tramp-tramp* of those unseen feet!

Electricity at that time was still largely a mysterious force up in the clouds and of little practical use except for telegraphing, so when night came our streets were as dark as the inside of a coal mine. What a miracle to see those marchers turn night into day; it was almost as if the sun had changed its course and come back to town in honor of the occasion. And long after they had gone by the atmosphere would still be heavy with their passing. I used to feel that the very air we breathed had been somehow hallowed by their presence. My loyal little heart would

163

swell until it felt near bursting with the pride of being an American. The human heart has to be young and elastic to take such a beating; in later years the strain would probably bring the mortician.

Father never marched. He was always one of the speakers. But once in a Fourth of July parade he rode on a white horse and carried his sword, the blade of which had such a funny smell. I was very proud to see him there on horseback, but I was secretly afraid that somebody would toss a firecracker and frighten the horse so that it would throw him off. Mother smiled when I told her that. She said that the first time she ever saw him he was on a white horse, coming back from the war, and after the way that horse behaved she would never worry again while he was on horseback.

Patriotism was no hollow-sounding word at our house. With Father it was the cornerstone of good citizenship, and he could talk pungently about it for hours without saying one silly thing about Old Glory, though he could not always control the emotion in his voice. We used to laugh about this vocal peculiarity behind his back, affectionate ribbing, of course, and called it "being eloquent." We were brought up to believe that life, liberty, and the pursuit of happiness were as tangible parts of everyday life as three meals a day, or the arrival of the *Democrat & Chronicle* on the early morning train. To hear Father tell about Paul Revere's ride was as good as "Hi-Yo, Silver!" any day in the week. His story of the Battle of Lexington and Concord was as exciting as any of the exploits of the James boys or Billy the Kid. He was thoroughly familiar with the Revolutionary campaigns, and if I had been content to listen to him I would not have been compelled to unlearn so many of the miraculous highlights then painted into the career of General Washington and some of the other heroes of the Revolutionary scene. It was no doubt

164

the magic of the printed word that misled me. How could it be printed in a book if it wasn't so?

Next to patriotism in my father's mind was a strong conviction of the majesty of the law. He never lost an opportunity to drive home the point that the law was always right. I don't suppose I ever gave a great deal of thought to the subject, but it was my firm belief that to break the law was as great a wrong as to break one of the Ten Commandments; greater, in fact, for if you broke a law you'd go to jail, and if you broke a Commandment you wouldn't go anywhere until after you were dead. Do not get the idea that we did not have the greatest respect for the Ten Commandments. We thought that for their size they certainly covered a lot of ground. But after all there were only ten of them, and there were tens of thousands of laws. To say of a man, "He does not remember the Sabbath Day to keep it holy," or "He takes the name of the Lord in vain," was to question his ethics, his piety; but to say, "That man broke the law," was to brand him as a felon and a dangerous citizen.

To us the Fourth of July took on just as much natal significance as Christmas. One was the birthday of Salvation, the other of Liberty. Both were inextricably involved with side issues. We sang sweetly about the child in the manger, while we were really interested in the three wise men bearing gifts. It was the same way with Independence Day; we endured the long orations on patriotism as the price we had to pay for our fireworks. Wherever the Fourth was celebrated there would be patriotic speeches; they were as much a part of the day as the fireworks. Personally I do not believe that an oration on patriotism has ever improved the citizenship of anybody but the speaker; and still the fires of patriotic oratory kindled during the Revolution burned brightly for more than a century, kept alive, no doubt, by relays of schoolboys demanding liberty or death, and by political orators who found patriotism a safe out-of-season subject and a sure-fire hit.

During my boyhood I sat through some stirring orations on patriotism, and they all affected me the same way—they deepened my resolve to have a bigger and better bonfire to celebrate the arrival of the next Independence Day.

Every year about as soon as the soldiers' graves had been properly decorated we used to begin our planning for that bonfire. Not that we actually started to gather fuel for it so far ahead, but we began plotting about it just as a gang of jailbreakers may begin plotting about a delivery for months before it occurs. Indeed, the plotting is a large part of the fun.

From the accounts in history books I judge that the original patriotic bonfires were kindled by the adults, not by the smaller fry. In the absence of radio, telephone, or telegraph the bright glow in the sky above a bonfire was a way of spreading good news to outlying districts. Wood was cheap and easy to get in the early days, and it did make a lovely light. It was probably when wood became more expensive and so scarce that it had to be purloined that the annual patriotic beacon was taken over by the younger generation.

Just when the bonfire took on its surreptitious character in our town would be hard to say. It was decidedly in that class during my boyhood days. And it must have been the same when Father as a young lawyer first hung his shingle in town, for his initial case as a cub lawyer was to defend some boys who, wanting to celebrate the arrival of the nation's birthday, had taken wrongful possession of several of the small frame buildings so necessary in those days of outdoor plumbing, and had made them a very prominent part of their bonfire. Without a certain amount of opposition the fine old custom might long since have died out, but the Village Fathers of one generation after another

166

have seen to this by prohibiting bonfires in the public streets and passing ordinances to the effect that anyone participating in such an affair would be prosecuted to the fullest extent of the law in such case made and provided.

Just why we never regarded the flouting of these ordinances as a violation of the *law* involves an interesting bit of reasoning. To us the law was a solemn pronouncement, like the Declaration of Independence, emanating from a great pillared hall filled with serious-faced citizens, mostly on their feet with one hand in the air, deliberating in the name of Almighty God and the Continental Congress. Unpatriotic resolutions and ordinances passed in a dingy room in the basement of the Town Hall by a handful of crabbed old curmudgeons known as the Village Board aroused no feeling on our part except the utmost contempt and an almost uncontrollable impulse to violate and disobey.

One of these ordinances would keep the spirit alive for about five years, and by that time the Village Board would usually get around to passing another to the same effect. The mere fact that the bonfire had been forbidden would give the occasion the proper tang of surreptitiousness to appeal to the younger generation, even if their patriotism was not strong enough to get them out of bed for a bonfire in the middle of the night.

At our house we always went through the same formality—we asked permission to go. And the answer never varied. Mother did not want her boys running around with a lot of toughs and the lawless element, carrying off people's property and burning it in the street. She had no objection at all to a bonfire; if we wanted to build one in our own backyard and light it at midnight, she would give her consent and Father would be on hand to watch it.

A *private* bonfire for Fourth of July! In our backyard! That was as much as a woman could grasp of the patriotic fervor burning in the heart of the youthful male. Father said nothing—just sat and smiled over his work.

We always refused her offer with scorn—and went to bed fairly early to "get rested for the next day," as we used to put it. From then on we would have a regular sentry go in our darkened bedroom until we were sure that Father and Mother had retired. Father never left us in any doubt about this; he never failed to look in upon us on his way to bed. He always found us in bed and properly covered, though we usually had our clothes on underneath. We would leave just enough garments on a chair by the bed to make a proper showing. As a general thing we were dressed, out of the window, and down a post of the side porch a few seconds after the light in their room was extinguished.

For years Stan and I put up with one of the worst rooms in the house just so as to have that post for use on a single night in July. A brand of patriotism, I dare say, which no longer exists. It was not really necessary. Friends on the outside would have come for us with a ladder as friends of Herb came for him, for his room had no window near the porch. One year they came for him so early that when Father went out to give our new dog a nocturnal airing he walked directly under the ladder without any indications of having noticed it. The dog was more observing. Another time, when Father saw at about nightfall on July third a short ladder lying inconspicuously behind the garden fence, he quietly exchanged it for a longer one that would surely reach to a second-story window.

The bonfire conspirators always used to meet at the same place—the old pointed-roofed bandstand which stood in the fork of the road and commanded a view of Main

Street. It was dark as a pocket here, except on concert nights, when the lamps would be lit, and there was plenty of shrubbery to shield our comings and goings. Here we laid our plans and sent out scouting parties in various directions looking for bonfire materials. The first place to look was back of the stores, for the merchants had a custom of throwing outside their back doors boxes and barrels which had been accumulating for some time. There was almost never enough of this material, and we would have to go foraging for fuel wherever it was to be found. Woodpiles, lumber, gates, fences—anything that would make a good blaze. More than once the boys had to resort to hencoops and woodboxes, and there was one occasion when they burned about half a block of planking from the sidewalk.

The traditional site for the bonfire was the most prominent corner in town. Here the boxes and barrels were piled as high as they would go, and promptly at the stroke of twelve the match would be applied and a war dance started around the fire. So long as the flames were leaping upward the bonfire would occupy everybody's attention; but as soon as it began to die down the East-enders and West-enders would take up positions on opposite sides of the street and bombard each other with Roman candles.

This was very exciting as well as dangerous. I can't understand why nobody was ever seriously hurt. Under ordinary circumstances, however, the engagement did not last very long, as we would run out of ammunition. It was the custom of all the stores selling fireworks to lock their doors for the night when the bonfire was lighted. But one year a merchant a little more progressive than his fellows left open the back door of his shop during the sham battle and kept us supplied with Roman candles as long as his stock lasted. When these were exhausted the contestants began to go into cannon crackers, and the war started in

169

earnest. When a cannon cracker came hurtling across the street with a lighted fuse you could never tell whether the fuse was long or short. If it was long you could pick it up and throw it back; if it was short you were due for a thunderous explosion underfoot.

When one of these lighted cannon crackers fell at Herb's feet he cautiously struck a match to see how long the fuse was. It wasn't long, but Herb thought it was long enough to throw back, so he quickly snatched it up and hurled it. Ordinarily he was a dead shot. He could pick off a man's hat from the other side of the street almost at will; but this time he took no aim and made a hasty delivery. Instead of landing at the feet of some boy standing in front of the store it went over everybody's head and crashed through the window. Breaking the window would have been bad enough, but that was not the half, for the cannon cracker had landed in a large display window full of fireworks.

For a moment there was an ominous pause—then a thunderous concussion, after which the inside of that store window began to look like the preliminary phases of a set piece that usually spells out HAIL TO THE CHIEF or some similar sentiment. Rockets swished from one end of the store to the other, flowerpots erupted their bright bloom of varicolored sparks, pinwheels hissed and squirmed under the counters and over the shelves, and all through the display there was a steady drumfire of cannon crackers and a confused rattle from the hundreds of small packs of firecrackers which had been piled in the window.

It had all happened so suddenly and so magnificently that some little time had elapsed before anybody realized that the display had been started by a cannon cracker thrown from the opposite side of the street; that is, anybody but Herb. And Herb was well on his way home before the display had much more than started. Both fire companies responded, arriving at almost the same moment, but they had no occasion for the fisticuffs which so often accompanied their arrival at the scene of conflagration, for they found the fire out.

The proprietor who had been in the rear of the store when the bombardment had started had dropped behind a counter to await the last shot. The moment the firing had ceased he seized a pail of water and ran around extinguishing the sparks, and when the firemen arrived he met them at the door with a box of cigars. He was apparently one of the few persons in town who did not know the identity of the boy who hurled the explosive, and he never tried to find out; for he came out of the mishap with a handsome profit. He received his insurance money, and then ran a fire sale for three weeks. He told Father privately that he had received good prices for a lot of old stuff that had been in his store for years.

The first time that Stan and I decided to sneak out and go to the bonfire we both fell asleep and did not wake up until long after midnight. We had no idea what time it was, but the house was quiet so we hastily dressed and went out the window. When we reached the scene of the bonfire we found it deserted. Not a human being was in sight with the exception of our two selves. We were sorry to have missed the tumult and the shouting, but after all, there in the center of the street was a huge bed of coals some twenty feet across throwing off a dull glow and lighting the store-fronts with strange ruddy colors and casting weird shadows which made the scene look strange and unfamiliar to us. We felt like little lost souls wandering in a half-remembered purgatory. Our footsteps grated harshly on the flagstones and the echoes of our voices were flung back at us from the dark grotesque buildings towering dimly just outside the circle of firelight.

We were really too young to go to a bonfire; we had no

171

business being there. And still, since we were there we did not want to miss anything. We climbed about half-way up the outside iron stairway which led to the tiny room above the bank where Father once had his law office. This was familiar ground and we felt a little safer here. Personally I wouldn't have minded slipping quietly off for home, swarming up the post and sliding silently—and safely—into bed. But we felt that we had a patriotic duty to perform in firing the firecrackers which we had brought along to add to the general confusion. We tore open a package, detached a few of the small explosives and put them to the match. They went off with a vehemence which astounded us and aroused a welter of echoes that came rushing at us from all sides. The noise also woke up a half-grown colored man who had been asleep in an alley back of the stores. He came out yawning and stretching, to see who was disturbing his peace at that time of the night.

At first we did not recognize him, and were afraid. But he spied us at once and started in our direction. We would have run away if we had not been paralyzed with fear. Even after we had recognized him we were not any too happy, for the youth had the reputation of being mentally deficient, and we did not know how he might act in a deserted spot at three o'clock in the morning—for the town clock struck three just as he rested one foot on the bottom step and said:

"So it yo' kids, hey?"

However, we needn't have worried, for our companion was the soul of affability. Since he was tongue-tied we were not always positive about the nuances of some of his re-marks, but we formed a friendly contact with the fellow that, so far as we are concerned, has never grown less. For our amusement he held firecrackers in his fingers and let them go off. This delighted us because it was something

172

we had never dared to do ourselves. He, too, was pleased, and after he had done this until the novelty wore off he proposed a new one—he would hold a firecracker in his teeth while it went off. To our enthusiastic approval he did this several times. Then he laid them on top of his woolly head while we touched them off, and as a last grand finale he stuck one in each ear and let us touch them off. Unparalleled act of bravery—or is bravery the word?

Breakfast on the Fourth of July was relaxed and leisurely at our house. There was no inspection and so no rush to be first on the carpet. Stan and I came tumbling down the stairs sleepy and bleary-eyed, our pockets stuffed with firecrackers and other noise-making explosives. We were both a little uneasy, as we did not know what might be said about the bonfire and we wanted to look as innocent as possible. As it happened, nobody said anything about the bonfire or paid any attention to us, for Father was already started on his usual Fourth of July breakfast table dissertation. He did not care how many firecrackers we shot off, but he wanted us to know what we were celebrating and why, with a reasonable grasp of names, dates, and places. And as usual he ended by telling us that there must be no firecrackers or other fireworks discharged either on the lawn or in the garden—and of course none inside the house or barn, but that otherwise there were no restrictions.

Mother's arrangements for the day's celebration were along quite different lines. She always prepared and brought out on the porch a first-aid tray containing a variety of bandages and a special salve for burns, with of course a large-sized bottle of Ozone Oil, the mere smell of which, Father often remarked, was more healing than a gallon of witch-hazel. He despised witch-hazel and never could look at the bottle without insulting it.

"Hogwash!" he would snort.

Mother would nod, quite undisturbed by the now familiar eruption.

"No more curative properties in the stuff than in a barrel of soapsuds—if as much!"

"Yes, I know, dear."

"But if you know, why do you have it around?" he would growl.

"Because some of the neighbors' children believe in it," she would explain patiently, "and when they get bumps and bruises around here I like to have them think that I'm doing something for them."

"Mental healing's all they'll ever get out of *that* bottle." He'd turn away.

"And there are some people who don't like the smell of Ozone Oil," Mother would call after him.

He would not answer that, and would pretend that he did not hear it.

16. Mourners' Bench

THE revival meeting was as much a part of our amusement life as the theater. As a matter of fact it was more so; the revival meeting was free, and we could go as many times as we wished, whereas a good show cost from ten cents to a quarter and we seldom had a chance to go more than once or twice in a year. As on the Temperance question, there was a slight difference of opinion in our household on the ethics of the revival. Father regarded it as a cheap, sensational appeal to the emotions which had no connection whatever with either religion or morals. He saw through the shabby tricks of the so-called evangelists, and despised them as parasites who preyed on the superstition and credibility of the young, the ignorant, and those who were not quite bright.

Quite often Father had inside information about these itinerant evangels. Board bills that had been jumped in other towns had a way of coming to him for collection, and occasionally there would be an appeal for restitution where a sizable loan had been obtained from some well-intentioned but unbelievably credulous widow-woman anxious to serve God by rescuing the evangel from the clutches of an imaginary loan shark about to thrust him into jail and ruin his career because of a non-existent debt.

The town was once very much puzzled over the mysterious disappearance of an evangelist who had packed the church for three or four nights and had worked his listen- ers into a high state of religious excitement from which a crop of converts was confidently expected. The fellow had come for two weeks and was really making a cleanup on a songbook racket. The books sold for a dollar apiece and were literally forced upon every individual who entered the church without one in his or her hand. The system was for the ushers to seat the victims well up in front, and after the church was filled and the meeting ready to go, to solicit them from every side. Young men went through the audience with instructions to put the pressure on the ladies, and the girl solicitors were all over the place using their wiles on the men. Even the audience had a part in the sales program, it being the custom for those having books to point out to the solicitors those who did not. Somehow the evangelist had created the impression that it was unseemly in the eyes of God for people even to try to worship without a copy of this hymnbook in their hands. This pre-meeting sales campaign was always con- ducted with a great illusion of speed. The idea was to con- fuse and fluster the prospects so that they would have no time to build up an effective sales resistance, and anyone who hesitated was given to understand that it was he or she who was delaying the meeting. A person who did not happen to have a dollar was in a bad spot—unless he was willing to humiliate himself by saying so. Solicitors did not waste much time over a prospect without the necessary dollar; that particular part of God's business was done on a strictly cash basis. The bookselling was a perquisite of the evangel—just an insignificant line tucked into his con- tract—and it was going full blast, with ten days still to run, when meeting time arrived one night and with the church packed to suffocation the evangelist failed to put in an appearance. Inquiry at the Inn developed nothing more than the information that he was not in his room and had not been seen since mid-afternoon, when he drove into the country to pray at the bedside of a dying woman whose name he had not mentioned.

The church authorities stalled proceedings as long as they could, but eventually dismissed the congregation with a sketchy explanation that the evangelist was unavoidably detained. That particular revival ended then and there, for the evangelist had dropped completely out of sight, and the church was never able to make contact with him even to turn over the money for the books sold on that last night.

Father chuckled over the affair and teased Mother about the fly-by-night character of journeyman evangelists, who, he insisted, were little more than psalm-singing gypsies. The fellow, he said, had been in his office that very afternoon trying to sell him a songbook. Wide newspaper publicity might have been given to the mystery but for one thing—an empty whiskey bottle was found in the hotel room hastily vacated by the evangel. This bottle might easily have been left by some previous occupant of the room, but when the church authorities learned of its discovery they paid his bill and hushed up the affair as quickly as possible.

It was many years later when Father told me the inside story of the man's hasty departure from town. As Father had taken such pains to say at the time, the fellow had come to his office songbook in hand, but he had come in answer to an urgent summons sent by Father, who wanted to ask him what he proposed to do about a girl he had left in trouble in one of the towns where he had conducted revival services earlier in the season.

The poor fellow seemed genuinely dismayed at the news of the young lady's difficulty. He could not seem to understand why she had not taken it up with him direct, as the

177

plan was that he was to go back and marry her at the end of the tour. However, since this had happened he would not wait until the end of his tour, but would go straight back at the end of the present engagement only ten days hence, and would make the poor dear his wife. Father took a long shot and asked him how his present wife would feel about such an arrangement. That, the evangel said, presented a new question about which he would like to go back to his room for prayer and contemplation. To this Father agreed, but he suggested that in considering the matter due weight should be given to the fact that the girl was not yet eighteen years old.

The evangelist nodded and said he would keep that in mind. Then he went out, closing the door behind him. Father heard him speaking to Libby Weston, his clerk and copyist, as he was passing through the waiting room, though Father was hardly prepared for what he discovered when he went out to give Libby some work a little later: the evangel had stopped just long enough to sell her a songbook.

Though Mother tolerated the revival meetings she was not enthusiastic about them. She thought them unnecessarily crude and undignified. It seemed to her that they could have been conducted just as successfully with a little more dignity; but after all, she used to say, the main thing was to save souls, and if the only way to save them was by using crude and tempestuous methods, she supposed that such methods would have to be accepted with as good grace as possible. She accepted them by letting us go to the meetings and staying away herself. Grandmother believed in them without any reservations whatever. The Devil had to be met on his own ground if he was to be vanquished. She understood perfectly that while all the ministry are fishers of men, no pastor could catch every fish in his particular pool. New bait, new lures, new methods of casting were needed to hook some of the wary ones, but once they were on the string it was comparatively easy to hold them there. Grandmother was not able to get out to the revival meetings, though she took a keen interest in them and used to ask us for a full report after every meeting. Naturally we would pile it on a little just to make a good story, and at the same time to shock Mother if we could. As we told the story it was the entire Bruce family who were rolling on the floor one night in a religious frenzy, and not just Anna who "got religion" so violently that nothing but the floor was big enough to hold her. We had old Alexander, her father, there on the floor rolling with her; we had Ma Bruce in her best black silk and the little black bonnet with velvet strings also rolling, but with ladylike restraint; we had her old maid sister on the floor, as well as her great, hulking, slow-witted brother George, all moaning and groaning and shouting, "Hallelujah! Praise God! I'm going to glory!"

I never could understand what got into Anna Bruce that night. The Bruces were good Presbyterians who attended church every Sunday and paid their pew rent in advance. They really did not need to be converted, and did not go there for that purpose. It is more than likely that they went only to be entertained. They were well-to-do farming people and substantial citizens who minded their own business and had money in the bank. Physically they were all large and powerful, not one of them being under six feet in height, moving with ponderous motions and thinking ponderous thoughts, if any.

It is to be remarked that the evangelist was in unusually good fettle that night. He had whipped his congregation into a high state of emotional excitement before he went into the story of the little child who just before breathing its last gets a preview of Heaven, and appeals to the de-

179

praved and wicked father to come to Jesus before it is too late.

Just what there was about the story to make Anna Bruce rise from her seat and stalk to the mourners' bench was never very clear. It was a sad story and all that. I may have shed a tear or two over it myself, though I felt no desire to go forward on the strength of it. Brother Burdick, the evangelist, hailed Anna's arrival with a shout of joy. He prayed and gesticulated and shouted that there was great rejoicing in Heaven over the return of this sheep that had been lost—and was now found. It may have been the enthusiasm of this reception that went to her head, for, upon hearing it, she rose to her full six feet, waved her hands frantically over her head, and without further warning fell down upon the floor and began to roll over and over and over.

Anna was not a Holy Roller. I doubt if she had ever heard of such a sect, if indeed it was then in existence. The speaker, however, had seen such things before and was apparently not greatly concerned. He told the ushers, out of the corner of his mouth, to carry her out, and attempted to go on with the service. But carrying Anna out proved to be a difficult job for the ushers. Anna preferred to roll, and when she wanted to roll, she rolled. Her sister was the first to go to her rescue—then her mother—then her brother, and eventually her father, old Alexander himself. At first individually and later collectively they tried to bring Anna to a standstill, but she out-maneuvered them. She first brought down her sister, and a moment later her mother. She did not actually bring down her brother; he got down by himself and wrapped one of his large and powerful hands around each of her ankles. He took hold of her as he would have taken hold of a steer, had one, by chance, been rolling there in a religious frenzy, and when she tried to kick herself loose he threw his weight upon her pedal extremities. The mother and sister whispered discreet instructions to him from the other end of the frenzied form, the arms of which they had seized and were struggling to hold. But in spite of them all Anna continued a convulsive movement back and forth as ponderous and as resistless as a steam roller.

People were by this time standing up in the seats to look, and the evangelist was having a hard time to hold the attention of his congregation even with the able assistance of the organ and the choir when Alexander stepped into the breach. He was too portly to get down on the floor, but he bent over and caught Anna by one arm and started for the door of the session room dragging her along as he would have dragged a log of wood. George let go of the legs, which stiffened out straight and remained as rigid as fence rails. Ma Bruce ran ahead and opened the door. Alexander made his exit followed by the others. As the door closed behind them the evangel raised his hands far above his head.

"When the Devil comes into us," he said, "he comes mighty soft and easy. But when he's *driven out*," he thundered, "he sometimes goes *mighty hard!*"

And the meeting went on.

It was months before Anna Bruce ever came into the church again; then she came for her father's funeral. After Alexander was gone the attendance of the family became more and more fitful, and at the end of a year or two they surrendered the family pew. Here was the chance for which Father had long been waiting. Our family had started with 62 and had overflowed into 61, immediately in front. This accommodated us nicely, but for years Father had been wanting to get the Bruce pew, which adjoined 62 on the left. He had tried to persuade Alexander to move to another pew. But Alexander did not care to move. He was occupying the pew his family had filled

181

since the church was built back in the forties; and why should he be asked to move a few pews ahead or a few pews back just so Sam Partridge could seat that big family of his in one long line instead of two short ones? There was good sense in Alexander's position. As for myself, I never could see much point in stretching the family out along a company front extending the length of two pews. It was an odd vanity of Father's, a sort of patriarchal pride, but one that was destined not to be fulfilled. For by the time the opportunity for fulfillment had come so many of the children had grown up and left home that we could fill only one pew.

Among the God-fearing folk of the town a genuine conversion was always regarded as having a little touch of the miraculous about it. It was as if God had singled out the convert for personal attention. In spite of all that had gone before here was a soul worth saving. There was none of this feeling over the Anna Bruce affair. Anna's position with the church was already secure; she did not need saving. The townspeople enjoyed the entertainment she had created, and talked about it for weeks afterward, but they did not misunderstand it. They recognized her case as an outburst of the religious hysteria, not uncommon during the excitement of a revival. As a conversion it had little standing in the neighborhood, especially since Anna had not seen the inside of a church for months after it had happened.

One of the most celebrated conversions we ever had was not the result of any religious excitement whatever, and no evangelist could claim a part in it since the convert had never attended a revival meeting in his life. It simply came out of a clear sky.

Old Tom Curtis, the convert, had been a client of Father's for many years. He was a hard-bitten old fellow who had been a horse-breeder and a follower of the races all his life. Very early in Father's career, Tom had come to him with a horse case, and the two had fought side by side through many a legal battle after that, largely over horses, but occasionally over other matters as well. Father had once defended for Tom a case brought against him for alienating the affections of a horse-trader's wife over in Wayne County. Tom had been a lusty fellow in those days, and off away from his family for weeks at a time he was sure to get himself into one scrape or another.

"I live to suit myself," Tom used to say. "That's my religion. If I want a drink—I take a drink. If I want a woman —I take her if I can get her."

Tom was a steady drinker. He always took a few jolts of whiskey every day, and yet in all the years Father had known him he had never seen Tom when he had had too much.

"Yes, sir, I live to suit myself, and I ain't sorry for nuthin' I ever done. If I do a thing, why, it's done and that's all there is to it. I don't see no use in thinkin' about what's past and gone. What good does that do? Just a waste of time. No, sir, I ain't sorry for nuthin' I ever done."

Tom was always ready to bet on a race of any kind. If he won he would spend the money freely, and when he lost he never had been known to whimper. For years he fought his only brother over the settlement of his father's estate. It was a hard and bitter contest, and more than once Father had urged him to make a settlement at a time when a compromise could easily have been worked out. But Tom had refused to budge an inch. "I don't give a damn if the lawyers get every dollar of the estate," he had declared, "so long as it is kept out of the hands of that psalm-singin' skunk who calls himself my brother." The most that Tom had succeeded in winning from the controversy was the undying enmity of his brother. "But I ain't sorry I done it," he never failed to add when speaking of the contest.

The Curtis family had been Methodists, and once a new minister sought to make peace between the two brothers. After one interview with Tom he dropped the subject and confined himself to trying to get Tom to promise to come to church. But Tom was obdurate. "You won't see me there until they carry me in with a set of nickel-plated handles," he said gruffly.

"But, Mr. Curtis, what do you do on Sundays while your wife is in church?"

"Breed mares, geld colts, and build hogpens. I can always find some pleasant way to pass the time."

"Don't you ever give a thought to your immortal soul?"

"Never! I ain't too sure I got one of the damn' things."

The man of God shook his head with stern disapproval. "Some day you'll be sorry."

Tom laughed. "I ain't never been sorry yet."

But for all his hardness Tom had one soft spot—it was for Tilly, his wife. Aunt Till, as everybody called her, was a little mouse of a woman who never in her life had weighed one hundred pounds. She adored Tom and took him just as he was. She put up with his drinking, and his coarse talk, and his swearing. She never complained when he was off on the racing circuit for weeks at a time. Aunt Till was a good Methodist, and was as meticulous about never missing a meeting as Tom was about never attending one. But she apparently knew that Tom had his limitations, and she respected them. Till never tried to put any sort of religious pressure on Tom until after the doctor had told her that Tom's long overtaxed heart was about ready to give out—that Tom was not going to get well. It was under the stress of that terrible moment that Aunt Till had sent for the minister. The thought of being in Heaven without Tom had unnerved her, she told Father afterward.

At first Tom wouldn't let the Reverend come into the room where he was. He just swore at him and told him to mind his own business. It was not until Aunt Till had come in and whispered that the Reverend just wanted to read the Bible to him that Tom had let him come inside the door.

"All right," he muttered, "let him read—but I don't promise to listen."

The Reverend came in and read some of the Psalms. After he had finished he asked Tom what he thought of them.

"Not bad," Tom admitted, "though they ain't exactly my kind of readin'."

"I suppose you know they're Aunt Till's favorites," said the Reverend. "They'll be about the only comfort she has left after you're gone."

This was too much for Aunt Till. She had held back as long as she could, and when a sob escaped her she slipped out of the room.

"The Lord is my shepherd, I shall not want—" the Reverend began, but Tom stopped him.

"That's enough," he said. "You don't need to say another word. I'm ready to give in."

"You mean—you're ready to repent?" asked the Reverend eagerly.

"Call it anything you want to."

"But you mean you're ready to put your trust in Jesus?"

"I'll do whatever Till wants me to."

By that time the Reverend was on his knees weeping for joy and thanking God fervently for "softening the heart of this sinner who now repenteth." It was the following afternoon when Father walked up the flagstones under the spreading maples in the Curtis front yard in

185

answer to a message from Tom to come and bring his
will. He glanced a little enviously at the round bed of
petunias in the center of the lawn. His own petunias
were not doing so well. He went up the steps leading to
the pillared veranda, and turned to look off down the
valley through which the creek meandered lazily, having once cleared itself of the high banks along the
Thicket. Down on the flats near the race track he could
see the walnut tree, a likeness of which had been carved
on the Hoskins family monument because young Nathan
Hoskins had fallen from it to his death some years before.
Father had turned and was reaching for the knob of the
old-fashioned doorbell when Aunt Till herself opened
the door for him.

Her eyes were swollen and there were traces of tears
on her withered cheeks—and still there was no mistaking
the expression of happiness deep in her eyes. They talked
for a moment in the doorway. Father asked what she did
to her petunias to make them grow like that. Aunt Till
had just remarked that she thought it must be the soil,
when Tom's voice came floating out to them from the
downstairs bedroom.

"The hell it is!" he growled. "It's the sifted horse ma-
nure I put on 'em that makes 'em grow."

"Tom—!" Aunt Till was gently reproving. "You
shouldn't speak like that." They went inside.

"I know it—it slipped out." Tom was a little shamefaced. "But if you'd been talkin' as I have for the last
sixty years—"

Father laughed softly. "So you've seen the error of
your ways, have you, Tom?"

"That ain't what I said," muttered Tom gruffly.

"And if you had your life to live over again there *are* a
few things you'd do differently?"

"Well," Tom admitted grudgingly, "mebbe so."

"No mebbe about it," said Aunt Till firmly. "If Tom had his life to live over again, he'd live it like a Christian —wouldn't you, Tom?"

"Yes, ma'am." The reply was prompt, but it struck Father as having a strange note in it.

"A great change has come over Tom in the last few days," Aunt Till explained. "At last he's seen the light— he's goin' to die a Christian—and a Methodist."

"Not unless you quit your everlastin' gab and give me a chance to talk to Sam in private," he said, humorously querulous. "Now you folks get outa here and stay out till we're through. Got my will there, Sam?"

Father closed the door behind Aunt Till and the nurse. "Yes, I've got it," he said a little testily, "but you're not going to change it. You know as well as I do that brother of yours—"

"Who the hell said anything about changing my will?"

"But you just asked me if I had it with me," said Father.

Tom stopped him with a wave of the hand. "Listen to me—I'm a-goin' to die. I ain't got long to stay and I know it. But I felt as if I couldn't go without explainin' sump'n to you. You heared what Till just said about me bein' converted. Prob'ly ever'body's talkin' about it by this time."

Father nodded. "Yes, Tom, I'd heard all about it. I want to offer you—"

"Don't offer nuthin'—just listen—I only done it to make Till feel good."

Father smiled.

"God's truth! There ain't nuthin' I wouldn't do to make her feel a little better after I'm gone. But I might as well tell you I couldn't go without explainin' it to somebody. All I want you to do is to keep it to yourself until Till's gone—and then I wish you'd tell my friends the truth."

187

"I'll do that for you, Tom," said Father, "if I should happen to outlive Till. Just what is it you want me to tell them?"

"Just tell 'em I ain't really sorry for nuthin' I ever done."

I never knew a revival meeting in our town to rescue anyone from the gutter. As a matter of fact, there was nobody in our gutters to rescue. Most of the converts were simply floaters from some other church who could not resist being saved all over again whenever a persuasive evangelist came to town. They derived a certain exhibitionary pleasure from going up and sitting on the mourners' bench. For a few weeks after a revival the prayer meetings would have a little better attendance, and perhaps the prayers would be a little longer and a little louder. That's about all the revival meetings ever accomplished in our town.

17. But Once a Year

THE burns of the Fourth of July had hardly healed on our fingers before we would begin to have vagrant thoughts about Christmas. After each of these major holidays was over we simply lived for the next. The ever-glorious Fourth may have aroused nobler sentiments in our breasts, but once the day was over—it was over. Christmas presents, on the other hand, often lasted for weeks and months. Sometimes a substantial present like a pair of skates or a scroll saw would last for years. It is one of the regrets of my life that I never received a scroll saw, for I feel sure I would still be enjoying it to this day. Whereas, the violin I did receive, which cost just as much, has spent the last forty-four years more or less in somebody's attic, and is at the moment in mine.

Mother had a very definite genius for Christmas presents. If I happened to remark in April that I wanted a certain kind of ball or a bow and arrow I was almost certain to find it in my stocking or on the tree at Christmas time. She almost never gave one of the children a present for which a desire had not at some time been expressed. Of course this did not apply to the smaller children, who did not have, or at least were not supposed to have, any preference of their own.

But it was not only mental notes that Mother made far in advance, she made actual purchases. It was not unusual for her to buy at the January sales presents for the next Christmas still eleven months away. These would be carefully locked up, and sometimes they would be so completely forgotten that they would not come to light until long after the Christmas for which they were intended. She did this once with a pair of skates she bought for me; she lost track of them for a year and a half and found them in the middle of summer. They were exactly the kind of skates I wanted some two Christmases before, but I had outgrown them and Stan got them, very much to his surprise, for he already had an adequate pair.

There was little useless giving in our family. Every present that went from one person to another was intended to have a practical value. We boys were not always meticulous about the recipient's interest in a particular article. Indeed, we made quite a practice of giving presents to somebody else that we ourselves wanted, and then bartering or bargaining until we had them back.

I will not say that we always had sleighing by Christmas time, but we sometimes did. I have very distinct memories of two such occasions: one when all of us children drove out in the woods in a bobsled with Uncle Albert to cut a Christmas tree; and the other, the night I wore my first pair of pants, which were of black velvet and made out of an old dress of Mother's.

It was about the middle of the forenoon when Uncle Albert drove up before our house in a bobsled drawn by his team of high-stepping carriage horses and announced with a great jingling of bells that we were all going over to Young's woods to cut our Christmas tree. This was, as I recall, the day before Christmas. Of course we all set up a clamor to go, even down to Leslie, who was just learning to walk, and Mother did not know quite where to draw the line.

Grandmother had no trouble at all in making a deci-

190

sion. "If anybody must go let it be the four older ones; the younger ones can stay home."

At that Herb began to bawl. He could always bawl without any apparent effort. Tears came naturally to him and could be turned on and off as with a spigot. For a few moments he bawled experimentally, feeling out the situation; but when Mother said, "Why, I think it would be all right for Herb to go," he shut off the tears in a flash and was instantly all smiles. As he raced out to get his overcoat and mittens Stan and I both tried to bawl, but we were no good at it—we couldn't raise a single tear between us. Herb was just getting back with his wraps when Grandmother spoke again.

"I wouldn't let any of 'em go if they was mine. Those horses ain't safe; the bells will scare 'em and they'll run away."

Now she had gone into Father's field. He knew about horses. "Those horses are all right," he said. "And Albert knows how to handle them."

"Nobody knows how a horse is goin' to act in the winter, and anybody who goes had better dress for an upset."

"Albert never had an upset in his life," Father declared.

"He never drove around with no eight children in his sleigh, singin' and hollerin'," said Grandmother imperturbably.

Mother was beginning to look anxious, but Father wasn't going to see the fun spoiled. "All right," he said cheerfully, "I'll go along with them myself. Leslie's too small, but all the rest can go."

Grandmother waved her hand ominously. "They'll all be upset—and prob'ly mangled."

Father smiled. "Well, I'll be there to pick up the pieces, if that's any comfort."

It was comfort enough for Mother, for she gaily

191

wrapped us in our warmest things. Father took us out and tucked us snugly under the buffalo robes in the box of the bobsled, and we went jingling off up the street singing *Jingle Bells*. We turned a corner or two and went racing out into the country, and after that I was geographically at sea. I recall riding through a barnyard full of cattle. I had never seen so many at one time, or seen them so closely. Then we went dashing down a little narrow road that I was told was the farmer's lane, at the end of which we found ourselves in a great rolling field. Across this the horses flew, throwing snowballs from their hoofs, but at the edge of the woods on the farther side of the field Uncle Albert pulled them down to a walk. I was surprised to see how many trees there were in the woods, and how they grew right up out of the snow. At first we didn't see any Christmas trees at all, and we drove on and on along a little winding road through the woods until suddenly we saw thousands of them. They were all around us. Some hardly reached up above the snow, and others went almost to the sky. We all jumped out and ran around trying to pick the perfect tree. Father told us each to make a choice, and then he would go around and select the one he thought was best. I felt pretty sure it would be mine, but the one he finally chose was Elsie's. He cut it down with only one or two whacks of the ax, and we all dragged it over the snow to the bobsled. Here Father wound a cord around and around the tree and made it look very small with the limbs entirely tied down. Then we all climbed back in, and Father sat up on the seat with Uncle Albert and held the tree straight up while we went jingling back home at a merry clip.

We spent the rest of the day decorating the tree and tying small packages on it. The big ones like sleds and wagons were piled underneath, and made a very sizable pile, for with fourteen people giving each other presents

192

we used to exchange between 150 and 200 gifts every Christmas.

Santa Claus had nothing at all to do with our Christmas tree. He handled only the stocking presents and then went on about his business. He understood perfectly that our tree was a private matter entirely in the hands of the family.

How Father would have appreciated the colored electric lights of today! Our tree was lighted by candles fastened to the branches with little metal clips, and Father was always fearful that the tree would catch fire and do some serious damage. Other people used to scatter little flakes of cotton over their trees to look like snow. But we never did that. Cotton was inflammable. Our tree was never lighted for more than a few minutes, and when it was Father stood right beside it with a pail of sand ready for the worst. No presents were removed while the candles were burning. We stood and looked earnestly at the tree and tried to get a visual impression that would stay with us. After the candles had burned as long as Father thought was safe he would blow them out and pluck them off the limbs. It was then that Father would begin to enjoy the tree and really get some fun out of the occasion.

From the time that we were old enough to know what we were about Mother used to let us select our gifts for other members of the family. I remember so well the first time I ever went off on a Christmas buying spree. I was given twenty nickels and turned loose in a Five and Ten in Geneva, New York. It was really no great task that confronted me. I had only fifteen presents to buy with all that money, and I handled my purchasing to such good advantage that after my fifteen presents were all bought and paid for I still had a couple of nickels for my own use.

That year I created a small family crisis by sending to a very old and very difficult relative in New York City a doll's five-cent nursing bottle complete with nipple on a long rubber tube. It was something that I very much wanted myself though I did not at the time know what it was. It came neatly packed in a box, and without showing it to anyone I printed her address on it and mailed it. After the explosion which followed I had a hard time explaining to the family what the present was. I remembered the name on the side of the box and that was as much as I could tell them. The words were "Biberon de poupée" but between my bad pronunciation and their poor translation they were a long time finding out the truth. The next year I took no chances on my present for her, and sent her something I was sure she would not misunderstand. It was a lovely cake of very fragrant pink soap molded in the shape of a pig. With it I enclosed a sentiment I had copied from a card that some boy had sent with a bunch of roses to one of my sisters. It read, "These make me think of you."

I was a long time getting over the fact that she did not like this present either. Mother seemed to know what she liked, for as soon as I began to consult her I never had any more trouble with unpleasant incidents.

In spite of all the work involved Mother loved Christmas. She far preferred it to the Fourth of July. She even liked it better than Easter, which was a holiday that caused her practically no trouble at all except getting the whole family outfitted with new clothes. There was something about Christmas which stirred her very deeply. No matter how busy she was with her shopping or how much she had to do she would always stop and linger over every store window that showed the little Christ child in the manger. From Thanksgiving Day on our entire household titillated with secrets and mysterious whisperings and errands. These always multiplied after a shopping trip to Rochester, for she kept the interest alive by showing each one of us in great secrecy presents she had bought for some of the others.

She needn't have taken the trouble to show me, for I used to pry into every package that was not kept under lock and key. It was a very rare occurrence for me to receive a single present that I had not previously seen. One year I had asked for a pair of Indian clubs. I was really not much interested in anything else. Indian clubs were being quite extensively advertised at the time for the development of the muscles of the arms, shoulders, and chest. I was very ambitious to have muscles like the man in the picture, and I had exerted all the pressure I could to give Mother the idea that if I did not get those Indian clubs my Christmas would be ruined.

Each time she went on a shopping expedition either to Rochester or Geneva I would, as opportunity offered, go over her purchases; but although several very likely-looking packages came into the house I was able to find no Indian clubs.

"Now be sure not to forget my Indian clubs," I reminded her as she was setting out on the last shopping trip of the year.

She smiled like the Mona Lisa. "I'll try not to forget anything on my list," she called back.

I was at the train to meet her when she returned, and none of the packages I was allowed to carry felt at all like a pair of Indian clubs. Once more I watched for my chance and searched the house from cellar to attic without turning up any kind of sporting goods except a hunting coat for Herb, which I had already seen, and a tan-colored bridle with martingale that Stan wanted for his old mare. This made me feel pretty glum. And yet, on Christmas Day when Father dug down into the presents

195

under the tree, as my turn for a present came around—naturally we used to get them in the order of age—he pulled up a large box containing a pair of Indian clubs for me. My surprise was so complete and the laughter of the others so hearty that I realized my industry in hunting for those clubs had not gone entirely unnoticed by the rest of the family. But the secret of the hiding place was simple—they had kept the clubs at the house of a neighbor, where, naturally, I had no opportunity to do any prying.

The Indian clubs, as it turned out, were not the muscle-builders of which I had dreamed. For nearly two years I swung them industriously for half an hour a day, and though I learned some very interesting movements I fell far short of becoming a muscular giant. It was really a great disappointment.

There was one curious fiction connected with Christmas at our house. It had to do with presents to and from Grandmother. For years she had not been out of the house, and much of the time she was not able to get out of her chair without help, and yet as surely as Christmas came, there would be a present for every one of us from Grandmother. And in going over our lists before Christmas Mother was always careful to see that there was a present for Grandmother from each one of us. It always seemed to me that Grandmother was about the hardest person on earth to give a present to. She did not want anything, did not need anything, and could not use anything that seemed like a Christmas present to me. The girls used to crochet little lace caps for her until she had enough of them to supply an old ladies' home. Eventually they had to think of something else. Handkerchiefs looked like a good bet, and they all began to initial or embroider handkerchiefs for her. She rarely used one and never lost one, and her handkerchief folder finally became so full that Mother had to call the handkerchiefs off. After that they began on aprons. It was Grandmother's custom to wear a white apron every day until four o'clock. Promptly on the hour she would remove the apron, and was then ready for a cup of tea. She never read anything but her Bible and the local weekly, *The Citizen*. There was a Rochester paper within reach of her hand all day long, but she never opened it even to look at the advertiscments. Once, however, I saw her poring over it for a long time and wondered if perhaps she was taking an interest in a murder case then on trial; but no, she was only studying the timetable, which in those days used to appear as news in every paper.

I finally hit upon the idea of giving Grandmother a bookmark, and every year after that, so long as she lived, I kept her in bookmarks. Grandmother was always very careful to thank each one of us, though she always seemed a trifle mystified when we tried to thank her. She would smile a little noncommittally, as if with her deafness she had not quite understood what we had said, and still, all things considered, there was no use in carrying the matter further. In time we all understood that Grandmother did not even know that she was giving us presents; and when she died Mother found her bureau drawers literally stuffed with aprons, and handkerchiefs, and little lace caps. She also found quite a collection of bookmarks.

Mother liked to have all the serious preparations out of the way before Christmas Day. She wanted that day to be peaceful, to take on a little of the delightful flavor of a Sunday, especially during the earlier part of the day before the excitement had whipped itself up to a high pitch. And I suppose she wanted us out from underfoot during the preparations for the big Christmas dinner. In any event she used to get the small fry, the noisy element, out of the house and keep them out most of the forenoon. Father, too, liked to enjoy some quiet on Christmas Day. It was one of the few occasions when he went around the house until nearly dinnertime in his slippers and velvet smoking-jacket.

Father always sharpened his two carving knives on Christmas morning. These were his own private tools. Nobody else was supposed to use them, and shortly after a dinner was over he customarily went to the kitchen to rescue them "before the hired girl had a chance to chop her wood with them." Father was a fine carver and a rapid one. He was one of the few I ever saw who could carve for a table of fifteen or twenty people and still have time to eat.

As he stood sharpening his knives one Christmas Day during the calm when the smaller children were out of doors and the older ones were in their rooms wrapping presents, Mother came to him in a dither and said the kitchen range was cutting up and the turkey was not cooking.

He continued to ply his whetstone. "What seems to be the trouble?"

"It simply won't draw."

That range was the one mechanical device he understood. He had learned while in the Army how to make a fire burn, and he never forgot. "It won't draw if you let the ashes accumulate on the grate."

"There are no ashes on the grate."

"What makes you think so?"

"I cleaned them out myself."

He smiled; he knew how she poked a stove. "I'll be right out."

To his astonishment Father found no ashes on the grate, and even with all drafts wide open the fire remained sluggish and the oven little more than lukewarm. He understood the whims and caprices of that kitchen range,

198

which he said was very much like a woman. There were times when it needed coaxing, and other times when nothing but a good shaking would do. This time Father knew at a glance that there was no whim or caprice about it.

"How long has it been balking like this?"

"It's been coming on for several days."

"That settles it—the chimney is clogged. I'll have to disconnect the stovepipe and clean out the soot."

Mother threw up her hands. "Oh, Sam! Not on Christmas Day!"

He shrugged. "Nothing else to do."

"But it will spoil our dinner!"

"We won't have any dinner if it isn't done."

"Can you—get anybody to come today?"

"Wouldn't ask anybody on a holiday." Father picked up the coal scuttle and small shovel.

"You aren't going to try it yourself?" Mother was alarmed.

"It's as simple as shoveling snow—though not quite the same color." Father shut off the drafts and disappeared up the stairs.

On the theory that it would heat the second story the stovepipe had been carried upward through a drum and entered the chimney a short distance below the ceiling of the second-floor hall. Cleaning the flue had to be done from the top of a stepladder and in semi-darkness, but Father tackled it without a murmur. I came in just as he had finished and was about to descend the ladder. He had shoved the stovepipe back into place, but had not yet wired it and was holding it with his hand. The coal scuttle, filled to the brim with soot, was still standing on the top of the stepladder, and Father, very much pleased with himself, called to me and said he would hand the scuttle down. He warned me to carry it carefully as it was heaping full. I took it and started for the stairs.

That back stairway was dark to begin with, and it was crooked; and as I reached the turn near the bottom I lost my footing and almost fell. I had the presence of mind, when I felt myself going, to set the bucket down, but it was now balanced precariously on the edge of one of the steps, and I was trapped in the corner so that I could not move without upsetting it. I called to Mother, who was passing, to lend a hand. Together we struggled for a little while and then she called to Father, but he was wiring the stovepipe in place and said he would be down in a few minutes. Meanwhile my leg was doubled back in a very uncomfortable position. Mother called the maid, but this only added to the crowd and spilled more of the soot, for she moved the bucket just enough to tip it part way over, but not enough to get the weight off my leg. Herb finally came along and extricated me by going up the front stairs and down the back far enough to lift the bucket out of the way. And he, too, succeeded in getting himself covered with soot.

We were standing in the kitchen, each one of us looking over his or her contaminated condition and feeling a little mad about it when Father, spotless and unruffled, appeared in the doorway. He smiled brightly when he saw us.

"Getting ready for a minstrel show?" he asked.

"Minstrel show!" said Mother, always a little slow to see a joke. "Does anybody know any good jokes?"

"I do," said Father gaily, "but they might not soot you."

It was the only pun I ever knew him to make.

That Christmas the girls were giving Mother a wonderful eight-piece set of bedroom china, something quite indispensable in those pre-plumbing days. It was pink with a gold band around it—washbowl, pitcher, slop jar, and other articles too numerous to mention. Indeed there were so many pieces that we could not put them under the tree and had to hide them behind the parlor door.

When the right time arrived all eight of us slipped into the parlor, and then came marching back in single file, each bearing a piece of the china set. The piece that fell to my lot was the slop jar, and just to make some fun I slipped it over my head. The caper made a great hit— but after the fun was over I found I could not get my headpiece off.

We all struggled valiantly for a time and then sent for

the doctor. He made a careful diagnosis and shook his head.

"Get me a hammer," he said.

It was Father who finally struck the blow. He held a flatiron against one side of my headgear and gave the other side a smart rap with the hammer. The crockery broke into a dozen pieces, leaving me a bit groggy from the blow—but free.

One of my brothers says that it was not a hammer, but a croquet mallet that Father used. Another says it was not a slop jar but some other piece of crockery. That was their recollection—this is mine.

18. Many Happy Returns

WE NEVER had birthday parties at our house. There were too many birthdays and they were not well timed. It was unfortunate that we weren't distributed over the calendar to better advantage, for seven of our birthdays came in the first three months of the year, and two of the children were born near the Holidays. I turned out to be a lone wolf who came in the summer. You could stay home from school on your birthday, if there was any school. In my case there never was—I was born in July. All through my childhood I was bitter on that point. I thought that parents were very inconsiderate when it comes to selecting birthdays for their children. I still think so.

In our family the mental concept of the birthday party was kept well in hand and consistently played down. Talk about the subject was not encouraged, and if one of the children happened to remark that So-and-so was going to have one, a negative attitude was at once turned on. Children could be spoiled by too much indulgence. It was a great misfortune for a child to get the notion that his coming into the world was an event of such importance that parties had to be given to celebrate the occasion. Only inexperienced people with small families were likely to fall into such an error. This deflation of birthdays, however, was not carried to the point of disregarding them, but simply limited their scope.

Each child found at his place at the breakfast table on his natal morn one cent for each year of his age—real money to us in those days.

From breakfast time on, all day long, the birthday child was free to follow his own sweet will. He could do anything he liked, go anywhere he wished, and stay up that night as long as anyone in the house was awake.

Another privilege he was allowed was to choose the dessert for dinner that day.

These birthday perquisites, an ingenious device worked out by Mother, were really very satisfactory. They had none of the disadvantages a birthday party for each child would have entailed in our big family, and yet they took sufficient cognizance of the day to personalize it for the celebrant and make it important to him. And not the least valuable feature of the arrangement was its inexpensiveness at a time when every penny had to be watched.

I don't remember which birthday of mine it was—it must have been a fairly early one—when in following the dictates of my own free will I elected to eat my dinner from the top of the stepladder instead of from my usual chair at the table. The decision caused some levity, no doubt, and probably made no little bother in serving me and in passing dishes up and down. But nobody sought to dissuade me, and to this day I recall how earthbound and insignificant the rest of the family looked sitting squattily down below, their plates resting on an ordinary dining-room table. They seemed so crowded down there, so packed in, so much in the way of each other, while I sat majestically up in the clouds with no company other than the flies, who, by the way, seemed very glad to see me and quite willing to share my repast with me. My one regret on the occasion was that I could not walk upside down on the ceiling as the flies did.

On one of Herb's birthdays he elected to sit at the table, but to sprawl his elbows out on it as far and as

wide as possible. He was determined to have one day when nobody could remind him of his elbows, at that time very much in evidence. Mother had to put an extra leaf in the table to make room for him. Stan on one of his birthdays ordered a large plate of toast, so that he could eat out the middle of each slice and leave all the crusts. Stan hated crusts and used to hide them in his pockets or balance them on a little shelf he had found under the table—from which the dog would sniff out and eat them with great relish later on. I was a little surprised at Mother's equanimity as she saw Stan punching the middles out of those slices of toast and leaving the crusts piled high on his plate. I did not think of it then, but I now have a suspicion that Stan helped to eat those crusts the next time we had stuffed chicken or "dead dog," a favorite dish of ours in which a large flank steak was rolled and stuffed with dressing.

I used to feel very much like a man-about-town as I sauntered out of the house on my birthday without so much as a "by your leave." It was not so important in the daytime, especially during the summer vacation, for after our work was done we could go where we pleased. We did not even have to say where we were going; and if we did say, it was usually not so and was said only to put somebody else off the track. We had a reasonable amount of liberty during the summer evenings, though we were not expected to go beyond the sound of the nine-o'clock bell. We were not allowed to go to the swimming hole after supper. There was an impression abroad that older boys who worked during the day would be there at night and that rough doings were likely—and there was no mistake about it. One of the best fights I ever saw occurred at the swimming hole on one of my birthday evenings when I had exercised my freedom of will by going for a swim with a tough gang of older boys. On another of my birthdays I witnessed a scene that under any other circumstances I certainly would have missed.

It was at a time of great Temperance activity. We had just gone through a very acrimonious election to decide whether the town should be wet or dry, and by a super-human effort on the part of the Women's League the Dry forces had won the day. The leader of the Wets, Tim O'Neill, was an experienced politician and a gentleman whose word was not worth the paper it was written on, as Father told Mother when shortly after the election she came to ask his advice about a deal which the Temperance forces were then considering.

The fact of the matter was that Tim O'Neill had felt so sure of winning the election that he had bought, at a price which he considered a great sacrifice, the liquor stocks of all his competitors in town. It will thus be seen that when the town went dry Tim found himself in a very unenviable position. He was a resourceful fellow, however, and even before the election he had taken steps to cover himself by obtaining an option on the license of an old innkeeper in Alloway, a small hamlet just across the town line. As soon as he saw that the election had gone against him he announced that he would move his gaudy fixtures and his now greatly enlarged stock of liquors to the Alloway tavern, where he hoped to see all his old customers and as many new ones as the barroom would accommodate. It was this announcement which had aroused the women of the Temperance League to action. They had driven the other saloonkeepers out of business, but the worst of them all was only moving to another location. The victorious women felt that they must do something about it—and what they did was to buy Tim O'Neill's stock of liquors so that they might stage a great victory celebration at which they would knock in the heads of the casks and barrels and let the liquor run in the gutters where the forces of Temperance so dearly love to see it. They had very little trouble in reaching an agreement with Tim. He was, in the back of his mind, none too optimistic about the Alloway adventure. There was more than an even chance that the women of the Temperance League would continue to harry him over there and might bring on another liquor election; so when he saw an opportunity to get back most of the money he stood to lose, he was not long in grasping it. He also signed an agreement not to reenter the liquor business inside our township or within five miles of its borders during any period when the town was legally dry.

It was this great spilling of spirituous and malt liquors upon which I stood and looked the night that I was either nine or ten years old. When I arrived on the scene the great oaken casks had already been lined up on the sidewalk ready for demolition, with grim-looking headsmen standing beside them, ax in hand. They made me think of the pictures of the executioners I had seen in Fox's *Book of Martyrs,* one of our parlor-table books. The streets were packed with excited people, and one of the high officials of the Temperance organization was making an impassioned speech. I do not know how long he had been speaking, but I had hardly had time to find out what it was all about when he brought his remarks to a dramatic conclusion by a thunderous shout to the axmen to do their duty.

The mad frenzy with which those men attacked the barrels frightened me. I had never before seen human beings swing weapons with such fanatical hatred. In my memory the affair still lingers as more of a pogrom than a jollification. The heads of the barrels collapsed beneath their mighty strokes, and the bright-colored wines and liquors came gushing forth and soon had filled the gutters to overflowing while the godly folk looked on with cheers and satisfaction, and the ungodly stood and licked their lips.

Usually on my birthday nobody ever said anything about my going to bed; but when I came home after the liquor-spilling, all excited over what I had seen, Mother kept asking me if I wasn't getting sleepy. She asked me so many times that I began to suspect they had some reason for wanting to get rid of me. So I pretended to start for bed, went upstairs and shut the door of my room with plenty of noise, and then I softly opened it and crept back to the head of the stairs to find out what was going on.

"I told you that you should have put a watchman over that liquor," I heard Father say. "I have positive proof that Tim siphoned off all the gin and most of the whiskey, and sold it in Geneva." His laughing interrupted him. "I've got the facts and figures. I know exactly where it went."

Mother's voice sounded angry. "But that *can't* be so! I saw the barrels opened—they were all full!"

"Of water!" laughed Father. "Of course he'd have to fill them up with something."

By this time Mother was good and angry. "Why, the man's no better than a thief!"

"That's what I told you in the beginning." I could see that Father was enjoying this. "Why will you get mixed up with these fool things? If this should ever leak out you and your League for Temperance will be the laughing-stock of the nation."

"But—but can't we have him arrested for theft?" Mother demanded.

"Of course—but would your organization look very pretty prosecuting a man for stealing whiskey belonging to the Temperance League?"

This silenced Mother for quite a few moments and then, greatly perturbed, she asked, "Does—does everybody know about it?"

"Nobody but Tim and the fellow he sold it to."

"But are thieves likely to boast about their crimes?"

Father laughed softly. "Not unless they want to go to jail."

"So if the story leaks out it will have to come from you?"

"Well," Father admitted, "that would be the natural inference."

Mother gave a great sigh. "Then I think we will let sleeping dogs lie," she said. "Shall we go up now?"

I hastily withdrew to my room and undressed in the dark so that they would not suspect that I had been eavesdropping. Naturally I kept the secret. It was one of my dearest possessions. I hugged it to my heart, and after I was in bed at night I used to lie and think about it. The mere sight of Tim O'Neill would thrill me. I would look at him and think that even though he did not know it, he was completely in my power. This was very nourishing to my ego until Tim was removed from my sphere of influence by dropping dead of heart trouble. For years I wondered about those sleeping dogs and why Mother wanted them to lie. I kept wishing that I might have arrived at the head of the stairs in time to hear what they had to do with the story. But all in all I think it was the most exciting birthday of my life.

Birthday presents were something that we were not encouraged to expect. I don't recall that as a child I ever received one. We children used to club together and give birthday presents to Father and Mother, though the inspiration for such a gift always came from one of the older children. One year we gave Father a sterling-silver napkin hook. It was about the size of the shoe buckles worn by our Puritan ancestors, and as practical as a watch fob. The idea of the hook was to hold a man's napkin under his chin. An aperture was provided to grip the corner of the napkin, and the hook went down inside the place where a man's collar button used to be. I must admit that the device held the napkin securely—especially when fastened with the little safety pin Father kept for the purpose—though it bunched the material in folds to be expected from any square of cloth suspended by one corner. Nothing could have been more ineffective, more inconvenient, and still it brought tears to Father's eyes when we gave it to him, and more than that, he used it for three meals a day for years and years. In time he formed the napkin-hook habit just as he formed his other habits, and when he sat down at table away from home he was lost without it. Once when he was trying a long will case in Rochester and was away for nearly three weeks he sent home for his napkin hook. I was old enough at the time to think that was pretty silly, and asked Mother a little scornfully if she was going to send it.

"Oh, yes," she said, "I'll send it on the first mail. If I don't he'll probably lose the case."

We seem to have been going in for silver at this time, for when Mother's birthday came along we decided to give her a silver spoon for her own personal use and marked in a personal way. We didn't want just the family name or initial, we wanted something more intimate, and after many whispered conferences we decided to have the word *Mama* engraved on the handle. The girls had already selected the pattern, and two of them went back to the jewelry store to give directions for the marking. The watchmaker, who was also the engraver, was an old German with more artistic than linguistic ability, and when on Mother's birthday the spoon was delivered to her by a messenger from the store we found to our great disappointment and disgust that he had marked it *Ma Ma*.

Mother took no apparent notice of the peculiar marking. It was Louise who discovered the mistake and called attention to it. We children of course were crushed, for we thought that once a thing was engraved it was final and could not be changed. And we all felt greatly relieved

211

when Herb, with his unfailing supply of tears, burst out crying. Father gave the engraving close scrutiny and said that without doubt the superfluous capital *M* could be erased and replaced by a lower case letter. Somehow this did not seem possible to us, and even if it were possible we despaired of being able to make the old German understand. Father laughed this off. He said he would handle the matter for us and would explain it all to the old watchmaker in German.

Father's German was a matter of great family pride. He had studied the language in school, and in addition to that he had a practical speaking knowledge of it. A number of his clients were Germans and whenever they met him on the street they would shout their greetings in their own language. He was able to give them as good as they sent, and we all felt perfectly confident that the old watchmaker was in for a severe talking-to and some very definite instructions. As it turned out, however, Father's German was not, typographically speaking, equal to the occasion, for when the spoon came back the lettering was all in capitals of the most ornate and flowing Spencerian script, *MAMA*.

19. Keeping Up Appearances

NEXT to saving our souls it seems to me that Mother was more concerned with keeping up appearances than with any other department of our upbringing. On second thought I am not so sure that appearances did not in many instances come first. Not that her determination to have us saved was any less, but that she was even more determined to have us saved with our best clothes on. My earliest idea of Heaven was that of a place where people were always dressed up to the point of being uncomfortable. I suppose that was the natural result of the extreme measures that were taken to get us to church in a state of sartorial perfection. There was a curious mixture here of the worldly and the devotional. She did not want our neighbors to miss anything, but primarily her intention was to glorify God by having us all look our best when we went to worship at His holy temple.

Around home when there was nobody but the family to see we could go in rags and tatters; but if Mother sent one of us to the post office to mail a letter he would have to change his clothes before starting, and on his return he was supposed to get back into his play clothes. We found this an almost insufferable nuisance, but it was a point on which there was never any compromise.

I remember so well my mother's reaction to my first request for a pair of overalls. The very sensible idea of

213

putting children in overalls had not then been thought of. Indeed, it was a rash and radical experimenter who first made a pair of overalls for boys. The overall was at that time the sign of the laborer, just as the silk topper was the sign of the gentleman. I must have been about twelve years old when I saw the first pair of boys' overalls. They were on a boy about my own age whose father was a day laborer. I admired the way the garment covered his clothes and protected them from nails and splinters and brambles, and I went right home and asked if I could have a pair.

Mother smiled and shook her head. "No, dear, I'm afraid that wouldn't do."

"But why not, Mother?"

"It wouldn't—well, it wouldn't look well."

"But Frank Barclay's got a pair and they look fine— they save his clothes, too. He said so."

"They're all right for Frank."

"They're all right for me, too. They fit just fine—I tried them on."

"Let me explain, dear— Frank's father is a laborer; he can wear such things. Your father's a professional man; you can't. Don't you understand? We have certain appearances that must be kept up."

This was a great blow to me; Frank was one of my best friends. I did not want to be put above him, and most of all I did not want Frank to think that I thought I was above him. We had always been on a basis of equality, and I wanted that to go on without any change. That it did change later on was Frank's fault, not mine. I did not get my overalls right away, but in time I came into a dollar and a half and bought myself a pair. I used to keep them in the barn so that Mother would not see them, and in my whole life I have never enjoyed a garment any more than those bootleg overalls.

I wasn't the only one to feel the rub of having always to keep up appearances; the whole family felt it. There were so many necessary things that we never had any money left for those that were unnecessary but highly desirable. For months at a time when I was a boy in school I never had so much as a penny that I could call my own, unless I held it out on the heathen to whom our Sunday School money went at that time. I used to see the other boys buying chewing gum and candy nearly every day, and would comfort myself with the thought that the sugar would decay their teeth and impair their digestion. The only time when I was reconciled to this situation was when one of the schoolboys died of sugar diabetes. There was a disease from which I felt singularly secure.

Once I found a dime on the sidewalk in front of the Presbyterian church, and while I never did really believe that another dime was going to be found in exactly the same spot, I could not help feeling that it must be a lucky place, and I rarely let a day go by without walking over it a dozen times or more with my eyes searching the ground for anything round and flat.

I must have been just entering my 'teens when the mysterious word "allowance" first came to my notice. A girl from Pittsburgh who had an allowance of a dollar a week was visiting in our neighborhood. I couldn't imagine what she did with all that money. I would have been a plutocrat on fifteen cents a week. The idea of an allowance for myself caught my imagination. I could not understand how it happened that I had never thought of it before. At the first opportunity I felt Mother out on the idea. I suppose that in their turn each one of the children had tried the same thing. She did not seem at all surprised to have me bring it up. It was a matter that she and Father had considered many times, she said. But they had long ago decided that it was not advisable under the circumstances in which we lived. The chief objection was that it would lead to the unwise as well as unnecessary spending of money. Whatever was really necessary for the good of the family, she said, would be provided. But for children to have money to spend indiscriminately—that was, for things which they did not need—was very harmful. It led to wastefulness and extravagance, and it gave the young a very wrong idea of the value of money. To know what money was really worth, she said, one must work for it, earn it.

I knew what that meant. We had only two ways of earning money around home. One was to read the Bible, all the way through. This job paid five dollars on completion, and would have taken me about six months. Nor was there any arrangement for payment on a *quantum meruit* basis. You had to carry through to the end or you would not get a nickel. More than once in times of need I had started in with a firm determination to go through with it; but I always bogged down after fifty or one hundred pages. One of my sisters, I think it was Cecilia, although she denies it, used to sit in church every Sunday and read industriously all through the service. Nobody ever stops one from reading the Bible in church, in fact, nobody realized what Cecilia was up to until she came to Mother one day and asked for her five dollars.

Another way we had of earning money was going without butter. There was a standing offer of one dollar to be paid to any member of the family who would go without eating butter at home for a year. In these days of vitamins and calories and dietary insufficiencies such an offer would be regarded as contrary to public policy, an invitation to incur the rickets, and might even be the basis of a charge of improper guardianship. But in the days I speak of butter was looked upon with some suspicion. It was regarded as the natural enemy of a good complexion, and although

216

my sisters ate it sparingly they would drop it for weeks at a time on the appearance of a tiny pimple on the face. When the girls spread their bread thinly—and they could put on the butter no thicker than a sheet of paper—it was not daintiness on their part so much as facial ambition. I was too good a trencherman even to consider becoming a dollar-a-year man at the expense of butter.

These were the opportunities open to me in place of an allowance. Not a cheering prospect. But once my mind had turned to finance I began to look around for some better way to earn a little money. Within a day or two I had come back to Mother with a proposition. I wanted her to furnish me with a dollar to start me on a newspaper route. She blew up. One of her boys selling newspapers! That was worse than wanting a pair of overalls. I kept on trying first one job and then another, and she finally with some misgivings allowed us boys to pick berries for pay. But it was not until I had landed the job of pumping the church organ at twenty-five cents a Sunday that I had employment that was really to her liking.

I could earn more money picking berries. Once I picked one hundred quarts in a day and earned myself two dollars, but the berry season was short whereas the organ pumping went on fifty-two weeks in the year. I had to lick another boy to get the organ job, but Mother never knew about that. If she had refused to let me do the work on the ground that it was menial I would not have been surprised. But she beamed with pleasure. She could not have been more pleased if I had told her that I had the job of organist.

As long as I held that job I was always in funds, for the organist was ambitious and used to practice three or four hours a week at ten cents an hour, which in addition to the regular salary sometimes ran my pay up to fifty or even sixty cents a week. I might have held the job longer if the sexton had only been a little more cooperative. Old John was a peculiar man. He couldn't get along with anyone—even his own wife. And when he found that I was slipping out of the back door of the session room to forage for apples during the sermon, he began to lock the door and keep the key in his pocket. That did not stop me, it simply changed my method of exit. I began to go out of the window. Then one day while I was outside he came along and locked the window. This was most embarrassing; for to get back into my pumping cubicle I had to walk the entire length of one of the aisles of the church just as the minister was bringing his sermon to a close. An explanation was required that day when I got home from church, and Mother spoiled the nicest part of the job by insisting that during the sermon I must in the future come out into the church and sit in the front seat—where she could see me.

To get even with old John I put a firecracker in the bent end of the crook-shaped metal tube with which he used to blow out the oil lamps along the side aisles during the closing hymn of the evening service.

The fuse ignited at the first lamp, and the firecracker exploded just as he was blowing into the tube to extinguish the second one. Most of the congregation thought the lamp had exploded, and one hero had the presence of mind to leap up on his seat and smother the flaming lamp with his hat while he heaved it through the beautiful colored glass of a memorial window. Not long after this I resigned as organ pumper and went back to sit with the family in old 62.

Sunday after Sunday through my childhood I used to sit in 62 and try to keep George Bruce from resting his elbow on the arm of our seat. The seats were separated by a sturdy walnut partition, but like theater seats they had only a single arm between them. George was, as I have intimated, a big fellow, and when he seriously placed his elbow on that arm it was likely to stay there. The only way I could ordinarily displace it was by using agility. If I could bump it suddenly when he was not expecting me I could usually knock it off. But one Sunday I had prepared a secret weapon before starting for church. I drove a long, sharp tack through a strip of cigar-box wood, and then strapped the strip of wood to my left forearm with the point of the tack aimed at the proper angle to jab George in the elbow when our two arms came into contact.

Herb helped me to adjust the weapon, though he had no idea I would be able to smuggle it through the rigid Sunday morning inspection without discovery. He made me swear that if discovered I would not involve him; but he needn't have been so careful. The slight swelling inside my left sleeve went through with no trouble at all. Father did notice, however, that both Herb and Stan were reluctant to take a place at my left side.

"What's going on there?" he asked sharply, for he did not like any horseplay in our preparations for church.

"Nothing."

He pointed a finger at my left hand. "Have you got a pin there?"

"No, sir." I opened the hand to show him.

"Very well," he said, "take your places. I don't want to have to speak again."

It was a narrow squeak. The boys took their places and the family procession arrived at church in perfect formation. We made our way to our accustomed seats, where a great disappointment awaited me—George Bruce was not there. In his place sat old Uncle Charley, a relative of the Bruces' who was not quite bright. I had seen the old man driving with them on occasion, though they seldom brought him into town. My feeling when I first saw him sitting in George's place was resentment. This quickly

219

vanished, however, and was replaced by a consuming interest when I noticed that the old fellow was shaking all over. His hands shook—his fingers shook—his arms shook —his knees shook. Even his head bobbed back and forth, twisting slightly from time to time as if balanced on a pivot.

I nudged Stan who sat next to me, to be sure he was not missing it, for I did not then realize that it was to be a continuous performance. But Stan had already discovered the phenomenon for himself and was watching it with eyes wide and mouth slightly ajar. In response to my nudge he poked Herb to call his attention to what was going on. The gesture was quite unnecessary; Herb was not missing a thing. After watching proceedings for a few minutes Herb wrote something on the flyleaf of a hymnal which he passed over to me. Mother was watching at the time, so I had to wait until she looked the other way before I could read the message. When I finally read it, all it said was: "St. Vitus's dance."

So that was it! I had heard of the disease before but did not realize how fascinating it could be. Grandmother trembled to a certain extent, but her case was practically nothing. Here at my elbow was something so rare and unusual that I had the feeling it really ought to be in a side show where everybody could enjoy it. I hardly took my eyes from old Uncle Charley for an hour or more, and by that time I had so thoroughly familiarized myself with his motions that I was anxious to try them for myself.

As I sat there dreaming of the fun I would have in Sunday School mimicking the old man for the amusement of the other boys my elbow strayed quite unconsciously to the arm of the seat. I had completely forgotten the concealed weapon prepared for George Bruce until suddenly old Uncle Charley took a notion to rest his elbow on that portion of the pew already occupied by mine. When, with all his shivering and shaking, he wanted to make contact with anything stationary, he had to go about it very firmly. It was for that reason, I suppose, that he slammed his right arm against my left so positively. In fact, his arm struck mine with enough force to knock it completely off the arm rest—and at the identical moment of contact Uncle Charley rose up out of his seat with the suddenness of a jack-in-the-box. A single high, strident monosyllable escaped him. To me his exclamation sounded like "Jees!" though other auditors in an equally good position to hear insisted he said "Whee!" He turned towards me with fire in his eye, but before he could attack or even denounce me one of those big Bruces had taken him in hand so firmly that the old fellow couldn't even shake as he was led out of church.

Nobody seemed to know exactly what had happened, but the general impression was that Uncle Charley had suffered an acute nervous seizure, not to be wondered at in a person in his condition. Even Stan and Herb, the only ones who knew of my secret weapon, were not positive that the old man had run afoul of it though they suspected as much. I wasn't worried about them; what worried me was the explanation Uncle Charley might have given to the Bruces. There was no way for me to rid myself of the incriminating evidence while in church and I felt almost certain that one of those big hulking Bruces would be waiting for me at the door. I sat and worried about this until the service was over and then made a dash for the exit farthest from the Bruces' pew. I could see old Alexander towering above the crowd in the vestibule, but I gave him a wide berth and managed to slip by unnoticed. I quickly retired into one of the church sheds where, watched only by a close-mouthed old horse, I divested myself of my concealed weapon, which I hid in the eaves. When I returned to church I was just in time to hear one of the Bruces explaining to a passing inquirer that Uncle

221

Charley was sometimes "took like that." I pressed in a little closer and heard, "He always thinks he's stabbed or pricked or sump'n, but of course we know better than *that*."

My spirits rebounded when I found that I was not even under suspicion, and all through Sunday School I kept the other boys giggling with my sly imitations of the old man. They were nearly all doing it by the time Sunday School was over, and Stan and I entertained each other with further imitations on the way home. Here Herb joined us with some of his more mature interpretations, and Cecilia, hearing our laughter, came into the play room to see what was going on. It was not long before she was doing it, too. Even Louise and Elsie took a fling at it, though of course they were too grown up to go on with it. When Mother discovered what we were doing she put an immediate stop to it and told us never to let her see us playing that disgraceful game again. She laid heavy stress on the meanness, the wickedness of imitating and mocking a poor unfortunate old man. She reminded us of the forty and two children torn by the two she-bears for mocking the prophet Elijah and calling him "baldhead." She did not actually threaten us with being torn by two she-bears, though she did hint at the possibility. And she spoke with emphasis of "the looks of the thing." She did not want people to get the idea that we had such a dreadful disease in our family.

We took her at her word and did not let her see us, though we played the game with as much hilarity as before. Father did not ordinarily interfere in such matters. His usual method was to let things run their course and die a natural death; but for some reason our imitation of the St. Vitus's dance got under his skin and he forbade us to make each other even the faintest sign in or out of his presence. This of course had the effect of adding an

222

element of danger to what was already delightfully contraband. If I passed Herb a plate at the table his hand would give an almost imperceptible flutter just before taking it. Stan's hand would give an extra flourish as he reached for the salt. Mine would tremble an instant as I raised it to scratch my ear. Father knew what was going on, and several times we were caught and disciplined. This did not stop us, it only made us more wary. It made Father more wary, too, and we found it increasingly hard when he was around to get in any twitches or tremors without being caught at it. The time came when Father was extremely irritable about his inability to suppress this game. He sent Stan upstairs to get his slippers one night, and just as Stan was going out the door called him back.

"What happened to your knee as you went through the doorway?" he asked.

"I don't know." Stan assumed a puzzled look. "Did anything?"

"After you bring down my slippers you can go to your room for ten minutes to think it over."

Of course Herb and I were bursting with laughter. We saw Stan twitch his knee and thought he was taking a pretty long chance. But when Herb took up the dice cup to go on with our game of pachisi and began trembling it Father sent him to the corner to stand with his face to the wall for fifteen minutes. Stan was delighted to find him there when he returned from his own exile. Such incidents as these were common, though we always claimed that they were slips or lapses of memory. But there was nothing accidental about what befell Stan a day or two later, for Mother caught him red-handed trembling like old Uncle Charley himself. He realized that he was caught and that there was no use trying to lie out of it, so he kept right on shivering and shaking and oscillating even after she had called to him to stop. He had a faint idea that if he kept on with it he might be able to make her laugh, and possibly wiggle out of the charge. But Mother did not see anything funny about it. She was suddenly struck with the terrible fear that he couldn't stop—that the disease had indeed been visited upon him to punish him for his wicked mockery. With her literal belief in the story of Elijah and the two she-bears she could easily credit such a performance on the part of the Deity. She led Stan into the house and eventually quieted him, though he continued to string her along with slight convulsive movements. Her tender heart and her constant watchfulness to keep her brood from harm made her the easiest person in the world to deceive. She was always ready to believe the worst.

She presented a troubled face to Father when he came home that night, but he smiled as she unfolded her tale.

"You think it's a case of just retribution for his mockery, do you?"

"I'm almost afraid to say—I really don't think the boy can help doing it—oh, what will people say!"

Father took off his coat and removed his detachable cuffs. "Well, I'll show you a miraculous cure," he said. "Tell Stan to go to the barn—I'll be there directly."

Father was as good as his word. I doubt if St. Vitus himself ever performed a more successful cure; for Father, in a single operation, eradicated the last vestige of interest in the disease from all three of us.

20. The Melody Lingers On

MUSIC was important enough to be a good deal of a nuisance in our household, though it was not important enough to interfere with going either to school or to church. With no radio knob within easy reach and no phonograph record to slip into place, all home music had to be produced by hand. Father thought that no well-regulated home could be any more complete without music than without books. He furnished the enthusiasm, the spirit back of our musical efforts, and drove home the idea that music was one of the great elemental miracles of Nature—but it was Mother who made the idea work. She hunted up a teacher and saw to it that we took our music lessons when we were supposed to take them. She it was who put up with the agonies of our practicing and who kept an eye on the time just to be sure that our lessons weren't being wasted.

It was a big day for us when the new piano came. We already had an old one, but it was an antique rather than a musical instrument, and it helped to furnish the parlor by taking up a great deal of room. You could play tag on it, but you couldn't play a scale. It had come down from Rochester with the family furniture and had stood in grim silence in the parlor until Louise was old enough to take lessons. Then it spoke in a thin and quavering voice as she sat before it, her black hair in a thick braid, her wistful eyes on the little black dots that for centuries have brought the musical imaginings of the masters within the grasp of the pupil.

"There's something wrong with our piano," she said. "It doesn't sound at all like the teacher's."

"The piano's all right," Father assured her. "It will sound just like the teacher's after you have taken a few more lessons."

So little Louise plodded on. Then one day when she was shut in with a cold and the teacher came to give her a lesson at home the true state of affairs came to light—the sounding board was cracked. The child could never learn to play on that piano.

Other members of the family may have known that the new piano was coming, but to me it came with all the unexpectedness of a childbirth. I couldn't have been any more surprised if Gra Richardson had appeared that morning and announced that we had a new little brother. John Erlish brought it on his truck, and with the aid of three stout assistants unloaded it and trundled it on rollers to the front porch, where the box was removed board by board. At last the piano stood there in all its glory like a monument, upright, black, and glistening. In very refined gold letters on the front it said Dunham Bros., New York. Whether this was the only piano Dunham ever made I cannot say. All I know is that I never saw one like it before, and never have since.

The old piano was detached from its legs and carried out, the new one was carried in, and a great musical revival began in the household with all three girls taking lessons at once. It is saddening to admit that not one of them turned out to be a first-line pianist, though there were certain imponderables of worth which derived from their musical endeavors, for the courtship of each of the three is inextricably interwoven with that Dunham piano.

226

What sweetly tender sentiments may have come welling up out of the ebony box I would hardly venture to guess, though I spied quite industriously upon all my sisters and saw from well-hidden points of vantage a lot of kissing and hugging that looked to me like silly nonsense. Some of it occurred while a swain stood turning the pages of the music, and some at the conclusion of a song while the last vibrant chords of the Dunham were dying sadly away.

Love was pretty sad in the eighties and nineties, and some of the current love songs were enough to bring on acute melancholia if not something worse. But there were brighter things ahead, for the college songbooks were just then coming into popularity, and night after night the Dunham would be surrounded by a group of eager young minstrels putting everything they had into *Seeing Nellie Home* or *Good-bye, My Lover, Good-bye.*

To me personally the box of the Dunham meant more than the piano, for it was put in the barn where I spent many happy hours climbing in and out of it.

Father had a genuine feeling for music. He could carry a tune with perfect pitch, and as long as he had any voice left he liked to sing, though he detested whistling even though it was on key. I do not believe that music meant much to Mother one way or the other. In her youth she learned to play a few refined tunes on the piano. The only ones I now recall were *Listen to the Mocking-bird* and *While Walking down Broadway*. Both were simple airs to which a few flourishes had been added. She always played them correctly, with a genteel touch and absolutely no expression. She had no ear for music, and so could not sing, but being a pious person she used to open her mouth and whisper the words all the way through every hymn that was sung during a church service at which she was present. Her lullaby songs were tuneless as well as wordless, but they had a repetitious quality about them that did the business.

There was, however, no temptation to go to sleep when Father sang a song. His rendition of *Lord Lovell* would reduce me to tears in no time. It made me sad to think that out of her lovely bosom "there grew a red rose, and out of his a briar-ar-ar." And still I used to tease him to sing it. Perhaps I was just hungering for emotional excitement, or it may have been that I liked to hear him sing.

His song about Nicodemus, the slave, had a delightfully somber quality about it, though the chorus always cheered me with its promise,

> There's a good time comin',
> It's almost here,
> It's long, long, long on the way;
> Go tell Liza to hurry up,
> And Pomp,
> We'll meet 'em at the gum tree
> Down by the swamp,
> And we'll plant Nicodemus today.

Father was one of the earliest enthusiasts of Gilbert and Sullivan, and no matter how broke we were, if an opera company came within driving distance offering any of the Gilbert and Sullivan productions our family would be well represented. I knew every song of *The Mikado* before I could do twelve times twelve, though I was past forty before I ever saw a professional production of any of the work of Mr. Gilbert and Mr. Sullivan. Father's favorite opera was *The Bohemian Girl,* and any time we wanted to get him into the parlor we had only to play *Then You'll Remember Me,* and no matter how busy or how concentrated he was he would always appear.

Sometimes just for fun we would let him get back to his desk and give him time enough to pick up the thread of his work before we would play it again. After the first few

228

bars he never failed to appear in the doorway. I don't feel any too sure that he always realized he was there; he could get out of his chair and walk around the room without losing the thread of an argument he was writing down, and it may have been just a matter of reflexes. We have tried him out as many as five or six times in an evening without a miss. Just what that song may have meant to him we never discovered, though I like to believe that it had some stirring sentimental association that he was powerless to resist.

I never really wanted to play the violin; what I wanted to play was the piano. But when I first became music-conscious and asked Mother if I could take music lessons she immediately started selling me the violin instead. She began by telling me what a noble instrument it was, how personal and individual, and how it became almost a part of the owner, reflecting all his moods and feelings. It was a worthy effort, but it failed. I still wanted to play the piano.

She shifted her position slightly and approached the subject from another angle. Had I noticed the difficulties the three girls were having in adjusting their schedule for practicing? I had, but it did not change my mind. I still wanted to play the piano. Mother did not refuse me, she simply said she would see. It was shortly afterwards that the "family lobby" began to operate. Not that I recognized it as such at the time, although perhaps I should have, for it was something of the same sort which had established the family tradition that I preferred the neck of a chicken or turkey. The family lobby was a powerful instrument of persuasion. Where only one individual was to be affected it made a perfect substitute for the ukase. Instead of using force against an individual the family lobby so shaped the individual's mind that he began to ask for whatever it was. Its methods were purely psychological, and leaned heavily on the side of suggestion and reiteration. To show the working of the system I will tell as nearly as I can remember how the violin lessons were sold to me when I preferred piano lessons.

The first step came in the form of some extended remarks by Father on the colorful history of the violin. He mentioned Cremona and Amati, and went at some length into the story of Stradivarius. He also touched on Ole Bull. Father had heard him play and had been greatly moved. But as soon as I began to ask questions he dropped the subject and went on to something else. A day or two later I heard him talking to one of my sisters. As I came up he was telling her that the violin was a man's instrument— there had never been any really great woman violinist. It would, he said, be a waste of time for any girl to try to master the instrument. That was all; the talk went on to other things, leaving me to suspect that she might have asked permission to change over from piano to violin. No such thing was said, of course. I was just left to imagine it. The next step was Father's little lecture on the difficulty of learning to play a violin. This was touched off by a question from one of the girls. Father had, he said, as a boy taken a number of lessons and had been able to learn to play only three simple dance tunes, *Money Musk, Charley over the Water,* and *Pop Goes the Weasel.* This had me wavering, but it was Mother's casually dropped remark that the new schoolteacher, under whose magic spell I had already fallen, was trying to start a class in violin playing, which brought me all the way around. But when I began teasing to take lessons she was not at all sure how Father would feel about spending all the money that a violin would cost. She said she would have to talk it over with him. The final fillip was when Herb came around with a sour face and said that Father had refused

230

to buy him a new banjo because he was spending so much money for my violin.

This method was used over and over again, but it was practically fool-proof and almost never failed to produce the desired result. Herb was a dirty-faced, disorderly boy at fifteen. He never washed behind his ears if he could avoid it, his hair was always disheveled, his hands filthy, and his fingernails gnawed. He had more trouble in passing the morning inspection than anyone in line. Then suddenly the lobby got after him. It began by giving him a new necktie, then noticing it frequently and speaking about the change that had come over him. In a week's time the dirty face had disappeared, the dirty hands followed shortly, and by the end of a month the boy was spick and span, and he grew up to become the most fastidious member of the family.

When I came home after my first lesson and began to wrangle with the new violin I could hear the other members of the family go stamping off upstairs and slamming doors behind them. But upstairs was not far enough away, and soon they began to leave the house with some slight emphasis. Even Mother remembered a call she had to make. After a little, with the exception of Grandmother, I had the house all to myself. Grandmother was too lame to go anywhere—and it was fortunate for her that she was hard of hearing.

I began to feel that the violin was an important instrument; no amount of piano playing would have emptied the house like that.

The initial period of punishment was short-lived, however, for with a teacher I was anxious to please I made rapid progress and was soon quavering out Schubert's *Serenade* to the relieved household. That is, they were relieved for the time being. But as I kept right on quavering out that same tune day after day and week after week

231

as I polished off the finer points of the composition they were at first bored, then pained, and eventually rather nasty about it.

I was not at all discouraged by their attitude, for by this time I had come to realize that every great artist gets ahead only by making sacrifices—and in addition to that I did not mind having the other children where I could put a little pressure on them. As one of the younger children who had to take a great deal of bossing from a large number of people I appreciated this opportunity to get back at them. Then suddenly the teacher switched me to another piece. I did not know until long afterward that Mother had gone to her and begged for mercy.

By this time the practicing situation at our house had become acute. Practice was prohibited after supper. Father wouldn't have it, though he did not care how early the practicing began in the morning. With a single piano and only two hours between school and supper-time, and three music pupils each required to practice an hour a day, it was plain that somebody would have to do her practicing in the morning before breakfast, for right after breakfast we all started for school. The girls used to take turns at the early morning shift, and they were con-stantly trying to exchange periods with each other when outside activities were interfered with.

"I'll swap you my four-thirty to five today for your six-thirty to seven tomorrow morning."

"No, I don't want to do that, but I'll give you my six to seven for your four to five."

"But I want my four to four-thirty for myself."

"All right, then you take my six to six-thirty and I won't have to get up so early."

When I heard them I was glad that I did not have to wait in line to get at my violin.

There was never a great deal of cheating on the prac-ticing, especially among the girls, whose hours jostled each other too closely for any worth-while time-snatching. With me, however, it was different. I could practice wherever and whenever I wanted to, jotting down my time on the bulletin board so that Mother could keep approximate track of it. I used to take my time from the dining-room clock as I went past, and one day when I was anxious to get out and join the other boys I shoved the clock ahead

233

three minutes and marked down my hour as complete.

This was so easy that the next day I shoved it ahead five minutes, and later shoved it back again when nobody was around. For a week or more I took great liberties with the clock, shoving it this way and that to suit my own convenience. Then I became careless and did not always remember to restore it to the right time. One day I had pushed it ahead ten minutes in a burst of recklessness and neglected to set it back. Soon after Father came home that night I found him standing in front of it, watch in hand.

"I guess it will have to go in for repairs, Mother," he said with a troubled look. "Twice this week it's jumped five minutes on me, and now it's jumped ten."

Mother looked up from her darning. "I don't believe there's anything the matter with the clock."

"You think my watch is off?" he demanded. He had carried that big hunting-case gold watch for years, and to challenge its accuracy was like challenging the sun—or the Rochester *Democrat & Chronicle*.

"Probably not."

"Well, what *do* you think?" He disliked rambling notions about anything.

Mother smiled. "Oh, I don't know—just an idea of mine. I'll talk to you about it later."

The next day an hourglass came into the house. Mother said it was to help her keep track of my practicing. It was filled with fine red sand, which completely ruined for me the old metaphor about molasses in January. I tried for years to find some way of beating that hourglass, and the only way I could ever get the better of it was to break a string. I could not afford to do that very often, for violin strings cost money. I never could get a good E for less than fifteen cents.

From time to time other musical instruments made their appearance at our house. Herb had quite a knack

234

with the banjo, and Cecilia could play very handsome chords on the guitar. At one time Stan used to moan melancholy off-key melodies on a superannuated flute. But we were not a musically harmonious family; we had no desire to play together. The truth seems to be that we were a family of soloists. Herb had a good voice and could sing very effectively, carrying an air with great authority so long as nobody else chimed in. But let a bass or a tenor or even an alto attempt to go along with him, and he would soon be singing bass or tenor or alto. He simply could not carry an air unless he had it all to himself.

Herb took singing lessons one year, but it was only because music lessons were popular and he did not want to feel neglected. But he was shy and used to do most of his practicing in the barn. All the neighbors' children were taking lessons on one instrument or another, banjos, cornets, flutes, and melodeons. The members of our family were busy with the piano and the violin, and Elsie was trying her hand at the pipe organ. Music lessons seemed to be in the air, and Sadie, who was with us at that time, came to Mother and asked if there would be any objection to her taking a few lessons on her "instrument."

When Mother inquired about the cost Sadie explained that one of the boys who played in the town band had offered to give her lessons free. With a number of preliminary stipulations and not a few misgivings Mother told her to go ahead and try a lesson or two just to see how the idea worked out. A few evenings later as Father was passing through the lower hall he was astonished to hear the rumble of a man's voice emanating from Sadie's room.

Somewhat perturbed, he reported his discovery to Mother, but she assured him that it was quite all right,

Sadie was just taking a music lesson on her "instrument," and had agreed that the door of her room should be left open so long as the music teacher was there. Father said no more at the time, but the next day he inquired around and learned that Sadie's music teacher was the bass drummer in the band. I never knew quite what it was that Mother said to Sadie, but whatever it was she never took any more lessons on her "instrument" so long as she remained with us.

While it is true that with all the years of study and practice we did not turn out one real musician in our family, it cannot be denied that the making of music added much to the gaiety of our home. It furnished rhythm for our dancing and accompaniment for our song, and it gave us a pleasant ambition with which to occupy our spare time. And it must have brought some satisfaction to Father, for while none of us reached even the concert stage, we were all, without exception, ready and eager to render *Then You'll Remember Me* as often as he cared to hear it; and no doubt many of his briefs and documents reflected the lilt of our rendition of *Three Little Maids* or *Buttercup* or some of the other inimitable ditties of Sir William and Sir Arthur.

21. Seamstress

THE country dressmaker was one of the permanent fixtures of my youth. She used to come to our house every spring and every fall as regularly as Easter and Christmas. Her name was not printed on the calendar, but it might as well have been. "The next time Miss Gilbert comes" was definite and certain enough for anybody. It wasn't always the same dressmaker; she might die or she might move away, but there was always another one ready to step into the breach. Still in those days nobody ever took up dressmaking voluntarily. A husband ran off with another woman; a father died leaving an aged mother to support, or lost all he had by endorsing notes for his friends; the family wage earner fell on the ice and was crippled, and somebody had to get out and earn a living for those children. Dressmaking was almost a natural career for a maiden lady without means. For a woman to be unmarried in those days was not the career it is today. Though it was not in all cases a calamity it was a state seldom entered upon voluntarily and not often envisioned in advance, being thrust upon one instead of achieved. Matrons were almost certain to regard spinsterhood either with compassion or with envy, according to their own marital contentment; but no man, married or single, could ever look upon an old maid without a feeling of speculative amusement. Being a seamstress required very little preparation; anybody could go into it at almost any age. It was not as desirable a job as schoolteaching, nor was it anywhere near as exacting in its demands.

Our dressmakers were never young, they were never good-looking, and with one or two exceptions they were not good-natured; usually quite the opposite—for if they weren't downright disagreeable they were at least difficult. Mother was always warning us to be careful about what we said when there was a dressmaker in the house.

"From what she has told me about other people," Mother used to say, "I don't imagine that she will miss anything that is going on around here."

This was not her attitude towards any particular one, it was the way she regarded them all. She felt sorry for them without any nice husband to support them and a horde of children to keep their minds from dwelling on unpleasant thoughts, but she never took them into her confidence, and she always tried to put her best foot forward so long as one of them remained in the house. I never knew what it was that caused the friction between Mother and Bertha Gilbert. I don't know that Mother herself ever quite understood what it was that aroused Bertha so deeply. But one year after Bertha had finished her spring sewing at our house and had gone on to some other place Mother began to receive reports from her friends that Bertha was talking about her. Usually this was a thing that happened when Bertha had been displaced by some younger or some better dressmaker. Then she would tell all. But Mother had not displaced her, and there had been no unpleasant incident during the two weeks that Bertha was sewing at our house. The strange part of it was that while she had not spoken of it to anyone Mother had been thinking about making a change.

The thought came to Mother one day that Bertha was getting old and set in her ways. She was over sixty and she no longer was quick about catching the little style hints that Mother picked up in Rochester. She was elephantine in her memory, and if she could only see a dress once she would remember the details of it ever after. But Mother felt that with the girls growing older style was becoming more important to them. The girls, too, were getting the thought and were complaining that old Bertha's dresses looked as if they were made for a barn dance.

Mother had in the house some new material for a silk dress for Louise, but she could not bear the thought of having the Bertha imprint on so bright and gay a fabric. This dress ought to be smart and jaunty, and she realized that nothing Bertha had ever made could by any stretch of the imagination be either. She could not seem to make up her mind just who the proper person was to make this dress, but assuredly it was not Bertha. Mother had never shown Bertha the material or mentioned it in her presence; and, indeed, when the first reports of Bertha's hostile talk came to her she had not yet decided where she was going to have it made.

Mother was a little disturbed at Bertha's hostility, but at the same time she felt a sense of relief; she could send Louise's dress to any dressmaker she wanted to; for since there would be no further commitments with Bertha there was no reason why she could not have the dress made wherever she pleased. She eventually placed it in the hands of a Geneva dressmaker, who made a specialty of frocks for younger persons.

Louise was a lovely slip of a girl at the time, seventeen and just coming into the budding charm of womanhood. She had started going to the college proms and dances and was much sought after by the impressionable youths. She also made enough of an impression on the wives of the professors so that one of them could write me more than fifty years later, "She was one of the prettiest and

239

most graceful girls I have ever seen on a ballroom floor, altogether charming and a great belle."

The first try-on of that dress when it was brought home was a sensation. It left both Elsie and Cecilia in a state of partial collapse. After a single glance at it neither of the younger girls could think of anything to wear in which she would not look like poor Cinderella amid the ashes of her chimney corner. After Louise had gone upstairs to take off the new gown Mother missed Elsie and began a quiet hunt for her, finding her eventually weeping in the back parlor, her face buried in the pillows of the couch.

Mother was troubled, for she knew exactly how Elsie must feel, and had been expecting repercussions. She refused to regard her task as entirely hopeless, however, and tried to cheer Elsie by making suggestions for brightening up some of her clothes so that she would not feel quite so hopelessly out of the picture. She finally promised to let Elsie wear her Spanish shawl and comb, which had never been entrusted to one of the girls before, and which were really lovely on Elsie. And having made that concession she fell back on the reliable old seniority rule.

"You must not forget, dear," she said, "that Louise is older."

"But is that any reason why she should have—the best— of everything?" sobbed Elsie.

"I'm afraid it is. Your turn will come next, dear, and when it does you will have everything that she is having now."

Cecilia was not the weepy kind. Nor was she one to lock herself in her room and sulk. When she saw Louise go upstairs to take off the new gown Cecilia walked out of the house. She strolled slowly up the garden path until she came to the old apple tree, from a limb of which hung the swing. Here she seated herself and swung slowly back and forth for some time.

The three sisters were inconveniently, almost indecently, near the same age. Only three years and three months separated the oldest and the youngest. I think that Mother was inclined to view this as a matrimonial problem from the time when she first started to let down Louise's skirts, and at the same moment she began to do all she could to hold Cecilia back and increase the spread. But Cecilia was a hard child to hold back. She was as smart as a whip at her studies, and more than Fabian tactics were required to keep her teachers from jumping her over grades. She was equally smart at picking up games, dance steps, anything which required a quick wit and dexterity.

Mother stubbornly continued to dress her in juvenile clothes until Nature took a hand and began rounding the beautiful Cecilia into curves that are not ordinarily found on the contours of a child. But Mother was not to be easily driven from the field even by the incontestable strategies of Nature, and though she had to give ground she retreated grudgingly, yielding a hem here, a ruffle there, a little fullness in some other place. She even conceded a small bustle, but there she stopped. That far she would go and no farther.

Cecilia took these various concessions in her stride. A girl with older sisters matures rapidly so far as the desire for grown-up appurtenances is concerned, and Cecilia was no exception to the rule. As soon as the "misses" bustle had been assimilated into her wardrobe and she had thoroughly mastered the handling of it, she at once started a campaign for a full-sized bustle. I was only a small boy at the time, but for some reason the bustle presented only its comic aspect to me. I used to drive my older sisters wild by leaping astride their bustles from behind and try-

241

ing to ride them like a pony. Bustles were at best frail contraptions made of fine spring wire bent into spirals some three inches in diameter and eight or ten inches long. They would give under the pressure of being slightly sat on, and spring back into shape when the wearer stood up again.

The "misses" bustles allowed to Cecilia had only two of these coil springs, while those of her sisters had four— and I believe that one of Louise's most extreme gowns even had six, but never having ridden on that one I cannot be sure. I will never forget the appeals and arguments Cecilia put up while waging her battle for the four- instead of two-spring. She was a persistent young lady who usually got what she set out to get; but in this particular instance she was met by a very stubborn resistance. Mother could be as stubborn as the next one. She held out as long as there was any need for holding out, and just when Cecilia began to detect what she thought was a weakening of Mother's defense, she discovered that the bustle was going out of style, and that woman's posterior was going to be treated by dress stylists very much as it had long been treated by Mlle. Nature.

It was of this bustle contest that Cecilia was thinking as she swung back and forth under the old apple tree. It had been a hollow victory. Only in her mind's eye had she ever been seen in a four-spring bustle. And now in her mind's eye she had been seeing herself in skirts which swept the floor, while in reality her skirts had never swept anything lower than her ankles. Perhaps this was her chance to get them down where they really belonged. She slipped out of the swing and started for the house. Mother found her waiting in the library when she returned from comforting Elsie.

"I feel perfectly terrible, Mother," Cecilia said.

242

Mother laid a hand on her shoulder. "What seems to be the trouble?"

"It's that dress of Louise's."

"What about it, dear?"

"It'll just kill off the rest of us—nobody'll even know I'm on earth."

Mother shook her head. "But after all, dear, this isn't your party. You can't seem to understand that you're not quite old enough to be really a part of the social affairs of the older girls."

"That's all very well to say, Mother, but you must have seen for yourself how all the college boys come around and ask me to dance with them. Am I ever a wallflower?"

Mother did not retreat. "Of course they would be polite to a younger sister," she said.

"But I can dance just as well as the other girls—and I'm entitled to have my skirts as long as theirs."

"But, darling—you're only a child!" Mother protested.

Cecilia's cheeks flushed. "I'm only a year and a half younger than Elsie—and three years younger than Louise."

"You must not get mistaken ideas, dear."

"I haven't any mistaken ideas, but when the girls ask me to help them entertain their men, I think you ought to let me be reasonably grown-up about it."

Mother was firm in her refusal, but Cecilia would not give in. "I hope you're not going to treat me like an infant forever!" she burst out.

"You must learn patience, dear."

"You think I don't know why I'm being held back, but I do."

"Your turn will come if you'll just be patient," Mother evaded.

"It's because you're so anxious to get Louise married off."

243

"Why should I be anxious?" asked Mother quietly. "Louise is only seventeen."

"You're worried all right." Cecilia started for the stairs. "Otherwise you wouldn't be so stubborn about keeping me in swaddling clothes."

It was not until Cecilia had gone to her room that Mother's conscience began to function. Was she being unfair to Cecilia in trying to hold her back? After all, it wasn't the child's fault that she had come into the world so soon after the others. Was Cecilia really too young for grown-up clothes? She certainly was not too young to be popular with the boys, and she was old enough to realize it. She was an independent child, not afraid to fight for her rights. That was like her father. What Mother really wanted, she kept telling herself, was the greatest good for the whole family, and she *had* thought that could best be accomplished by not letting the two younger girls crowd Louise too closely. But in the end it was her conscience which won, and she told Cecilia she could let down the hem of her blue challie as far as it would go. She hoped it would not go all the way to the floor; but Cecilia had seen to that when the dress was being made. She had turned the hem herself and knew that there was plenty of it to meet all possible contingencies.

Cecilia never thought of herself as a little girl again.

Sadie, our musical maid, was away when Louise's new dress came. Indeed, her "instrument" had maintained a stolid silence for two full weeks while she was off on a vacation that was intended to reinforce her for the rigors of the Hobart College commencement season, which seemed to me at the time to be a vast series of jollifications and parties taking place in, at, through, across, over, and around our house. I did not then realize that the college itself had any other part in the gaieties than the furnishing of the male personnel. I could always tell when com-

mencement was coming by the way our house used to fill
up with girls: cousins from New York and Rochester,
school friends from all over, and a few visitors who seemed
to be nothing but company. Stan and Leslie and I would
be shoved up into the attic to sleep on cots under the tin
roof, among the trunks and boxes and the broken or dis-
carded furniture. We always had to have extra help in
our house during commencement week, for with all those
people to feed, the piles of dishes used to reach halfway to
the kitchen ceiling. But Mother had some old stand-bys
who would come for a week though they would not take
a steady job.

Sadie had offered to swear on a stack of Bibles that she
would be back the day before the festivities were to begin.
Mother thought the oath slightly profane and said she
would prefer to take Sadie's word. But Sadie's word appeared to be unequal to the task, for the day came and
Sadie failed to appear. Since she was momentarily expected no effort was made to find a substitute, and in spite
of all the Sister Annes who kept watching the road down
the hill it seemed as if the festivities would have to open
without the assistance of Sadie, who had been counted on
to serve a sort of state dinner for the visiting ladies and
their escorts.

The guests had arrived and were now scattered around
the big front veranda waiting for dinner to be announced.
Louise had received them in her new gown, which had
proved to be a real sensation. No two members of the
family can seem to agree on either the material or the
design of that dress. In the absence of a picture I will simply say that it was a vibrant shade of red and followed
the contours of Louise's figure faithfully. There was something about Louise in that gown which reminded the beholder of a rosebud plucked in a sequestered garden at
the most enchanting moment of a sweet dewy dawn. One

look must have been enough to spoil the pleasure of any other girl at the party.

The dinner was being delayed as long as possible in the hope that Sadie might still get there in time to serve it. Usually our family crises were kept from the guests, but on this occasion with so many sharing the secret even the passers-by in the street must have known about it. All day long persons in the household had been asking each other, "Has Sadie come yet?" and when the guests arrived for dinner that was the first query from most of them. But Sadie had not then appeared, though she arrived before the guests had gone in to dinner. And when she did come it was the bright eyes of Cecilia who had first discovered her; she had recognized the horse which belonged to Hillary Babson, a beau of Sadie's, as they came driving slowly up the hill. At the hilltop Mr. Babson plied his whip and drew up before our front horse block with a flourish that was plainly intended to indicate that they had come in a great hurry. It should not be forgotten that our house was on a corner, and Hillary could just as well have drawn up at the side where Sadie's debarkation would have been invisible to the group of young people on the front veranda.

At the first glimpse of them Cecilia turned to Elsie, who stood near by and said, "Here comes Sadie." Elsie quickly relayed the information to Louise, "Here comes Sadie." Louise turned and passed the word to Mother, who had just appeared in the doorway, "Here comes Sadie." Then everybody began doing it. "Here comes Sadie—here comes Sadie—here comes Sadie." The news was all over the veranda in no time.

All eyes were on Sadie as she stepped out on the horse block . . . dressed in a gown that was the exact replica of the one Louise had on, color, pattern, style, even the accessories. Sadie paused on the horse block for a moment

246

while Hillary handed down to her a parasol exactly like the one that was lying on Louise's bed at the moment. Sadie did not open the parasol, but tucked it jauntily under her arm. Then she turned, flashed a smiling good-by at Hillary and came hurriedly up the broad flagstone walk which led from the gate to the veranda.

Sadie had a marvelous complexion in a day when complexions were either natural or non-existent. She had a figure that would have won a rating of "elegant" in any company. It was a shade more developed than Louise's, and there was a little more of it. Her manner was one of becoming modesty, as if she could feel all eyes upon her, but must go ahead anyway and make the best of her opportunity. As she came up that walk she was a sight to take any man's breath away.

The general effect of her coming was not unlike that of a head-on view of an approaching locomotive in the movies, which comes sweeping on until it seems that nothing can keep the beholder from being ground under its wheels—and then suddenly it swings off to one side and goes by with a big noise but no damage. A few feet from the steps of the veranda a narrow walk led around to what now would be called the tradesman's entrance, and just when disaster seemed most certainly impending Sadie swung on to this narrow walk—went by with a devastating swish—and disappeared behind the house.

When the audience could breathe again and had recovered sufficiently to look at one another, Louise was gone. In a very short time she was back again in a different dress. Mother met Sadie at the kitchen door, hurried her into a white uniform and apron, and announced that dinner was served. Later she found the fragments of Louise's new dress scattered all over her bedroom. Louise had literally torn it from herself in ribbons. But Louise's temper was like Father's; an outburst, if of sufficient in-

247

tensity, possessed vast cleansing power and was almost instantaneously followed by a period of great calm and sweetness. Louise was never any more charming than in her old dress that night.

Father nearly expired of laughter when Mother told him later what had happened, for he had been in the library and knew nothing of it. But it was he who directed an investigation of the affair into the proper channels. He started with the assumption that Sadie was innocent of any wrong. Only a reckless or a stupid person, he said, would walk into the lion's mouth as Sadie had done, and most assuredly Sadie was neither reckless nor stupid.

When asked where she got her new dress Sadie said that it was a secret she had promised faithfully not to tell; she did tell, however, that the entire outfit had cost her hardly anything at all since it was part of the wedding raiment of a girl in Geneva. The story was that the girl's trousseau was all finished, and then the girl had a fight with her intended and the match was broken off. The bride-to-be was crushed, of course, and never wanted to see her trousseau again, so it was broken up and sold for what it would bring.

Sadie kept her promise. She never did tell where the dress came from, but Mother gleaned a clue here and there which satisfied her that Bertha Gilbert was the deep, dark plotter back of it all. Mother established the fact that a very homely woman came into the Geneva shop where Louise's dress was made, posing as a mother who was buying a trousseau for a daughter who, she said, was about to be married. The woman greatly admired Louise's dress, which had just been finished, and though she looked it over with care she bought nothing and left without giving her name. It was also a very homely woman who bought at one of the Rochester stores the peculiar shade of Milan straw from which both hats were made. Mother had finished Louise's hat before Bertha Gilbert's last visit at our house, and had put it with the parasol and gloves in the bottom drawer of the bureau in the guest room, where the material for the dress was kept. But she had taken great pains never to open that bottom drawer while Bertha was in the house.

However, the drawer was never locked, and Father's deduction was that during one of the periods when Bertha was alone in the guest room, which was being used for sewing, she had done a bit of snooping and had come

249

upon what she regarded as conclusive evidence that she was about to be superseded. Mother would never let herself believe that Bertha was snooping. She did not doubt that the woman had opened the bottom drawer, but her confidence in Bertha's character made her believe that it had been done by mistake.

"Even after the dirty trick she has done?" asked Father.

"Yes, even after that," said Mother. "I've known Bertha for almost ten years, and I should be doing her a great wrong if I should say that I ever knew her to do anything dishonorable."

Father smiled. "Whenever your conscience and your common sense come into conflict," he said, "your common sense never wins."

22. Croquet Gives Way to Tennis

THE exodus from the farms and small towns to the large cities had not yet set in with enough force to be felt to any extent in our town. It was a country town with a very strong attachment to land values. A well-to-do man was one who owned good farms. Banks and factories might fail, but the land would stay right where it was. Most of the people who left town in those days went west, where they thought they could get better land and more of it for less money.

Many of those who went came back again. Not that they did not find plenty of good land off to the west for quite a little less money, but they were lonesome out there. The farms were too large, and too far apart, and the great treeless expanse of landscape made them feel isolated. Trees could be made to grow in most of the localities, but life was too short to wait for them. They wanted a place where they could walk out in the yard and pick apples, and where they could cut a winter's supply of firewood without going more than forty or fifty rods from the house. A single windmill on the far-off horizon was a poor substitute for the tree-dotted landscape where they had been brought up. They craved closer quarters.

Back in the eighties people did not want to get away from the small towns because they were small. Given time they would probably grow large. Life there was leisurely, and competition, if it existed at all, was not of the cut-throat variety of a later day. I can count on my fingers more than twenty-five families of substance who lived on or near Main Street when I was a schoolboy. Almost without exception they owned the homes in which they lived, and additional real estate as well, either farms or business buildings in the village. Both were thought to be sound. Many of these properties had been in the family for more than one generation. One or two of them had been grants for services in the Revolutionary War, which, though they had been divided up, had never gone out of the family.

Most of the families I am referring to had children, some of them more than we had in our family. The average of the group, I should imagine, would be around four. To have only two was to be practically childless.

This group of old families made a delightful nucleus for social life. Some of the men had been away to college, and some of them had gone no further with their book-learning than the local academy. This didn't matter much, for the social status was determined almost entirely by family. Upstarts had a tough time climbing the social ladder, though it could be done, and occasionally was. It was much easier to be born into it, and much more secure; for at the first slip the upstart would be "snubbed" and people would fall back on the reliable old saying that blood will tell.

There were occasional small parties, dinners for eight or ten, or two tables of cards, but the usual type of social affair was to throw one's house wide open for the entire social register about once a year. The main feature of the party would be a huge supper, and often a fiddler or a two- or three-piece orchestra would furnish dance music for the young folks. For the older guests eating and talking were regarded as sufficient entertainment, and an occasional "square set" would give them an opportunity to dance off any heaviness that may have been accumulating from an abundance of substantial food and a complete absence of any form of alcoholic stimulant.

Once a great wave of dominoes went over the place. This game was thought to be a little safer than cards, and people who would not touch a playing card did not hesitate to spend an entire evening over the little oblongs of wood with the spots on them. I have heard twenty or thirty tables of them clicking at once.

These were not the piping times of Prohibition and the common man did not share the somewhat Victorian idea of the socially elect in our town. When he invited his friends for a barn-dance, a harvest home, or a house-warming—and every new building from a pigsty to a mansion called for a house-warming—he would set out a barrel of hard cider with plenty of large tin cups, and if a man did not get plenty of liquid refreshment along with his other entertainment it was not the fault of the host.

Nearly every winter the Masons would throw open their lodge room for "The Masonic Ball," long the social event of the season. This, too, would be for the old and young together, and the round dances and the square would alternate throughout the evening. The young people always managed to give one or two big balls or assemblies every winter, to which the older generation was admitted only as spectators. And every winter when the sleighing was good there would be moonlight "straw rides" to some neighboring village, where a hot oyster supper would be served.

These straw rides were already losing favor by the time that I was old enough to take part in such affairs. They were still talked about, however, and occasionally we would generate enough energy to promote one. I went on only two that I can recall, and each time I met with disappointment if not disaster.

The mechanics of the straw ride were simple. An ordinary country bobsled with a team of horses and driver would be engaged. It was customary for the boys of the party to chip in and defray the expenses of both the equipage and the supper. The box of the bobsled—actually the box of an ordinary farm wagon in summer—would be well filled with straw on the erroneous assumption that straw in the box of a vehicle is warming to a sitter on a cold winter's night. I will admit that straw has a certain cushioning effect, but otherwise it is a nuisance. On top of the straw an abundance of buffalo robes and heavy blankets (usually smelling very horsy) would be spread to keep the passengers warm. The couples alternated, facing each other with backs resting against the sideboards of the bobsled box.

Theoretically the arrangement appealed to me. I liked the idea of snuggling under a big fur robe with the lady of my choice and jingling joyfully across the moonlight countryside to a hot oyster supper waiting for us in a warm and hospitable inn at the end of the ride. To tell the truth I imagined that it was going to be quite a little like bundling, and I went into the affair with the keenest anticipation for a pleasant time. The omnipresent chaperon would be with us, of course, but she would be tucked under her own robes and would stay there. In any event she could not be everywhere at once, and she wouldn't know what was going on under any robes but her own.

All the guests were warned in advance to dress warmly, as there is no sport known to man, with the possible exception of ice-boating, that is any more chilly than sleigh-riding in a bobsled filled with straw. On the first occasion I discounted this warning, being, as I imagined, a hardy perennial in type—and from the start I suffered from the cold to such an extent that I spent all my time both coming and going in beating my hands together and wriggling my toes to keep them from freezing. I also caught a ter-

254

rific cold, and in addition suffered from chilblains for all the rest of the winter. I had nobody but myself to blame, however, and the following year when a straw ride was proposed through the winter moonlight, I went prepared. I put on just about every warm garment in our house.

This time I certainly did not suffer from the cold. I had warned about the cold the girl I was escorting and she had likewise gone well prepared for blasts of polar intensity. The result was that we were so well bundled against the weather that we were completely insulated against any other kind of bundling, even of the most inoffensive and unobjectionable character. My arm around the lady of my choice felt as if it were encircling a bale of hay. Amiable enough hay, I will admit, encouraging and receptive hay perhaps, but hay that was, alas, impenetrable and unfathomable.

As the moonlight glistened on the sculptured snowbanks and the bells on the prancing horses filled the night with their silvery jingling, as the steel-shod runners glided swiftly over the crunching snow and the half-buried farm houses floated silently past us as in a dream—I was working industriously down under the robe to get one of her mittens loose. We were only a mile or so from home when I finally got it off and held *her* bare hand in *my* bare hand. What a thrill that was! It seemed almost indecent at the time. . . . All too soon the prying lights of the town shone down on us, and we put on our mittens and showed our hands conspicuously outside the robe.

This time there was no frostbite. I did not come down with a cold or suffer from chilblains. But my zest for moonlight bundling in the dead of winter was forever extinguished.

I did not realize it at the time, but the social order in the small town was already breaking up by the time I was old enough to go away to school. The love of land had

255

begun to slip when the first of the old families sold its ancestral acres to a hard-working young Hollander who wanted it not because of any sentimental associations, but because it was good land for farming. The transaction was treated as a sacrilege, almost a scandal, at the time. The sellers were looked down upon because they had not preferred their land to money. Father had no ancestral acres of his own, but he shook his head over the situation and wondered what it meant. It was not so very long before he found out; for once the initial impact had worn off it became much easier for others to follow suit.

Another form of social activity that was popular in town during our childhood was the private theatrical. I found among my father's papers a short time ago the cast of *Mrs. Jarley's Wax Works* as the performance was given back in the days when Rutherford B. Hayes was President. My mother was cast as a waxen "dancing girl," and to my astonishment my father was playing the part of the loquacious Mrs. Jarley. His introductory remarks containing a mixture of mythology and local hits sound strangely unlike him.

Attractions at the local opera house were few and far between. This or that "Opera Company" used to come to town for a week during every season, with a ten-twenty-thirty organization. Occasionally an elocutionist would be billed, and "Blind Tom," the Negro pianist, was a regular annual miracle. The high spot of the season, however, was *Uncle Tom's Cabin,* for this usually had a street parade. And from the same little stage with its oil-burning footlights, which had to be blown out by the janitor to dim the stage, I once saw Joe Jefferson play *Rip Van Winkle.* Joe was an old man by this time. His voice was pretty well gone, his gestures were made with the exaggerated intensity of old age, and his memory was slipping occasionally on his lines. But it was such a performance as that stage had never seen before and assuredly never will again, since it has been torn down and rebuilt with an eye to the exhibition of motion pictures.

There was always at least one fine theater in Rochester, but there was no after-theater train, and to see a show there meant to stay all night. The Smith Opera House in Geneva came a little later. This was only eight miles away with excellent train service. You could leave home on the six-twenty and come back on the "late train" at ten-twenty —which would permit you to see practically the whole show, that is, everything but the last act. I often took advantage of this service and came to know most of the current road shows thoroughly—all except the last act. For considerably more than forty years I have been wondering how some of those plays came out.

Hardly a season passed without one or two amateur productions, which required many weeks of preparation for a single performance. Originally these were invitation affairs, though later on they were given as church benefits, or to buy new uniforms for one of the volunteer fire companies, with a general admission of ten cents and a top of twenty for reserved seats. The members of the Lotus Club, as they called themselves, were not awed by the big names or brilliant performances of others. They attempted everything they could get their hands on short of Shakespeare. *The Rivals* and *She Stoops to Conquer* were probably given oftener than any other plays, not only because they were more popular, but because they had the parts all copied off and ready to use.

Mother never took an acting part. She would occasionally be an angel or a sorrowing mother in a tableau, but she refused to take any part in which she would have lines to speak. Father, on the other hand, usually had one of the leading roles. He spoke his lines well, and no doubt

257

he was convinced that with a little more practice he could become another Edwin Booth. I saw him in a part only once and thought him wonderful. But by my day he was too much buried under the details of a large if unremunerative legal practice to have any time to study lines and rehearse. He was usually called in, however, as a coach for the last few rehearsals.

The amateur theatricals had begun to play out a bit by the time our family had reached its quota. They did not last long after the older children began to poke fun at them, and to tell their elders what terrible hams they were. Occasionally the younger generation would be inveigled into "putting on" something for the benefit of this or that, though they preferred to have a professional come to town to take the lead and do the coaching. Once they had a soubrette who called herself Lillian Helmer come and put on a benefit performance of *Child of the Sea*. As it turned out, this performance was mostly for Lillian's benefit, and she got herself terribly talked about by her goings-on at the Inn, where she was being put up. Several times an old German comedian named Charlie Collins came there to produce and coach *Fritz Stein,* a Civil War comedy drama in which Collins played the title role.

As far back as I can remember, croquet, picnics, and boating were the most popular of the summer diversions. Croquet was genteel and ladylike, and it could be played in the most formal of costumes. There was accordingly a set on every lawn in town. Boating had not quite so much to recommend it. It was after all a sport to which one had to dress down, and it was dangerous; still everybody whose property bordered on the creek maintained a large flat-bottom rowboat which would accommodate from five to eight persons. I used to be taken out in one of these by my sisters as soon as I could walk. I am sure my mother knew nothing of this, as she had an inborn fear of the water. But the girls had me on their hands, and if they were to get in their boating they simply had to take me along. Once when I was riding in a little triangular seat in the bow and somebody said, "Oh, look at the perch!" I looked—and fell overboard. The boat passed completely over me and I was rescued by Louise, who was seated in the stern. She caught me by my long hair, hauled me up, wrung the water out of my clothes, and told me not to lean so far over the side when I wanted to look at a fish.

Every summer would see a succession of picnics, usually at some pleasant spot along the creek and far enough out of town to make walking impossible. We would drive out in carriages, or sometimes in a hay wagon well lined with clean hay or straw. These were usually all-day affairs that would last until an hour or two after sunset, and then the picnickers would drive slowly home along the dusty roads singing old favorite songs for their own pleasure and the entertainment of the country folk living along the way. However, the amusement pattern of our lives was in for a bloodless revolution after Louise had been away to school for a year or two.

She came home with ideas which caused our household to seethe like boiling oil. She redecorated the back parlor, giving it some of the flavor of a Turkish seraglio. She rearranged the furniture in the front parlor, discarding certain items entirely and replacing them with other items from the attic, so placed as to focus the interest on a small table containing our Rogers Group called "Neighboring Pews." She renovated and reorganized the arrangements and service of the dining room. She augmented and enlivened the dreary Sunday night supper of bread and milk; she met some resistance here from Grandmother, but managed to put it down. However, the most far-reaching of her reforms, renovations, introductions, and

259

installations took place not in the house, but in the back-yard, where she induced Father to plow under a large part of our ample garden and build a tennis court. That tennis court completely changed the tenor of our lives.

To begin with, it threw gentility out of the window and effectually banished the ladylike game of croquet so far as our family was concerned. It brought us a fresh, new language—"fifteen all"—"forty love"—"volleying"—"set"—"deuce." It brought us a new fashion in wearing apparel introducing the striped blazer, white flannels, the knitted jersey, the rubber-soled shoes, the ankle-length skirts and an unheard-of freedom of movement for women, and eventually the shirtwaist. It brought us a host of college students. It resulted in the formation of the Alfresco Tennis Club, which moved the younger social set right into our own backyard.

Louise never got to be much of a tennis player herself, but she walked off with the best of them all and led her champion from the service line straight to the altar.

Until the coming of that tennis court I had spent my summers along the banks of the creek, fishing if the fish were biting, boating when they weren't, swimming when-ever I could find anyone to swim with me, tramping, hunting, making things hot for the furred and feathered creatures. I was a rough fellow, a woodsman, a sort of Daniel Boone until tennis came into my life, but after that the lone, wild places knew me no more. All I could think about was developing a deadly service, and perfect-ing my forehand. I made a fair though never a champion tennis player, but I still believe that the wilderness and waste places lost a distinguished guide and voyageur when I took up the tennis racquet.

If Louise had not gone in for tennis she would have taken up something else. She was a crusader, an organizer, a go-getter. Later in life she was the moving spirit behind the organization of several other clubs. Without knowing a niblick from a stymie she organized a thriving country club and sold many people the idea of playing golf. At another time somebody pointed out to her a place which he said would make a fine location for a yacht club. So without a halyard to her name she organized one and took the tiller of it herself. Hardly any of the members had yachts, but she mastered the vocabulary and so long as she remained the skipper it was a great success socially.

Other tennis courts were built in town, but not until we had had ours for a year or two. We had the edge on the sport when hardly anybody in town had so much as seen a tennis racquet. With Louise's marriage the Alfresco Tennis Club began to wobble as an all-year-round social organization. It would hibernate and come to life only when Louise and her husband returned to spend the summer at home. For eight or ten weeks it would flourish, but as soon as they went away in the fall the club would go back into the mothballs. Then came a summer when Louise was busy sewing on baby clothes. She did not come home that year or the next. When she did come she found people playing on their own courts, and the Alfresco Tennis Club had become only a memory. Our court ran down some, but it was kept in active commission until I went off to school. The following summer when I reached home for my vacation I found it knee-high with green corn, which always seemed to flourish best along the base lines and around the place where we used to keep the marking machine full of powdered lime.

The court was gone, but it had played a very definite part in our family life, for it had marked the passing of one epoch and the arrival of another. Croquet with its billowing skirts was gone. The tennis court and the tennis racquet had come, with skirts "all the way up to the ankle, by George!" And over the horizon, though nobody would have believed it, were the service ace and the passing shot —with girl players in bare legs, bare arms, bare backs, and *shorts!*

23. Tripping the Light Fantastic

DANCING never was a sin at our house. There was nothing in the Bible against it, and so far as I know the local Presbyterian church on the whole regarded it as a pleasant and probably harmless diversion. Usually the evangelists who were imported during the winter months to liven up the spiritual affairs of the community dealt the subject some stinging blows, but that was only because it was part of their stock in trade with the material all ready for use. It was almost the equal of reading a good sex novel to hear an evangelist describe the various steps leading from the ballroom to perdition.

I was very much puzzled by this the first time I heard an evangelist tell the intimate details. I had been dancing since an early age, but had not realized that all this interior fermentation was going on within the heart and soul of my partner. The dancing I had participated in was conducted along the most decorous lines. The Devil had never guided my hands into any of the sly indecencies so graphically indicated by the expressive gestures of the evangel; nor had the Evil One caused my body to weave with sinuous suggestiveness against the palpitating form of one of God's purest creatures as she was stealthily overpowered by the savage rhythm of the ballroom band, which soundeth sweet in the ears but stingeth like an adder in all other parts of the human anatomy.

The development which brought this great blast from the pulpits of the land was the swing in popularity from the square dance to the round. I can't remember when my sisters could not waltz and schottische and polka, but at the public dances it had been the quadrille, the lancers, and the Virginia reel which had predominated.

Nothing could have been easier to learn than those old square dances. They were simple evolutions in which opposite couples participated to march time, and consisted largely in swinging either your own partner or the opposite lady, though occasionally just to vary the proceedings you would swing at the corners. The ordinary square dance could be as stately as the minuet, or it could be as rowdy as you please. Sometimes instead of taking the lady by her fingertips and swinging her gently about before returning her to her place, an enthusiastic youth would seize his partner around the waist and whirl her a dozen times with her ample skirt billowing from the floor in a way that was considered graceful but slightly immodest.

I have recently been looking at an old dance program from a ball given in 1883. It starts with a grand march, and proceeds to alternate quadrilles with lancers for the next eleven dances. Then comes a Virginia reel, and after that an intermission for refreshments. The quadrilles and lancers are resumed in earnest after the intermission and continue until the twentieth number, which is an Old Dan Tucker. Number twenty-four to my astonishment was a waltz to the tune of *Home, Sweet Home.*

This was not at all out of the ordinary at the time. The old square dances really were a lot of fun. They required no practicing of complicated steps. Anybody who could walk could be steered through a quadrille or lancers by an experienced partner, and after going through a few times would require no more assistance than the "calling off" by the musician. Much of the time only two of the couples would be in motion while the other two, awaiting their turn, could stand and converse, flirt, gossip, or otherwise pleasantly pass the time.

It was the custom of the Evangelical clergy to deliver an occasional blast against the old square dance even when the professional revivalist was not around. I never could understand how dancing a quadrille could be any more arousing to the passions than a game of "musical chairs." Indeed, I have seen some pretty daring fumbling done in that eminently respectable game. But the preachers wholeheartedly approved of musical chairs, and even gave the game a religious flavor by calling it Going to Jerusalem. So far as I know the wickedness inherent in musical chairs has never been exposed or even discovered by the evangels, even those most rabid against the staid and innocuous old quadrille. I have wondered if the periodical sitting down could have had anything to do with purging the game of the inference of wickedness. It would have been quite possible for square dancers to sit down during their idle moments in the evolutions. As it happened, however, their time for sitting down more or less permanently was not far off.

It happened just as the old high bicycle was being displaced by the "safety." I do not mean to intimate that these events were in any way connected—just that they occurred at about the same time. It may have signalized repressed womanhood blowing off some of its stored-up Victorian reserve. A female in hoop-skirts cannot be anything but reserved. Nor are women in bustles going to be any too skittish. In our family the bustles went up in the attic with the arrival of the tennis court in the backyard. No woman with a bustle on is going to chase a little rubber ball around the landscape trying with no thought of personal dignity to whack the thing back over the net. Our tennis court did more to make natural, normal human beings out of our girls than any other single influence I can think of, though I must admit that the round dances were a great help.

The so-called "tennis dances" of the Alfresco Tennis Club consisted exclusively of the round dances with a single square dance called the Saratoga lancers, then very much in vogue, usually danced to airs from *The Mikado*. The round dances with which the Alfrescans began to disport themselves were the waltz, two-step, polka, heel-and-toe, gavotte, schottische, and galop. It was the usual custom to go right down the line, and to be socially adequate one was supposed to know them all and do them reasonably well. There were other round dances current, such as the racquette and the mazurka, but they never achieved any great popularity in our town.

If, however, a man went to a dance knowing only the waltz and the polka, he would have a great deal of "sitting out" to do; and sitting out was one of the arts in which my sisters took little interest. They were all fine dancers and they wanted to dance. It was hardly their idea of a good time to go to a dance with an escort who knew only a few of the steps and was unable to perform whenever he happened to be needed. And they worked out a very practical way around the difficulty. At our house there was always a space available for dancing, and somebody could always be found to provide adequate music; and my sisters saw to it that any boy who was showing signs of asking one of them to a dance was able to cope with the dances likely to be found on the program.

I have sawed away on my violin by the hour while some handsome youth, otherwise acceptable but with uneducated feet, was taught to dance his way through a ballroom program. Often a boy would already know one or two of the steps. With this start it would not be difficult for him to pick up a working knowledge of two or three other dances in just an evening or two. Dancing was in the air, and soon the college boys began coming around, not to learn, but to teach the girls some trick step they had picked up somewhere.

However, the old square dances did not succumb without a struggle. They had many friends who refused to give them up, and though fighting a losing battle they hung on in the rural districts for many years—and in some places still do. When our youngsters gave a dance they scheduled nothing but round dances, though they usually ran in as "extras" a square set or two during the evening to keep the chaperons happy. Parties given by the older people went just the other way. They had all square and no round, with the possible exception of a waltz to begin and end the festivities. And among those old-timers there were almost as many different kinds of waltz as there were dancers on the floor; I remember watching the "speel" in which the dancers glided about as if on skates, and one old couple used to rise high on their toes on the count of three. Hopping on all three counts was also quite common.

In time all the talk about the dancing craze reached the pulpits and brought about a deal of ominous thundering and disapproval. I don't know that the opposition ever reached the proportions of a movement. But the evangelist who came to our church that winter painted perfervid pictures of the vice and debauchery that were the almost certain outgrowth of unladylike, immodest, and often indecent conduct of the daughters of the best American homes when allowed to frequent the ballroom floors. We children began to wonder if Mother wouldn't fall under his spell and put an end to our dancing as she had to our playing cards. All the children had been flocking to the revival meetings as the children of today would flock to the movies if they were free. We had attended several meetings before Mother went at all, and the first night she did the revivalist quite outdid himself in the fierce vulgarity of his attack on what he called "flirting with the Devil on the ballroom floor."

On the way home we asked Mother a little nervously what she thought of the evangelist.

"He's a powerful speaker," she said slowly, "and I hope he does some good here; but he has the same mistaken idea about dancing that so many people have who have never danced."

We breathed a little more easily, though we took the precaution of doing no more dancing until the revival meetings were over and the evangelist had left town. Our house was really ideal for dancing. We could easily dance a square set in our front parlor, one in the back parlor, two in the dining room, and one in the library. The music for all would come from the front hall, where we would have the piano and perhaps another instrument or two. Wide doors joined the two sides of the house both at the front hall and at the dining room, and for round dances there would be a counter-clockwise movement, making a wide circle of the four rooms. It was not often that we had enough dancers to fill all the rooms, but on occasion it has been done with great success. The night Father and Mother celebrated their twenty-fifth anniversary the house was so crowded that there was not room for another couple on the floor.

Father had had about twenty heavy sustaining posts put in the cellar, but with forty or fifty people dancing at once the house used to swing and sway like a ship at sea. Several times during the evening when a large number were being entertained I have seen Father walk down into the cellar to assure himself that his sustaining pillars were properly in place. Occasionally he would take one or two of his friends down "to look at the foundations," and they always came up wiping their mustaches and talking loudly of props and lally columns.

Many a time I have felt the house swaying gently as I dropped off to sleep while some heavy-footed Freshman was learning the military schottische or the two-step.

The house was lighted with oil lamps in those days, which ordinarily hung low over the table in the library and dining room. For dancing these lamps would be hung close to the ceiling, and there they would swing slowly back and forth as the dancers went surging and swooping underneath them. I think Father was always a little nervous about those lamps. He was afraid that with the vibration one would jar loose and go crashing to the floor, spreading the burning oil in all directions. The thought so possessed him that he finally had Mr. Beach come to reset the hooks if necessary. Mr. Beach carefully took down a lamp and threw a rope over the hook, by which he hung suspended and swung back and forth. But when he tried the same test on the other hook it broke off and dropped him in a heap on the floor.

Father always believed that by his foresight he had saved a serious accident and possibly prevented the house from burning down, and when Mother suggested that Mr. Beach was somewhat heavier than the Rochester lamp Father smiled and said it was just as well to be on the safe side.

As the dancing craze went on new steps kept multiplying until Louise could boast that she was proficient in twenty-two round dance steps. She once gave a party at our house where the same dance did not appear twice on the program, but there were only sixteen dances in all. I could do most of these myself, though I was not old enough to be allowed on the floor. But like every other fad that is overworked a reaction soon set in, and the move to simplify the round dance situation went so far

269

in the other direction that by the time I was in college we were dancing nothing but the waltz and two-step at any of the college proms.

So long as any of my sisters remained at home dancing was one of the important diversions of the household, though even at that time the social flavor of the town had begun to evaporate. The silk-hatted, broadcloth-coated, silver-headed-cane era was already gone. The word "aristocracy" had lost all sense of elegance and taken on many of the characteristics of an epithet. Family was not wholly unimportant, though it was becoming more so every day to the young democracy that was coming up strong in the belief that if they could shout down the social consciousness of a lot of old fogies over thirty they would be able to prove that all men were created free and equal.

24. The Discovery of S—x

TO ME, or to any boy brought up in the country, the mechanics of reproduction were commonplace. Things didn't just grow—they had to be planted. Some seeds went into the ground and some went into other places. But there must always be seeds. And if there was to be a mother there must always be a father. For our cat to have kittens was no more of a miracle to us than to have radishes grow in our garden. I was well aware of the preliminary steps in either event. In the case of our cow even the guesswork was taken out. Her affairs became vital statistics written down on a paper and tacked to the side of her stall. The name and residence of the father was there, his age and nationality, the date of the marriage, and even the probable birthday of the offspring. Father was a wizard at guessing a calf's birthday. He never missed by more than forty-eight hours.

All this seemed as natural as the rain that fell from the skies or the wind that rustled the leaves of the trees. Nothing lived forever, and if life was to go on there must be young to take the place of the old. I realized that this was as fundamentally true in our house as in our stable or our chicken runs—and still there was a great and mystifying difference between the two spheres of reproduction. Goings-on at the stable and the henhouse could be freely discussed, but there never could be even the slightest mention of the reproductive facilities or functions of human

271

beings. It was quite all right for Father to say to me at the breakfast table:

"I think you'd better begin to give the cow a little warm bran mash every day. She'll be having her calf in about two weeks and we want her to have plenty of milk when she comes in."

It was regarded as equally good taste to discuss the prospects of a setting hen. But nobody could warn us children of the impending arrival of a new brother or sister. If we were old enough to be good at guessing we might suspect something of the sort, though it must never, never be put into words. I was aware of this difference for a long time before I learned the word for it. The word, once I caught it, proved to be short and easy to remember. It was "Sex."

At the time I learned this word I had never seen it in print and thought it must be among the unprintables. If I had chanced to see it written in chalk on the sidewalk along with the four-letter words I would not have been surprised. The *Youth's Companion,* which was my periodical haven at the time, apparently had no occasion to go into such matters. And Mr. Alger and Mr. Castlemon, with whose works I was then more or less involved, were likewise sex-unconscious. My astonishment can be imagined when I came upon that word in a library book. Never before had it occurred to me to look it up in the dictionary. It was not as unprintable as I had supposed and I learned that officially Sex is "the sum of the peculiarities of structure and function that distinguish a male from a female organism." Not much enlightenment there, but a little further on it says, "a process evidently of great but not readily explainable importance in the perpetuation of most organisms." Small as the word is it must have great power when Noah Webster admits that even to him it is not readily explainable.

272

As I branched out in my reading I began to come across the word oftener and oftener, and slowly it dawned on me that while its use seemed to have become respectable in print it was still unspoken in polite society. I never heard anybody say, "What is the sex of that child?" The question was, "Boy or girl?" There was no "sex problem" as such. Men and women had their troubles, of course, but they were "marital troubles," and even the lawgivers, who delight in calling a spade by its first name, codified the statutes dealing with marriage and divorce under the prettified if ambiguous title of "Domestic Relations Law."

In spite of their evasion of the word sex our parents never lost sight of the fact that the young people of their day were, after all, only human and subject to the same desires and temptations that had been plaguing and delighting mankind since the dalliance of Adam and Eve there in the garden. I never could quite understand whether the theory was that every man was a probable seducer, or that no girl was able or willing to defend herself. The strict chaperonage of the period could have proved the case either way, though of course it was not put on any such ground. Propriety, pride, custom, the looks of the thing—any reason but the real one was given, though the indispensability of chaperonage was constantly impressed on a girl from the time she ceased teething. The only places to which our girls were allowed to go without a chaperon were to school and to church. They were permitted to run over to the near-by homes of other girls in the evening. If the distance was more than a block one of the boys would have to go along as an escort, for the streets were at this time unlighted and as dark as a pocket. I can remember being sent off on these escort jobs when I would much have preferred to go on with my own affairs, which might happen to be a game or perhaps a bit of carpentry. I would go grumbling and growling along until I got her

273

to the place where she was going, and then after staying to see that she got inside the door I would go racing home to resume my own business. But even so the job was only half over, for somebody would have to go and get her. There were no telephones, and such matters had to be arranged beforehand.

Mother was very careful not to relax her chaperonage requirements. It was her firm belief that any girl who went to a formal party unchaperoned deserved to be treated as an adventuress—and undoubtedly would be. My sisters had no ambitions in that direction and would never have dreamed of going to a formal affair without a chaperon, though I used to hear them telling Mother that the other girls in the neighborhood were allowed to do this or that by themselves. Mother tried not to be unreasonable with them, though she realized that exceptions were dangerous, since one was almost certain to lead to another. One year the girls did their best to get Mother to let them go with some of the other girls to meetings which a Gospel mission was holding in a vacant house on William Street, and which were at the time—and long afterward, indeed—the talk of the town. Mother knew all about the fact that there is safety in numbers, but she shook her head.

"I'm afraid you'll have to get some older person to go with you."

"But *six* of us girls are going together!"

"It's much better to have an older person along."

"But, Mother, you forget this is going to church. We don't need a chaperon for church."

"This isn't quite the same," Mother argued. "This is a—well, a very different kind of church. It isn't even in a sanctified building."

"But it's a Gospel mission. It moves around from one place to another."

"See if you can't get Alice's mother to go with you."

Mother knew very well that these Gospel meetings were a good deal of a circus. They were led by a band, and every night the lights were switched off for a period of repentance. The Gospel Fathers had learned from experience that people who would sit glum and silent under the lights would repent in the dark. Every night there had been some dramatic or perhaps comic confessions, and people were flocking to the place in droves. They packed the downstairs rooms to suffocation, and the overflow began taking seats on the stairs. Indeed, these seats on the stairs became the most popular place in the house for the young people to sit. They said it was because they were higher up and could get a better view of what was going on. This may have been true, but there were other advantages as well, for during the period of repentance when the lights were off adoring couples found it easy to slip away for a few kisses and caresses in the unsanctified darkness of the upper story, where some of the members of the mission maintained temporary living quarters.

Sometimes these little incursions into the upper chambers were so prolonged that the lovers failed to get back to their places on the stairs until after the lights had come back on, and to avoid becoming conspicuous they were obliged to wait in the dark until the meeting was over. Then in the confusion caused by the departure of the congregation they could mingle with the crowd and obviate discovery. But something went amiss, and one night just as the lights were turned out for the period of repentance a body of masked men armed with shotguns took over the meeting and placed guards at both front and rear stairs. They dismissed the congregation but detained the Gospel Fathers in a small room while the house was submitted to a careful search. People were found hiding under beds and in closets, and one hysterical lady was seen to leap from a second-story window. She was found in the yard below with a broken leg.

The Gospel Fathers concluded their engagement that same night and moved on to an unnamed destination, but for weeks the town argued about what had taken place. Some people said it was a holdup pure and simple. Others insisted that the Fathers had been driven away by thugs in the employ of one or more of the local churches, all of which were known to be hostile to the enterprise. Father was one of the few who knew the facts of the case, and I found jotted down in his little black book the names of all persons involved.

It was no holdup, nor were the men hired thugs. They were indignant fathers and husbands, for things really had been going on. One girl under eighteen had been so seriously "compromised" that the young man who had been escorting her regularly to the meetings took her before a justice of the peace and married her that same night while her irate father, gun in hand, witnessed proceedings from outside through a window. The lady with the broken leg had a hard time explaining to her husband, but she eventually convinced him that she thought it was a holdup and had run upstairs to get away from the masked men with the guns. All the other cases were classified as "Suspicion clearly justified by surrounding circumstances but unsupported by actual evidence. Husband will handle discipline at home."

The general public suspected the worst, but knew few of the particulars of the raid by the masked men. It is doubtful if Mother ever knew any of the real details of the affair, though she must have heard an endless amount of gossip. The girls had been unable to get Alice's mother to go with them, and so had missed the most sensational episode that had happened in town in a decade. They were crushed and disappointed and for several days never lost an opportunity of bemoaning the cruel fate that had kept them away. Mother, however, was quite complacent over her part in the proceedings.

"You ought to be thanking your lucky stars that you were not there," she said to them. "Think how you would have felt if those masked men had held up the place and you had been there without a chaperon."

"If Mother has her way," complained Louise, "we'll soon have a chaperon with us when we go to the well for a drink of water." She turned to Father. "Surely, Papa, you aren't in favor of having an old hen go clucking around after us every time we move."

Father who had been having a hard time to keep his face straight pulled himself together. "I don't blame you for not liking it, my dear, but until our streets are lighted it isn't safe for any girl to go out alone at night."

This was one of Father's theme songs. As soon as he had succeeded in getting a town water supply piped under the streets he had started a crusade for better street lighting. Up to this time the town had made no pretense of furnishing lights for its streets. Lighting his way when he went abroad at night was a man's own business. The town had no more reason to light a man's way than it had to polish his boots or button up his overcoat. At least that was what Father reported as the attitude of the authorities. Lampposts, it is true, were to be seen here and there, but they were privately maintained for the convenience of the person on whose property they happened to stand. The lamps in these beacons required a daily refilling with oil, and it was not unusual for people to neglect to fill them or forget to light them. And occasionally if they had been lighted the wind would blow them out, or a small boy with a snowball or a baseball would fail to miss the large glass top which made an almost irresistible mark.

Night life did not flourish to any great extent at that

277

time and place, and still there were bound to be occasions when people had to be out at night. Just going across the street on a dark night was an adventure to the girls. They rarely returned from visiting their friends on the other side that they did not come running in panting and squealing with a wild tale of having been chased by a drunken man. Father had been agitating the subject of street lighting for years without substantial success. Indeed, it was not until he had had an affray in the dark with an assailant from whom he had absorbed quite a little punishment that he made any progress at all. Then all he succeeded in getting from the town was a lamplighter to go around daily and fill and light certain of the street lamps belonging to private citizens, which happened to be located at such intervals that one could be seen from the next.

Father's encounter in the dark, though it left him with numerous bruises and contusions, was not without its humorous aspects. He was postmaster at the time and was coming home with the day's receipts about ten o'clock one Saturday night. The other places of business—with the exception of the saloons—were already closed for the night, and most of the inhabitants were either in their beds or in a washtub in front of the kitchen range, though a few may have been in the rubber bathtubs current at the time which hung suspended between two straightback chairs. The night was as black as the inside of an Ethiopian sarcophagus. Father was carrying his receipts and certain reports and notations appertaining to them in a metal strongbox, which he had taken no pains to conceal as he was passing the brightly lighted thirst parlors. But he did not think of this until he came to the part of his journey which was not lighted at all. All went well until he was passing the Harger place, a handsome brick structure standing some distance back from the street, when the

278

sound of stealthy footsteps came to his alert ears. They seemed to be approaching from the front, so he stepped over close to the picket fence, which he knew to be on his right, although it was of course invisible, thinking that he would give the approaching pedestrian plenty of room to pass. But the pedestrian did not pass. He was not in front. He was coming from behind, and when Father slowed up his pace to see what was going to happen, the maker of the footsteps came rapidly upon him from the rear, collided quite violently with Father and immediately embraced him with a bearlike hug which pinned Father's arms to his sides.

Father instinctively threw the strongbox over the fence into Harger's yard. This accomplished he challenged in a gruff voice:

"Who are you?"

There was no answer, nor was there any relaxation of the powerful grip in which Father was held. Father still cherished a faint hope that he might have been seized by mistake, and thought that he had better investigate that angle before actually starting hostilities.

"What do you want?" he demanded.

Still there was no answer.

Nothing so angered Father as the failure to answer him, and his temper began to rise. "Take your hands off me or I won't be responsible for what happens to you."

Far from removing his hands the assailant only tightened his hold. Then Father's temper blew up entirely. He was not a large man, but when aroused he was something of a "coalheaver." He was a fast thinker and usually knew what to do next before most of his opponents knew what they had done last. With a sudden wrench he seized the arms that were around him, gripping them so that they could not be taken away. Then he quickly bent forward, at the same time giving his posterior a violent jolt towards the rear. As he felt his opponent's legs give he put everything he had into a terrific heave which rolled his assailant up over his back like a bag of flour, catapulted him over his head and landed him prone on the ground with a very reassuring thud. In an instant Father was on top of him, and then the fighting began. For some time they rolled around on the ground pummeling each other and kicking and slugging until finally Father got his man belly down—with one arm behind him. Then he began to twist the arm in a way that all good "coalheavers" would readily understand.

At the first twist the fellow let out a piercing scream, and he continued to scream so long as Father applied the twisting tactics. Suddenly a light showed in the Harger house. A window opened and Charley Harger asked what was going on. When Father told him Charley scrambled into his pants and boots and came out equipped with a lantern, a heavy cudgel, and some stout cord.

"Who you got there, Sam?" asked Charley.

"Don't know yet," puffed Father. "Swing that lantern over here and let's have a look."

"Can you hang on to him?"

"You bet I can. He won't get up until I'm ready." Father put a little pressure on the arm and was rewarded with another scream.

Charley poked the captive with his cudgel. "Quit your damn' hollerin' or we'll give you something to holler about. Let him get his face up out of the dirt, Sam, so that I can see who it is."

Father removed his hand from the back of his assailant's head as Charley flashed the lantern in his face.

"Good Lord!" he chuckled. "Let him up, Sam—it's Dummy Dixon!"

The fellow though powerfully built was a harmless deaf mute. He had accidentally bumped into Father in the dark, and convinced that he was being attacked he had hung on to the best of his ability. The post-office funds had really been in no danger at all, and on the whole no particular harm had been done except to give Father a very rough workout. It did show the kind of affrays that might be expected on unlighted streets, however, and it had resulted in a lamplighter. As soon as the people had become accustomed to the lamplighter Father started a vigorous campaign to get more and better lamps for him to light, and eventually succeeded in having a good oil street lamp placed on every important corner along Main Street.

As soon as electric lights had become practical he tried to interest the people in a town lighting system, but found them singularly unresponsive. After a little he discovered that practically all of them were afraid to have the electric wires around the town. The strongest argument seemed to be that if the wires came down they'd kill people. There was also an unconfirmed rumor circulated that electric light was very injurious to the eyesight, and one strong obstructionist before the Village Board based his entire argument on the assertion that the lights would attract the bugs, and then would kill the birds that came to eat them.

When, shortly before the turn of the century, the electric light plant finally came it arrived not as a forward-looking public improvement but as a makeshift to keep a mill from being abandoned and a water power from falling into disuse. The town couldn't afford to lose an industry simply because the patent flours and cereals had made the local stone-grinding of grain no longer profitable.

The new lights so illumined the streets that not only could people recognize their friends passing at night on the other side, but they could actually read their papers by the light of the arc lamps as they sat on their porches of an evening. Women lost their terror of being grabbed by an unseen assailant as they walked along at night. Schoolgirls were allowed to go around unescorted, if that was what they wanted. Life seemed better and safer, and even the tension of chaperonage was considerably relaxed. My sisters, however, were not there to enjoy this new-found freedom. It had been so long in coming that they had married and moved away. Cecilia, the youngest, and the last to be led to the altar, was a bride of a year before the first flash of current was turned on, while the band played *Hail, Columbia, Happy Land.*

But progress when it comes is not likely to be confined to a single line of thought. Electricity was ramifying from the arc lamps and the chandeliers; it was heating the stoves and flatirons, it was bringing voices over the telephone, it was firing gas in the cylinders of the first sputtering automobiles—and soon it would be projecting pictures on the screen, hurling great sleeper planes through the skies, and overloading the interstellar spaces with megacycles, but the ferment of progress was rising all over the world. Science and invention were remaking the planet. Men were probing and reexamining the old truths and philosophies. Women were emerging from the cocoon shaped for them by a man's world, and were shouting for individual property rights and even the right to vote, as they elbowed their way into business and the professions. And eventually the great upsurge of progress got around to our little three-letter word—and turned it over like a pancake.

At this time it was romantic love that made the world go round. Under the refining influences of the Victorian age love had become so purified and rarefied that it bore little resemblance to life. It had become so rarefied, indeed, that love was now treated as an emanation of the soul not necessarily involved with any physical implications whatever. The mere fact that romance ordinarily led up to certain physical demonstrations was regarded as beside the point. In everyday life such things were not discussed, and in books matters usually went no further than the altar. Thus at the turn of the century romantic love was safely ensconced in the American home with writers of the Laura Jean Libby school of thought seated comfortably at the head of the table. But the first year of the century had not yet ended when the big eruption came, and *Vogue*, one of the leading women's magazines of the day, tossed Laura Jean Libby out of the window and came brazenly out with the statement that there was no use deluding ourselves any longer; so-called romantic love simply had no existence unless founded on sex.

Though *Vogue* was the first of the respectable magazines to take the plunge, splashes could be heard from coast to coast of periodicals and newspapers anxious to be in the swim. Father nodded his head in approval. The new idea was no novelty to him; he had known it all along. Mother was horrified. She wouldn't have a copy of "that awful magazine" in the house—she wouldn't even mention it by name. Perhaps it was just as well that she did not live to see her granddaughters grow up—she would have had to eat so many of her predictions of depravity and disaster, though I am sure that she would never have lost the impulse to leave the room whenever the word s—x was spoken.

25. Teaching Us Manners

MANNERS were painfully important at our house. Mother began her "please" and "thank you" training as soon as she caught an infant experimenting with sounds not connected with simple bawling. And the "yes, sir" and "no, sir" and the "yes, ma'am" and "no, ma'am" were drilled into us with the persistence of an army sergeant. While theoretically Mother may have held to the tenet that cleanliness comes next to godliness the question of good manners was always right in there putting up a fight for second place. Mother believed in good manners in the same tenacious way that she clung to her belief in the efficacy of prayer. If your faith was great enough you could get things from God, and if your manners were good enough you could get things from men. In spite of all the evidence around her to the contrary she clung with child-like faith and bulldog pertinacity to the conviction that without good manners you had very little chance of success in the world.

Having been brought up in the silk hat and long-tailed coat era, Father had charming manners. A little courtly for the modern age perhaps, but he would have been a great success in the days of the minuet. In court I was always astonished to have him hurl a verbal thunderbolt at opposing counsel or a lying witness, but it was as much part of the game as a savage smash at a tennis ball. He was never unnecessarily rude, and preferred to win by brains rather than lung power. He backed Mother in her efforts to teach us good manners, though he was always fearful that she might carry her efforts too far. All that he ever hoped for from us was that we would "act reasonably civilized."

Most of us fell into the "please" and "thank you" routine without much difficulty. Father had devised a little scheme for the use of "please" which really put teeth into it. If at the table one of the other children asked me to pass him anything, the bread or the butter, say, and neglected the "please"—I did not have to comply unless I happened to feel like it. There was nothing compulsory about such a request. If, however, he said the "please" I was supposed to stop what I was doing long enough to accommodate. There was, however, another string to this sort of request. In addition to the "please" the request must be addressed to a definite person.

"Please pass the bread," sung out by one who couldn't reach it was very likely to produce no results whatever. But "Stan, please pass the bread," required a courteous compliance if Stan was within reach of the bread.

Occasionally one of the children would take a dislike to a rule and would try to wear it down by persistent violation. Herb could say "ma'am" without a struggle, but he hated to say "sir." I have heard Father prompt him on the subject half a dozen times at a single meal.

"Shall I put gravy on your meat, Herb?" Father would ask as he was doing the carving.

"No." Herb wasn't gruff or surly. The reply was respectful in tone, but it simply did not come up to the rules.

Father would look at him. "No what?"

Usually Herb would quickly add the "sir" as if he had just remembered it, though there were occasions when he

285

carried the play a little farther and replied, "No gravy."

This was almost certain to be received with a sustained silence from the head of the table and a complete cessation of service until the proper response had come through. Once when he was feeling a little out of sorts Herb simply disregarded the silence. He was expecting another demand for the "sir" and when it did not come he began to hope that at last he was making some progress. Give him time and he would break down the silly rule. He kept his eyes turned away, but presently his ears told him that Father had resumed operations, and he was content. That is, he was content up to the point where he discovered that he was the only person at table who had not been served. Plates for the three younger boys had been shunted down the other side. Mother took up her fork, the signal for all hands to turn to, and with most elaborate disregard for Herb we began to eat, to make a clatter with our knives and forks, and to force animated conversation in which no attention was paid to Herb.

I sat right beside him where I could watch him, and for a moment I thought he was going to burst into tears. I am sure he was tempted—he hated to miss a good excuse to cry. Tears, however, would have brought on another complication—anyone who wept had to leave the table, and having left the table could not return during the meal. So Herb decided not to turn on the tears. Instead he looked appealingly at Father.

"Father," he said, "you haven't given me anything to eat, sir. And if you please, sir, I don't care for any gravy on my meat, sir."

At the first "sir" we all pricked up our ears. At the second we laid down our knives and forks, and when he came out with the third we rewarded him with a fine shout of laughter. It was one time when Herb did not come off second in the process of becoming civilized.

Especially among the younger boys there was a great deal of raillery continually going on. It was not so annoying to our elders away from the table, but during meals Father had little patience with the practice. If a boy was reprimanded for a slip in table manners—licking his knife, spreading his bread on his hand, using his finger for a pusher, in fact, any little social error—he was quite sure to hear from the other three boys. Little clucks, coughs, cheeping sounds—anything to make the miscreant uncomfortable. At one time the popular gibe was "pleep-pleep," and we pleep-pleeped at each other until the grown-up members of the family were driven nearly to distraction. Father was the first to break under the strain.

"Just a moment!" he said ominously one day at dinner when Stan and I were ribbing Herb over some slight rebuke he had received. "I don't ever want to hear that noise again at the table from any of you. The penalty will be to leave the table and not return."

We could see that he meant business, so there were no more pleep-pleeps at the table from that time on. However, we had found a new one by the following day, and at the first opening where a bit of raillery was called for we came out with "deet-deet!"

Father overlooked it for a little while to see if we would not tire of it by ourselves, and when we didn't he again put his foot down.

"Now let's have this understood," he said, "so there can be no claim of ignorance of the law. From now on there are to be no more words of derision during a meal. Is it understood?"

"But those weren't words," Stan complained. "They were only sounds."

"Very well," said Father, "we'll enlarge the rules to include all words or sounds of a derisive nature."

The next day we were back with another new one—the

rule did not forbid signs. We leveled one finger for a first offense, two for a second, and so on. Father did not catch on at first, though he must have known from the suppressed laughter at our end of the table that something was going on. It was not long, however, before he caught the drift, and then the prohibitory regulations were enlarged to include "all words, sounds, and signs, of every name, kind, and nature denoting or implying derision." This covered practically everything and spoiled one of the most entertaining as well as most objectionable of our mealtime sports.

To goad Father beyond his endurance was always a temptation, because when he lost his temper he put on such a good show. With his strong likes and dislikes he was a merciless prosecutor even when the object of his dislike was trivial. He regarded gum-chewing as slightly less reprehensible than wife-beating or assault with intent to kill. He simply could not abide the stuff, regarded the use of it in public as atrociously bad manners, and would not knowingly remain in the room with anyone who was chewing it. On one occasion, although his witnesses were in court, he had the trial of a case put over the term when he discovered the court stenographer chewing violently on a wad of gum. The thought of having to work for two or three days in full view of those champing jaws completely unnerved him. He was afraid he would become so irritated that he might lose his case. Gum-chewing at our house was indeed a hazardous occupation. We used to think Father could read our minds, for if I had gum in my mouth I could not even walk through the room where he was without being caught in the act. Of course we all tried it at one time or another, but I never knew of a case where a culprit escaped detection.

Mother was not at all touchy on the subject. Indeed, she would chew an occasional piece herself just to keep us company. Sometimes when we offered her a stick she would take it and drop it into her sewing basket for a rainy day. And rainy days at just that time were often quite eventful at our house. The tin roof was beginning to rust through but it was the wrong season to replace it, so we had to put up with the leaks and do our best to keep them from damaging the plaster and the furnishings. It was not at all unusual to have pans and tubs and pails spread around in the attic to catch the drip. One night, however, in a terrific downpour a hole opened up through which the water came so rapidly that the large receptacle which had been expected to handle the intake until morning overflowed its sides and started a babbling brook in the attic. This poured down through the floor with a pretty purling sound and soaked through the ceiling of the room where Father and Mother were asleep. To make matters worse it began to drip directly on their bed. It had soaked through the bedding and reached the sheets before it woke up Father. He was a little puzzled at first to know where the dampness had come from, and as he raised himself up on his elbow to investigate, a drop of water struck the top of his bald head. No more than that single drop was required to put him in a fighting mood. He leaped out of bed, hurried to the kitchen for a lantern, and went stalking into the attic in bare feet and nightgown.

Mother listened to the rattling of pails and pans up there as long as she could stand it, and then she put on her dressing gown and rubbers and went up. She found Father standing at the foot of the ladder which led to the hatch in the roof above.

"What are you doing?" she asked.

"I'm going up."

"But you can't. Listen to the wind—and the rain."

"Got to. There's a stream of water coming in as large

289

as a small river. Ruin everything in the house if I don't dam it."

"But you'll be soaked through!"

"Can't be any wetter than I am."

"Oh, Sam, you'll kill yourself going out on that roof—"

"Never have yet."

"But it's so slippery—and that awful wind!"

"I won't go near the edge. The leak's in the flat part. I'll have the lantern with me anyway. Got to find that hole before I can plug it. That's the trouble with a tin roof. Rusts through at the worst possible moment."

She knew that he couldn't be stopped, so she said no more and up he went. The wind howled and the rain beat in as he raised the scuttle. His nightgown filled like a balloon with the uprush of air. A less determined man might have changed his mind at this point. But Father never wavered. He gripped his lantern and stepped out into the gale—while Mother stood in the dark and prayed. She said later that she could not help thinking of a neighbor who climbed a tree on Sunday and fell to his death. She was glad this was not Sunday.

It wasn't very long before she saw Father's bare feet reaching for the top rung of the ladder. The nightgown was no longer blown up like a balloon. It was sticking to him with the adhesiveness of courtplaster. Soon he was standing before her dripping like a wet dog but glowing with an idea.

"I found the hole. So big I can stick the end of my finger right through it, but I think I know how to fix it. I read the other day of a man who stopped a leak with candle wax. Now if I can just light a candle and let the wax drip down into that hole—"

"How long do you think a candle would stay lighted in that gale?"

"No, I don't suppose it would do this time," Father ad-

290

mitted. "But it's a good thing to remember. How about a piece of cotton? If I could jam that down in the hole it would slow up the water."

"Sam—I have it! Wait here. I'll get something." Mother rushed downstairs and in a few moments came back tearing the wrappings from something she had in her hands.

Father peered at it. "What have you got there?"

"Chewing gum."

"That stuff! In this house? Throw it out."

"It's just the thing to stop the leak!"

"Chewing gum never did anything useful. It's worthless."

"You know how it sticks."

"Never knew it to stick to anything but the underside of the table."

"It's waterproof, too. Put this in your mouth and chew it."

"Me—!"

"Yes, and here's another stick. You'll need a good-sized lump."

He stood holding the two sticks of gum in his hand. "Why, Mother, you don't realize what you're asking me to do."

She turned her head. "Just listen to the water coming in that leak."

For a moment they stood listening to the steady stream pouring into the tub. Then Father clapped the gum into his mouth and began to masticate noisily as he took his lantern and clambered back up to the roof, leaving Mother again in darkness. After a little she noticed that the stream of water had slowed down to a trickle—and finally to a drip.

Then Father's face appeared in the hatchway. "Is it any better?"

"It's all over," Mother called back. "Now come right down before you catch your death of cold."

He closed and hooked the hatch and came shivering down. "That's great stuff," he said. "Sticks like pitch. It is a kind of pitch—comes from a tree. But, Mother," he gave her an insinuating look, "how did *you* happen to have chewing gum?"

"Why, it's some—well, I took it from the children."

"Um-m-m—so that's it. I wondered."

Mother hurried him downstairs to get off the saturated nightgown and put on some warm clothes while she ran to the kitchen to heat water for a hot drink. We children howled with glee the next morning at the breakfast table when Mother told us how Father had hung the lantern on his arm like a freight-train brakeman and disappeared into the night champing on two sticks of gum, his nightgown inflated like a balloon.

"I'm afraid I've never been quite fair to gum," Father admitted. "It hasn't the disagreeable taste that I expected, and I certainly recommend it to anybody who wants to mend a tin roof in a gale, but I still think it the acme of bad manners to chew gum in the presence of another person."

Other boys I knew did not seem to be greatly bothered over manners, and for several years I had the idea that all this drilling over good manners was just a family idiosyncrasy. The idea of rising when an older person entered the room was particularly distasteful to me, especially if I happened to be occupying the most comfortable chair and had been put to some pains to get it away from one of my brothers. But most distasteful of all was the requirement of raising one's hat to a lady. This was a thing Mother was insistent about when we happened to be with her, and she would warn us far in advance so that there would be no mistake about it. "Here comes Mrs. So-and-so. Now, boys, be sure to raise your hats before she gets by." Mother even made us raise our hats to girls of our own age, which was most embarrassing. When she was not along, however, it was quite a different matter. If my hat came off in passing a lady, young or old, it was because some fresh boy had knocked it off. I did not get the idea that raising the hat was a mark of respect until I learned it from a man whose name I never knew, the day of Jerry Billings's funeral.

Jerry's death had come as a sudden blow to our family. We knew Jerry had been ailing, but nobody had thought that he was seriously ill. Father was very much broken up over the news when he came home to supper.

"Some of the neighbors are already there," he said to Mother, "but we must go to Jerry's house at once and see if there is anything we can do."

"Supper is all ready to put on," said Mother. "We'll go right over just the minute we're through."

Father, too upset to eat, served the rest of us and then sat looking at his empty plate.

"Well, Jerry is gone, and I've lost a friend," he said finally. "A friend that I was proud of. I don't know who Jerry was or where he came from, but I do know that he was made of good stuff. It took good stuff to spend nearly ten years in jail for a crime he did not commit, and then come back and live on friendly terms with the very people who sent him there."

"Don't you suppose he ever felt any resentment towards the people who put him in jail?" asked Mother, her conscience now troubling her because she had never been able to like Jerry.

"He did at first, of course," replied Father. "His letters were bitter. But ten years is a long time to harbor ill-will."

"But I should think that every year would have added to his resentment."

"It probably would if he had not reasoned it out for himself that it was no individual, but the people of the state, the government, which were to blame."

"He was always so sullen before he went to prison," said Mother.

"But not after he got out," Father reminded her. "He was genial and as agreeable as any merchant in town.

294

Have you ever heard one word in criticism of his conduct since he came back?"

Mother shook her head. "No, I don't think I have."

"I offered to help him get started in some other town," said Father, "but he wouldn't have it that way. He wanted to come back here and shame the people who had wronged him; he wanted to show them that even with his record as a convict he could be as good a citizen as any of them. And he succeeded. I don't believe there is a person in this town who would hesitate to say that Jerry had completely reestablished and rehabilitated himself in the eyes of everybody."

"That's true," said Mother. "There's no doubt about it—but I keep wondering if people will go to his funeral."

Father looked puzzled. "But why wouldn't they?"

Mother shook her head. "I don't know, but people are funny about funerals."

As it turned out they needn't have worried about it. Everybody wanted to help, and when it came to the funeral nearly the whole town was there. I wasn't allowed to go, but in walking past the house I could see that it was packed, and even the dooryard was full of people who stood there all through the service. The streets were lined as the funeral procession passed through town and wound its way down the hill, across the stone bridge, and on up to the cemetery. I had never before seen people walking in the street behind a hearse, and I was so absorbed by the sight that I did not notice that the onlookers were uncovering their heads until a man behind me touched my shoulder.

"Take off your hat," he said in a low tone, "and show your respect for a real man. Ain't you got no manners?"

I snatched off my hat in a hurry, feeling very much ashamed to think that somehow I had failed my old

295

friend Jerry. But from that moment manners had an entirely different meaning to me, for I began to realize that they were not just a form of household oppression and irritation, but that they had a substantial standing in the community.

26. The Family Grow Older

WHILE both Father and Mother believed in a college education for their boys they based their views on slightly different grounds. Mother thought that college training, in addition to teaching them things, would help them along later on in a social and business way. Father, on the other hand, thought that a liberal education would widen their horizon and bring them greater opportunity for happiness from life. "Give me time," he used to say to us, "and I'll give you all the education you can absorb—but you'll have to take your turn."

Mother could not bring herself to approve of college for the girls. She felt that colleges gave too little supervision and not enough discipline for girls of tender age, and their educational facilities seemed far in excess of any real need. The belief was general at the time that girls had very little use for more than a fundamental education. What was really desirable was training in the household arts, music, and perhaps in poise and social adequacy. Of course if a girl wanted to be trained for a teacher the more advanced study was necessary.

Then as now education cost money, and with the burden Father and Mother were already carrying the vision of the long pull ahead must have broken their spirit had they not both been slowly anaesthetized by the Micawber philosophy that something would always turn up. We know now, as all except the Micawbers knew then, that while this philosophy is a sure cure for the worrying habit, it has about as much of a basis in fact as a belief in fairies. The only other advantage that it possessed in the case of our family was that it had never failed to work.

So long as we could attend the local school no serious educational complications arose. One child crowding another from behind made very little difference. With the three girls so near the same age they were continually stepping on each other's scholastic heels. Two in the same room at a time was not uncommon, and there was a day when three in the same room seemed quite possible. The numbered grades had not yet been introduced at our school, the pupils in each room being divided into an A Class and a B Class. The trouble came when the children had finished at the town school and were ready to go into the upper educational reaches, the cost of which had to be carefully counted. Thad was only halfway through his college course when Louise finished at the public school and was ready to go on to something else. She was a brilliant student, and to hold her back for two years while Thad was finishing his upperclass work would have been a real hardship. It seemed inevitable, however, since there simply was not money enough for them both, and the household rules decreed that Louise, being younger, must await her turn. It looked like a real impasse until the Micawber theory went into its beneficent operation.

The "something" turned up when Thad went west for a vacation at the end of his sophomore year. What turned up was that while there Thad fell in love with a Western girl and lost all interest in his college education. A few lines of Latin on a bit of sheepskin no longer attracted him. Day and night the sound of wedding bells rang in his ears. When fall came he did not return to college, but seized upon an opportunity to go into business in the West—and Louise went off to her finishing school.

A similar collision was looming when Elsie was graduated from the public school, and again the financial principles of Mr. Micawber saved the day with a joyous jingling of wedding bells—this time Louise's—leaving the way clear to Elsie. And thus it went straight down through the family. It was not always wedding bells, though something always did turn up. As each one left the nest the home burden became lighter, and by the time that the academic procession had narrowed down to the last three boys the matter of waiting for one's turn had become unimportant, or at least it was no longer critical. Stan was in preparatory school while I was in college, and by the time he had reached college I had gone on to law school. Father had paid out enough for our education to set each one of us up in business. But he never begrudged a penny of it—not even when our reports were poor and our marks low. He had a strange notion that no more than half the value derived from a college education came from the classroom.

Thad's sudden decision to make his home in the West was a great disappointment to Father. Though he had never mentioned the subject to Thad, Father had always expected that eventually Thad would become his partner. Ever since Thad was a little fellow Father had been watching for qualities that would show an aptitude for the law. He looked with approbation at evidences of the boy's courage as well as his magnificent gall. Both would be useful in a lawyer. As Thad grew older Father noted his straight thinking and logical approach to any problem he attacked. And always Thad was articulate. If you did not know where he stood on any subject that chanced to come up it was just because you did not happen to be listening. It was a bitter pill to Father to see Thad throwing away

299

such fine legal ingredients for a life in the marts of trade. But he tried to accept it philosophically, and began to look for legal possibilities in Herb.

Herb had an analytical turn of mind that at times was a nuisance; nobody wants every single statement to be taken apart and the pieces spread out on the floor. And from the day he was born Herb was argumentative. I can easily imagine him giving the nurse and doctor an argument over his weight as they took him off the receiving scales. Father considered Herb's temper calmly and shook his head over it. He knew from his own experience how much of a nuisance a quick temper could be, especially in litigated work. If Herb was to go into the law there would be plenty of work to do on that temper of his. But Herb had no desire whatever to go into the law. He detested the very thought of public speaking, and any proposal to adopt it as a means of making a living would have received a very cool reception from him. But happily for Herb he received an offer of a job from a business friend of Thad's and departed to make his fame and fortune in the West before Father had even approached him on the subject of the law.

It was not until some time after Herb had gone that I discovered Father was measuring me with his eye as a possible candidate for his mantle. He was following the familiar pattern and looking us over according to age. Soon after I made this discovery the family lobby began to operate. There was talk about all the years Father had spent building up his practice. Too bad that Stan wasn't more studious and hadn't more of the temperament of a lawyer; it would be a fine chance for him. Of course Leslie was too young to tell what his leanings might be later on; but after all Father was not getting any younger. I had other ideas for myself, but they were gradually cut from under me, and soon I found myself faced by a family understanding that of course I was going to study law and become Father's partner.

Mother beamed with satisfaction when I began to make my plans to go to law school; for she knew that if I studied law I would go in with Father—and if I went in with Father I would not be moving off to the city to live. Up to this time her plans for family solidarity had not been working out very well. Of the five children who had preceded me only one had settled in the old home town—and it was in the cards that she was not to remain there. Thad had slipped through her fingers with a running start. It was a great blow to her when he wrote that he had lost his heart in the land of the setting sun and would not be coming back. For weeks afterward a look of sadness would come over her face every time his name was mentioned. Father was more successful in covering up his disappointment and was continually trying to put a cheerful face on the situation.

He reminded her that in leaving home and family and striking out for himself in a new place Thad was doing just what they themselves had done. And in time he succeeded in convincing her that Thad's opportunities for success would be greatly enhanced by his settling in a new and growing country. It was, after all, Thad's happiness that she had in mind, though she had to keep reminding herself of that fact for a long time before she became reconciled to the idea that he had gone away from home to stay. However, she had learned her lesson; if she wanted to keep her brood together she must shape future events so that the drift would be in the direction she desired. She must leave nothing to chance. Thad's sudden maturity, his taking matters into his own hands, had caught her off guard, but she promised herself this should not happen another time—and suddenly it came to her that another time might be even then in the making.

Louise was growing up and was developing immense popularity. Admiring youths and sad-eyed swains had flocked about Louise since she was a child in pinafores, and it was only a question of time—perhaps a very short time—when young men would be coming with proposals of marriage.

Mother would have scorned the idea of being a matchmaker. In her mind that role was associated with the mothers of "commonplace" daughters unable to attract admirers by themselves or, having attracted them, incapable of bringing them to the fusing point. Mother felt that matchmaking was beneath her, far beneath her. She was fully and unalterably determined that each of her daughters should make her own choice of a husband. In only one particular would Mother even hint at using her influence, and that was in the matter of domicile. She did want her girls to marry home town boys—and she could see no reason why she could not bring a certain amount of inconspicuous influence to bear in case a youth from a distance seemed to be getting the upper hand.

There was nothing that Mother abhorred like scheming. She regarded it as deceitful and wicked. There should be no scheming or plotting to advance the interests of this young man or that; but she could see no wrong in giving preferential treatment to an entire group so long as she attempted to make no choice of an individual within the group. She had just succeeded in convincing herself on this point when Louise returned home from her school blushingly conscious of an engagement ring she had accepted from an admirer whose sole disqualification was that he lived at the other end of the state. Parental objection could not withstand the entreaties of young love—and so they were married, and the home town boys had no choice but to dance at the wedding and throw rice and old shoes to bring the newlyweds good luck.

Elsie was not so precipitate as Louise, though she was equally sure of her own mind. She felt that she was capable of handling her own love affairs, and she neither invited nor received any parental cooperation that she was aware of. It may have been the doings of the laws of probability and chance, and it may have been something else, but Elsie married a local boy, settled down only a block from the old home, and started a family of her own.

Then Mother went to work on Cecilia, and Cecilia at the same time went to work on Mother. It must have been an amusing contest, though I was not old enough to take in the finer points. Basically it was a repetition of the battle of the bustles and the skirmish of the skirts. Cecilia had her heart set upon an outlander, and it was an outlander that she eventually married—that is, as soon as *she* was ready.

With Cecilia gone the Dunham stood silent and deserted in the back parlor. For weeks at a time it would be opened only to be dusted, since nobody in the house could play. With only boys left at home the character of the place changed rapidly. Baseball bats and shinny sticks stood in the corner where parasols had been. Dogs overran the place. Bicycles were parked on the porch. Balls and gloves—the mitt had not yet been introduced—were everywhere underfoot.

Herb developed a penchant for guns. He came around first with a small muzzle-loading pistol with a brass barrel. He never fired a shot from it, though he carried it around in his hip pocket and reached for it at critical moments as if he had forgotten that it was not loaded. He traded this, with some other valuables, for a four-barreled derringer. This was a much more formidable weapon than the first, but for some reason he also distrusted the derringer. He used to snap a cap in it occasionally, but he never charged it with powder and ball. Herb's next weapon was a navy pistol of 1812. This had a bore the size of a nickel, and an attached ramrod with which to hammer home the charge. It was a practical weapon, though it must have had a kick like Big Bertha. Herb never found out, for he was afraid to fire it, and after a little he swapped it off for a bone-handled revolver of comparatively modern vintage. Here was a gun that he could shoot, and did, though the first bullet struck an apple tree, deflected, and buried itself in my thigh. We picked it out by ourselves, but Herb was chary about revolvers after the experience and swapped it, with a pair of rabbits to boot, for an old Civil War musket. What a gun! It would shoot a slug completely through an oak tree a foot in diameter and would undoubtedly have dropped an elephant in its tracks. Big game, especially elephants, was scarce in the neighborhood, so Herb traded the musket for a twelve-gauge shotgun. He left this behind when he went west to make his way in the world—and I don't believe it was ever fired again.

Stan went in for livestock. He started with a dog that cost a quarter and kept trading until he had a serviceable though not very handsome mare which used to draw us all over the township and occasionally to an adjoining town for a band concert on Saturday night. He was probably the only horse trader in town who ever beat the gypsies on a deal. The boss gypsy must have thought that there couldn't be a worse horse than the one he was offering. But there was, and Stan had it. The gypsy horse was blind in one eye, but it could navigate. Stan was the only one who could keep his horse on its feet for more than one hundred yards, and when the gypsies were ready to move on they had to leave it behind.

I went in for bicycles, starting with the old high-wheel "ordinary." I bought, repaired, and bartered several of them. A fancy rider who came to town taught me many of his tricks, and several we learned to do double. He wanted me to go on the stage with him. I was perfectly willing, but for some reason the family did not want me to go. I guess it was just as well they were firm about it, for the professional found a lady partner, which was what he wanted all the time; and he went off in her company without even saying good-by to me. In spite of this disappointment I never lost my love for the bicycle, though I always preferred the high-wheel to the safety. At about the time when my professional career as a trick rider came to an end I found a new interest—making a collection of birds' eggs.

We were as a family not much given to making collections. Soon after Herb got his shotgun he began a collection of stuffed and mounted birds. He could not have finished with more than three or four of them before Mother discovered that his specimens were being eaten by moths. She expected Herb to make a scene when she told him that he would have to move his museum to the barn; but Herb did not mind at all. He had tried taxidermy and found it not quite suited to his taste. For almost a year Leslie gathered and pasted in a book what he thought was to be the world's greatest collection of stamps. It might in time have rivaled that of President Roosevelt or even the famous collection of King George V if Leslie had not swapped it for a billy goat.

I was determined that my collection of birds' eggs was really going to amount to something, so I began to read books on the subject. From these I learned that it was best to start a really serious collection with the eggs that were most difficult to get. The easy ones, it said, could be picked up at any time. So after mature deliberation I decided to begin with the eggs of Corvus *brachyrhynchos*

Brehm, known to the nonprofessional and particularly to the farmer as the "crow."

My first move was to choose a piece of woods about a mile from home, which I knew was frequented by crows. For days I skulked around the place trying to catch a crow in the act of building a nest. But crows are wise birds; they never came around so long as I was anywhere near. Then one day I stood off at a distance, and instead of looking for crows I looked for nests—and almost immediately found one. It was firmly constructed in one of the highest crotches of a giant ash tree some seventy-five feet from the ground. The tree looked rather formidable, but I knew a boy who had a pair of homemade climbers and asked him if I could borrow them. He said they weren't very good or very strong, but I took them just the same. I got Stan to go along with me so that he could make noises and scare away the birds if they should attack me. This proved to be an unnecessary precaution, as the birds flew away the moment I started up the trunk and did not return so long as we were anywhere around.

It was a tough climb. The trunk of the tree was large around and the lowest limb was some forty feet from the ground. The climbers were dull, and as I went up they became duller. Occasionally one of the spurs would lose its grip and give me a bad scare, but after a long hard struggle I got myself a limb, where I sat down for a good rest. The remainder of the climb was easier. It took time, but I eventually reached the nest, the size of which astonished me. It must have been fifteen inches across and was lined with what looked like the soft inside bark of a dead tree. In it were four greenish buff eggs irregularly blotched and spotted with brown.

The custom in handling large eggs is to put them in a box and lower them to the ground with a string, but I did not know about that and so had neither box nor string.

I had intended to carry the egg down in my mouth, not realizing that a crow's egg could be so large. After a single glance at them I realized that the big question was whether I could or could not get one in my mouth. I looked them over and selected the one that seemed to be the smallest. When I picked it up I was surprised to find that it was still warm. I opened my jaws wide and softly pressed the egg against my mouth. It slipped inside without breaking—and at just that moment Stan began to shout up to me.

"Any eggs in it?"

I slowly nodded my head.

"How many?"

No answer.

"What color are they?"

I waved impatiently for him to be still, and started to clamber down. I found it almost as hard to go down as to go up, and much more dangerous, for I could not see what my feet were coming to and had to go by feeling.

As I made my way precariously down, the steady stream of queries came floating up from below. Then suddenly the climbers slipped and I slid some distance before they caught again and I was able to stop myself. Stan halted his questions just long enough to caution me to be careful. "What's the hurry?" he shouted. "Take it easy or you'll break your neck."

I had just stopped myself after one of these paralyzing slides and was clutching the bark about ten feet above the ground when I heard him say:

"What do you think you are, a squirrel? Lemme tell you nobody can come down a tree as fast as that, and if you don't take your time you're gonna get hurt!"

As I clung there catching my breath and wondering what to do next Stan called up with enthusiasm:

307

"This is darn good fun. I think I'll start a collection myself. How many of the eggs did you take?"

"One—" I started to say impatiently, when suddenly I felt something give way in my mouth. At the same moment my climbers lost their grip and I went slithering down, clutching for my life, all the way to the ground on which I landed with a terrific impact. Judging by after-results I should say that if I had not removed it from the nest that egg would have hatched out a little black crow within the next day or two. Stan never could understand why I blamed him for the breaking of that egg. But from that day he lost all interest in birds' eggs. He never began his collection, and I never went any further with mine. We just were not the collector type, I guess. In any event I went away to school soon after that and never again had the opportunity for another start.

27. A Belated Career

ALL her life Mother had had a suppressed desire to be an artist. At school she had taken a few painting lessons and had been told, of course, that she had "real talent." It was at this point that love had come in at the door and art had gone out of the window. But though art may go out of the window readily enough it seldom stays out, or if it does, it keeps peering sadly through the pane for years and years and years. Mother never knew quite what form her talent would have taken. She never could look at a piece of sculpture without imagining that her hands had molded the surfaces and graven the forms. If she looked upon a pastoral of cows lying on the greensward or standing in lush grasses she could always see herself just outside the frame sitting before an easel on a little canvas stool, her thumb protruding through a hole in her palette, and long-handled brushes bristling in her hands. Had she lived at a later day she might have satisfied her artistic craving with pyrography on leather, engraving linoleum blocks, or modeling in soap. These art forms not having come into popularity at the time when she was ready to resume her long-somnolent artistic career, she found herself in a position where she had no choice. Instruction was available in only one of the innumerable branches of the graphic arts. She could take it or she could leave it.

As one by one the children grew up and went away

Father and Mother began to feel a little lost in the big house. Father was still busy with his practice, perhaps doubly so, since he was trying to teach me how to handle some of it, but for the first time in many years Mother, with no diapers to change, no pants to patch, no clothes to make over, found leisure on her hands—and remembered her thwarted ambition. The town was without a drawing teacher, a painting teacher, an etcher, or a sculptor. But there was a woman who painted china, and Mother went to her and suggested the formation of a class.

Not long afterward peculiarly colored ashtrays began to appear in the house. Father encountered one on the library table and automatically knocked cigar ashes into it before he noticed the strangely painted symbols on the side. The decoration had a nonprofessional look about it and the design, he noticed, was slightly lopsided. He surreptitiously emptied the ashes into the waste basket, and having wiped the tray with his handkerchief replaced it on the table.

"What's this?" he asked as Mother came into the room. "A new ashtray?"

"Yes. How do you like it?"

"I like any ashtray—if it's big enough."

"But the design—rather nice, don't you think?"

Father was now playing safe. "Quite unusual."

"Colors are a little muddy though."

"Muddy? Hardly that, my dear. Subdued, let us say, but certainly not muddy."

"Then you like it?"

Father had turned it over and was looking at the bottom. "It better be good," he said. "It's Limoges."

"Notice anything else on the bottom?"

He looked again. "F. A. P. You mean to say you did this?"

She nodded. "What do you think of my belated talent?"

Father laughed softly. "I think you show great promise —for a beginner," he said.

A few days later he noticed that his old bronze pen tray was gone from his desk, and in its place was a long shallow china dish with crossed pansies hand-painted on each end. Not long afterward he found the covered brass jar in which he had kept his cigars was missing from the table and its place taken by an open-top bowl obviously intended for a flowerpot, though now decorated with a sprig of what he took to be appleblossoms. He did not move the cigars which were in it, since they had already dried out, but in the future the cigars he smoked were taken from a box in a drawer of his desk.

For years Father had been keeping his library matches in a little glass boot on the table, but one night when he reached for a match he found the glass boot gone and a pale green cup decorated with blackberries in its place. For a creature of habit like Father no evening cigar lighted with a match from anything but that little glass boot would taste quite right. I saw him eying the green cup with disdain every time he took a match from it; but he made no complaint. At about this time Mother had turned her hand to a set of bread and butter plates, and for the next few weeks Father's old routine was not further disturbed. Mother found the "detail work" of a set of plates tiresome, however, and when she had at long last finished six of them she again turned her hand to single pieces.

One day when I dropped in she showed me a hair receiver and a brush and comb tray that had just come from the firing oven.

"She's doing a matching set," Father volunteered, "to harmonize with the color scheme in each of the bedrooms."

"Not a bad idea," I said.

"It was your father who thought of it."

I turned toward him with a smile. "Are you taking up interior decorating?"

"Well, no, not just that; but it seemed like a good idea."

From his standpoint it must have seemed like a perfect idea. Even in his own room he could not have been greatly bothered by the arrival of a new hair receiver and matching brush and comb tray since his hair was all gone but a little fringe of gray around the back of his head. With so much practice Mother was developing facility, and the bedroom project was finished within a very short time. When I asked Father one day what she was going to do next he shook his head and said, "Heaven only knows." A day or two later he told me with obvious relief that she had started in on vases, urns, and ewers. These were the first really sizable pieces she had attempted, and she was very much excited over them. Every time I went to the house she showed me new pieces that had just come from the oven. They were of every conceivable size and shape, and she had them perched on every mantel, table, and bookcase in the house.

Up to this time Mother had been a little doubtful about her ability to cope with large pieces, but after her success with one or two capacious urns a wave of self-confidence swept over her and emboldened her to undertake a project which had long been tempting her—the decoration of a large platter with matching vegetable dishes. She wanted something that would do for Sunday dinner and for the special occasions when the grandchildren gathered around and the dining-room table was again extended until it sagged slightly in the middle and had to be steadied while Father was carving. And she especially wanted something to show off at the reunions when all the children came home. Of course by this time each of us had received as a Christmas present some example of her belated talent, but evidently not enough to satisfy her.

Father could find no fault with the large square platter we already had. It was roomy and deep and trustworthy; he knew what he could and could not do with it. The fact that it did not match the rest of the set had never been considered of material importance during the three or four decades that he had been using it. It was not customary for him to let an old and satisfactory household article be taken from him without a struggle, and I was all prepared to hear a vigorous protest. A real explosion would not have surprised me; I had seen some violent ones with much less provocation. But he took the new platter without a peep, shallow though it was, and oval, and inconvenient. He spilled a little more than usual on the tablecloth the first time he used it, but not enough to bring any pained exclamations from Mother's end of the table. Indeed, he seemed to have himself so well in hand that it came to me the years were actually toning him down and taking some of the dynamite out of his spirit.

I was even more aware of this when Mother went on to the next stage of her artistic career, which turned out to be an almost mural type of decoration on large-sized jars and jardinieres. He made no complaint when a huge crockery container the size of a beer keg was placed on the floor in front of the library window so near his line of march that he stumbled over it almost every time that he went to or from his desk chair. This stumbling habit was nothing new. Ever since I could remember he had stumbled over things whenever he was concentrating on his work. I can't remember that he ever fell, but if he walked past a chair while he was trying to think something out

313

he was almost certain to get his feet mixed up with it. It is just barely possible that he did not realize that the jar was new and supposed that it was one of his regular stumbling places. But this could not possibly have been so with the hand-painted tile that Mother presented to him in place of an iron umbrella stand in which he had kept his walking stick and his umbrella as far back as I could remember.

He looked a little dazed when she pointed the new one out to him. "What did you do with the other one?" he asked.

"It's up in the attic."

"You don't expect me to keep my cane and umbrella up there, do you?"

"Hardly," said Mother with a smile. "I expect you to keep them in the new tile. That's what it's for."

I was a little worried about it when he put his walking stick in the tile and went into the library without another word. Indeed, I was so uneasy about it that I brought the matter up the next time I saw Stan, who by this time was married and living in Rochester.

Stan laughed over the whole affair. "He's just stringing her along," he said. "One of these days she'll carry things too far, and when she does he'll blow up all over the place."

Not long after this, in reaching for a match, Father managed to knock the hand-painted match-holder from the table and broke it into a thousand pieces. Irritated and angered by his awkwardness he let his vocabulary get out of hand and before he could stop himself he had ripped out some very potent if profane language. Mother's sharp protests left him shamefaced and regretful. The accident, she said, was regrettable, but his language absolutely inexcusable.

314

She picked up the matches, and having no better container for them, brought out the little glass boot. It was the expression on Father's face when he saw it that gave him away, and I would at that moment have been willing to wager that there would be further breakages. It was accordingly no surprise to me to hear that on the following day he accidentally broke the cigar container on the library table, and got back his old brass jar. Not long afterward he dropped a paper weight on the hand-painted pen tray on his desk—and reclaimed his old bronze tray once more. In between these self-serving crashes he managed to knock over a vase or two, which may or may not have been in the nature of a red herring. I never happened to be around when he disposed of a vase. But I was there the day he finished off the umbrella tile and stalked out of the house swearing not wholly under his breath.

Mother had stuffed her fingers into her ears to keep from hearing him.

"It almost prostrates me to hear him say such things— and the awful part of it is that it's all my fault."

"Your fault that he's clumsy?"

"But he isn't clumsy. I don't know what's come over him. Until a few days ago he never broke a piece of china in his life—and I feel so guilty about it!"

"*You* feel guilty?"

"I'm really to blame for every word of his profanity— it's just as bad as if I said the words myself—and it's terribly on my conscience."

"Oh, that conscience of yours," I said. "How can you be guilty of his cussing?"

"Because I'm the real cause. If it weren't for me he'd never be saying those awful things. The only time he swears is when he breaks a piece of my china."

I had a hard time keeping my face straight, Father's plan was working so perfectly, but I managed to suggest that she could put the china where he wouldn't bump into it.

She shook her head. "It couldn't be done. In his present state of nerves he'd go out of his way to bump into it."

"There's always the cupboard," I said. "He can't bump into it if it's locked up."

"You don't think he'd feel hurt if—if I should put it away?"

"He might not even notice it if you do it gradually enough."

The next time I was at the house I saw that the hand-painted china had begun to disappear. Within a week or two not a piece was to be seen. One day I asked Father casually what had become of it.

He smiled. "Oh, I guess Mother must have become tired of seeing it around," he said.

"She doesn't seem to be painting any more."

He shook his head. "Seems to have satisfied her artistic urge. In the Indian summer of life artistic urges are somehow more easily satisfied."

Mother never painted another dish. It was the end of her career as an artist. Fully a year later when I was at the house one day I found her cleaning out the china cupboard. The hand-painted ware, she said, was taking up too much room and she was moving it to the attic.

She held up an ornate rose bowl and eyed it critically. "Quaint, isn't it?" she said. "It hardly seems possible that I could have painted that." She laid it on a stack of plates and turned to get down another of the large pieces.

"I'll carry up an armful for you," I said, "if you'll tell me where to put it."

"Oh, just set it down by the chimney," she said, "any-

316

where where people won't tumble over it and hurt themselves."

Themselves—not the china! As Father had said, her artistic urge had been satisfied, and it was now being laid on the attic floor along with the piles of dishes. There was no doubt about it.

28. Among the Pines and Hemlocks

A S MOTHER saw her brood growing up and scattering to the four winds she must have realized the utter impossibility of holding them together in actual propinquity, for the time came when she ceased to make any attempt to keep them in town, and centered all her efforts on the development of the strongest possible emotional attachment among them. Family loyalty had been instilled in us from the cradle. "Remember he's your brother!" It was like reminding a man of his oath of office or his pledge of allegiance to the flag. A boy might criticize and correct his own brother, he might even chastise if necessary—but nobody else could lift a finger against him. So long as we were all together family affection and family loyalty were assured. It was the problem of keeping these feelings alive and eager through the months and years of separation that was now facing her. The system she had built up for home use had to be geared to operate at long distance, and she could think of nothing that would so animate the interest as an intimate knowledge of what was going on.

When children were away at school and college she had insisted on a letter every week, each of which she answered with promptness and enthusiasm. Family news, family activities, family interests, had been so thoroughly covered that an absentee knew almost as much about family affairs as when he was at home. By the time a child had finished his schooling and was ready to go out into the world on his own responsibility, the habit of weekly letter-writing had been so firmly established that there was little difficulty in carrying it on. Mother was very exacting about it—no absent member of the family could skip a week without hearing from it. There was never any compromise with this system, and with Mother acting as a clearing house there was little family news that did not get around. If one of Thad's children had croup in Minneapolis, Louise, in Westchester County, knew all about it within a few days and was perhaps writing Thad direct to tell of a new method of treatment she had heard about. And when Elsie was expecting, the distant members of the family were aware of the news sooner, no doubt, than if they had been at home and left to themselves to find out what was going on. The outstanding feature of the few faded letters in this family correspondence that still survive is the small amount of space devoted to the weather, and the pages and pages given to the discussion of health. Emma's pleurisy (Emma was Mother's sister) came into so many of the letters one winter that it was almost as if the distant members of the family had it right in the house with them. Another item that was never neglected was the food; in mentioning a party or picnic, or even a family dinner, a detailed account of the food served to the guests was never lacking. Familiar household apparel— Mother's "fur-lined circular," Father's old gray shawl, worn about his shoulders in winter and pinned with a giant safety pin. Family jokes were referred to from time to time, and any indisposition or caprice of the dog was sure to be mentioned. Daisy, our old white horse, figured as much in the letters as any single member of the family,

319

and once a year Jessie, the cow, claimed a place among the vital statistics when she dropped her annual calf. Nobody was ever allowed to get the feeling that because he was far away the rest of the family were not interested in what he was doing. He knew very well that all were interested, and he went to some pains in his letters to Mother to see that they were kept well informed.

The success of the letter-writing must have been a great consolation to Mother, and still she had realized from the beginning that she could never be completely satisfied without seeing the children in the old home nest from time to time. She tried not to be unreasonable in her demands, not to insist upon their coming at intervals that would be too much of an effort or expense, for the family were soon so spread out that they spanned half the continent. She would have preferred to have them all come at the same time, but she realized that people cannot always do what they would like when they would like to. It did not seem quite the thing, she told me once, for so many people to have their lives regulated to suit the whims of a single individual—even if she was their mother. She finally hit upon five years as a reasonable length of time, and as one after another the children left home she exacted a solemn promise that so long as she lived each child would come back to see her at least once every five years.

It was a promise that was never broken, though there were times when the family was scattered from San Francisco to Paris and intermediate points. And curiously enough, though there had been no insistence on our all coming at once, that was the way it worked out.

Thad, the first to leave, was the first to come home for a visit. After three years in the West he came on for Louise's wedding, the first reunion of the eight children. Both Thad and Louise returned when Elsie was married some three years later. We next came together when the

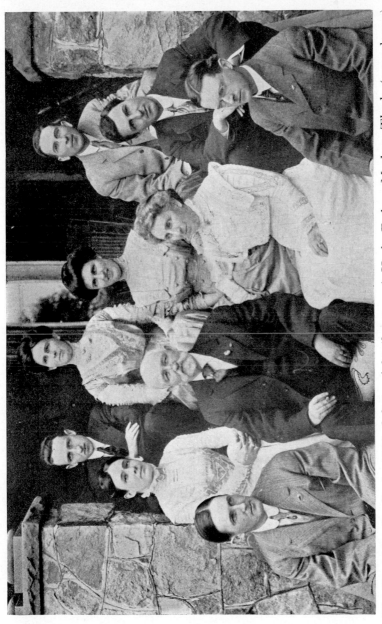

The Partridge family in 1909: *left to right* (front row) Herb, Father, Mother, Thad; (second row) Louise, Cecilia, Stan; (back row) Leslie, Elsie, Bellamy.

wedding bells were ringing for little Cecilia, youngest of the three sisters. And so it went. Running true to family tradition we were married in the order of seniority all the way down to the youngest child, and for each nuptial event all the brothers and sisters came together at the old home.

By tacit understanding we always came unaccompanied on these pilgrimages, leaving husbands, wives, and children to come some other time. Mother never failed to invite them, but we all understood that what she wanted was to have her own brood back, to see them all together again, and to live once more in retrospect a little of the past. The visits usually lasted from three days to a week, and were festive rather than sentimental in tone. While we were at home the old rules were rigidly enforced. We got up with the rising bell and went on the carpet for inspection, trying all the old methods of cheating the inspector, though we were almost invariably caught. The antics at morning inspection usually got the day off to a hilarious start. At meals we were served in the order of seniority. And at night we went to bed when the clock struck ten. We did not always stay in bed, but at least we went when the signal sounded. On one of these visits Father brought home some legal papers for us to copy; and he insisted afterwards that it was the poorest job we had ever turned out.

The breaking up of these reunions was always sad, for the fear was present that there might never be another. It was Leslie's wedding which brought us together for the last of the festive reunions. We were all there to see the marriage of the youngest child. The next time we gathered at home it was to mourn the first break in the family circle as we laid Father to rest among the pines and the hemlocks on the sunny hillside where so many of his old friends lay waiting for him.

After half a century at his side Mother could not believe that he would be contented without her. She complained little about her health, and though she seemed to be growing weaker she maintained a cheerfulness which alarmed us as she went about putting her house in order as if about to leave on a long journey. At Easter time, with the buds all bursting with the vehemence of spring, she went to join him. She felt that we were grown up and established, and no longer had need of her; that her earthly work was done. Without Father she had the feeling of being incomplete and useless—and she went so calmly, so happily that we could not greatly mourn her going.

I do not believe that Mother ever knew to what extent each one of us had pirated her ways and methods of raising a family, and were adopting her solidarity methods to weld it together. She must have known that our children were brought up under the same rules and chastised to a certain extent with the same punishments. No doubt she knew that they were sung to sleep by the same tuneless lullabies and amused by the same jingles, but I have many times wondered if she ever realized that the most lasting and important of her contributions to the rules of conduct would be her invention of a villain.

"This can't be *my* little boy," I once heard Thad's wife saying to one of her misbehaving tots. "This must be little Charley Beverwyck!" She turned to me and added in an aside, "Whoever *he* is. It's what Thad always says to the children."

Little Charley Beverwyck! My memory staggered. Charley Beverwyck had been the worst boy in town when Thad himself was a little chap—forty-five years before and a couple of thousand miles away. We had all been brought up not to be like little Charley Beverwyck. But Charley

Beverwyck had long since grown up to be staid and re-spectable. I knew him as a middle-aged man with well-behaved children of his own. Charley Beverwyck has been dead these many years, and his name is all but forgotten in the town which gave him birth. But in the outlying districts, wherever a root of our clan has dug in and there are young to be born and brought up, little Charley Beverwyck is still very much alive, and there is still a magic power in his name; for to this day no child ever wants to *be* little Charley Beverwyck.